ERIC ENGLAND:

THE PHANTOM OF PHU BAI

TURNER

Books By J. B. Turner:

Alamance: Birthplace Of Liberty

Eric England – The Phantom Of Phu Bai

High Humor Of The Hills

Victim Of Valor

White Boy In The Colored Section

ERIC ENGLAND:
THE PHANTOM OF PHU BAI

J. B. TURNER, Ph.D.

Nathan House Books

SPECIAL LIMITED EDITION

THIS BOOK IS BASED ON THE LIFE AND ADVENTURES OF ERIC ENGLAND, AS WELL AS THE EXPLOITS OF SEVERAL OTHERS WHO HELPED TO CREATE THE SNIPER MYSTIQUE. SOME CHAPTERS RECONSTRUCT EVENTS, DIALOGUES AND SCENARIOS FROM BEST AVAILABLE ACCOUNTS. IN SOME CASES ERIC IS DEPICTED REPRESENTATIONALLY IN MISSIONS AS THEY COULD HAVE BEEN. BUT HIS COMBINED ACTUAL ACCOMPLISHMENTS FAR OUTWEIGH ANY AMOUNT OF WRITTEN ACCOUNTS... OR BARRACKS BULL'ONEY.

Printing History:
SEVENTH EDITION
PRINTED IN USA

v

DEDICATION

To My Father,
Dr. James Harry Turner,
Our Family's First Marine,
Who Inspired This Book
And Events Depicted Herein...

To James M. Brown, Jr.,
Edward Mauney Turner,
John Jarrett Turner,
And C. Preston Turner,
WarriorsWho Have
Sure Been There...

To Gen. James S. Harkins, Ph.D.
Legendary American Hero...

And To All The
Distinguished Shooters

CONTENTS

PROLOGUE

The Appalachian Mountains have produced many remarkable figures in American history, such as Daniel Boone, Davey Crockett, Meriwether Lewis. But few such men ever actually set out for fame's trail.

Rather, they seem to have followed the path of modest dedication and intuitive propriety—yet in looking back, discern that they have blazed a trail of greatness for others to follow.

Such a man is Eric R. England. Reared in the wilds of Appalachia, yet nurtured by the hearthside of family devotion to principle, he has drawn deeply from the well of soul...

He found true his mark in the world, magnified his talents, uplifted his fellows, served his nation and community, gave credit to others, and fulfilled the lofty callings of friend and kinsman. He is a hero of the hills.

TRIBUTES TO ERIC ENGLAND

"I'm proud to be related to Eric England, and that Choe Stoe blood flows in both our veins. (*Choe Stoe is the Cherokee name for the Appalachian area they grew up in, and which their forebears pioneered.*) Eric was the main reason that I joined the U. S. Marine Corps. I always thought he was the sharpest, most squared away Marine that I had ever seen. I wanted to be like him. I also wanted to be able to shoot like him, but only a very few could do that.

When I read articles in *Reader's Digest* about 'The Most Unforgettable Person I've Ever Known,' I think of Eric. This ole Marine mountaineer is one of a kind. They don't make men like Eric any more.

Here's one way to look at it: I joined the Marine Corps because of Eric. The Marines are the main reason I was disciplined enough to become Governor. So Eric is the reason I became Governor. Thank you, cousin."

[ZELL MILLER, Former Governor of Georgia; U. S. Senator; Former Marine Rifle Instructor; Noted Author And Lecturer; Public Benefactor; Fellow Mountaineer.] [UPDATE: Zell answered Taps on 23 March 2018.]

" I think what added to Eric's greatness as a Shooter were his traits of steadiness, loyality, reliability, and above all his levity during difficult situations. He was such a pleasure to be around—there were a couple of times when the Rifle Team got bumped and his attitude would hold the team spirit together—then he would go on the line and save the team with his score. He could be counted on to get anything done and to deal with any challenge, being respected at every rank of the Corps.

No matter how miserable things got, he could walk up and have an entire company laughing merrily at one crack of his dry wit. Yet he is a modest man who magnifies the simple pleasures and modest virtues of life. He could have wiped out an entire regiment of NVA, and would not have batted an eye; nor would he so much as boast of it to a single person. Eric is still on record as the highest scoring Shooter in our nation's history, but most importantly he was a great Marine and always a pleasure to be around. He's as big as the North Georgia Mountains that produced him."

[NORMAN A. CHANDLER, Lt. Colonel, USMC, Retired; Co-Author Of The Acclaimed Death From Afar Series; Founder Of Iron Brigade Armorers; Creator Of "The Carlos Hathcock Sniper Rifle;" Renowned Firearms Consultant And Military Historian; Distinguished Shooter]

"Eric England—what an outstanding rifleman! And such a fine individual. His spirits were always positive and kept you cheered. And when your team needed a score, you could always depend on him. He was never rattled by anything. He always held himself and the team together. He is a very fine person and a great Marine. I liked him very much and always looked for him for putting a team together. I hold him in the highest regard, and there's no one with whom I would rather associate."

[WALTER WALSH, Colonel, USMC, Retired; "Father Of Modern Shooting." Triple-Distinguished Shooter]

"A great Shooter—a hero—yes. Eric is all that. But what really made him great in the eyes of those around him was his amazing wit, team spirit and total loyalty. He could do just about anything on earth, do it like a pro, and walk away like it was nothing... then give others the credit. You just never forget a guy like that."

[NEAL CRANE, USMC, Retired; Distinguished Shooter; FBI Staff]

"Eric was always as solid and dedicated as any Marine ever was. As a Shooter, he is without rival. As a savvy strategist—cool under fire and masterful at arms—the spirit Eric helped promote was in keeping with the finest tradition of the Marine Corps. Eric's talent goes beyond mere shooting, although he exemplifies shooting to its greatest state of refinement. But he also has that certain sparkle of wit and camaraderie which hold a unit together; that is what he was known for in the Corps. He inspires men to be their best. I am proud to be numbered among his friends."

[JOHN BOITNOTT, Sgt. Maj., USMC, Retired; Pioneer Of Modern Sniping; Veteran Of 23 WWII Battles And The Korean War; Co-Founder (With Gen. Paul Tibbits And Pres. John Kennedy) Of The National Military Command Center; Distinguished Shooter]

"I can't imagine my career being what it was, without the presence of Eric England. We were shooting partners all through our careers. The Marine Rifle Team was as tight a unit as the world has ever seen, and men like Eric helped mold them together and function as one. His secret weapons were friendship, dedication, and an awful lot of talent! I am proud to call him brother."

[DON BARTLETT, Major, USMC, Retired; All-Time Champion Of Champions, Distinguished Shooter]

"Eric and I go back many years, to the beginning of my career. Jo and I consider him the finest and most good-natured of friends. He was an inspiration to all us Shooters, and has the admiration of all the greatest. Eric England is a great man, a great Shooter, and a great Marine!"

[CARLOS N. HATHCOCK, II, USMC, Retired; World's Best Known Scout-Sniper; 1965 Wimbledon Nat. Champion; Subject Of Many Publications; Distinguished Shooter]

"Eric is my lifelong friend. Top rifle teams—Vietnam—We did it all. I saw him set the all-time National Open record in 1968, despite war stitches ripping out. I had just beaten Don Bartlett's national record, then twenty two minutes later Eric fired a .998 and set a new one, while enduring a festering war wound!"

[JERRY KOZUCH, USMC, Retired; ATF Technical Researcher; Former National Open Champion; Renowned Firearms Analyst And Consultant; Helped Develop "The Carlos Hathcock Sniper Rifle;" Distinguished Shooter]

"Eric is one straight Shooter, all around! I've even trusted him with my race car. Eric England— a true mountain fellow. I'm glad to know him!"

[BILL ELLIOTT, Legendary NASCAR Driver; Great Guy; Fellow Mountaineer]

" Master Sergeant England's contribution to the Corps is still remembered a quarter-century after his retirement. I was proud to have served in the same cause with him in time of war. He also kept the spirit of the Corps alive and well in times of peace. He was and is a true Marine."

[GEN. CHARLES KRULAK, Commandant, USMC]

"Dear Master Sergeant England:

I would like to take this opportunity to thank you for your dedicated service to our Corps.

Though it has been many years since your retirement on 31 May 1974, today's young men and women of the Corps are continuing to follow the footsteps and traditions carved throughout history by Marines such as yourself. Your accomplishments in long-range rifle competition and combat set the standard for others to strive to attain. Please know that your dedicated service and continuing pride in your Corps are truly valued.

Best wishes for continued success.

Semper Fi, L. G. Lee ~ 31 July 1996"

[L. G. LEE, Sergeant-Major OF The Corps; Advisor To The Commandant]

"My years of service were so much more enjoyable, thanks to the example of a remarkable Marine like Eric England. We crossed paths many times: rifle teams, Vietnam. It was always encouraging to be on a team with him, either as a Shooter, or as armorer. He was like my big brother. My time at Phu Bai went much easier, having a buddy like Eric there. I know for a fact that as a Sniper, he was unequalled in his duty. He caused the enemy much reason to fear!

But I think what I admire most was watching him intentionally disqualify himself from an historical National all-time record in the 200 yard rapid-fire competition, which had already been credited to him, but which he adamantly refused to accept. He cleared his weapon, and discovered he had not fired his 20th round! He took the judges to task. They told him to accept the honor, as he had it coming with all those rounds dead-center. But he would not. Eric formally challenged the score, as unjustified. Finally Col. Williams walked over and told the judges, 'If Eric England says it, then you can take his words to church!' Eric won much more than a score that day. Now, that is my idea of a hero!"

[TED HOLLABAUGH, USMC, Retired; FBI Staff; Distinguished Shooter]

"Eric England—now there's a name to remember! We were part of a great moment in Marine Corps history. We all knew it, and shared the greatness of it. Still, I feel Eric's part in it goes beyond all description. But of all the compliments I could make about Eric, I would just say that he is a great friend. That's what he is best at, and that's the best thing a person could ever be: a friend like Eric England."

[DON BARKER, USMC, Retired; First Sniper To Record A Confirmed Enemy Kill In Vietnam War; Distinguished Shooter] [Author's Note: Don States He Shares Credit For His Famed First Kill, With His Co-Shooters]

"We did a lot of great shooting together, on a lot of famous teams. I was glad to run into him later, at Phu Bai. He was always an asset, and always there when you needed him. I also admired him because we were both mountain boys. Eric is a backwoods genius who 'made good.' There was never anyone equal to him, his skills, or his character. I'm proud to be his friend."

[ROGER KNAPPER, Colonel, USMC, Retired; Stalwart Warrior; Distinguished Shooter]

CAVEAT

A strict biography of Eric R. England is a nigh-impossible task. It is too multifaceted, too full of adventures. His life and career accounts must be an amalgam of many faces, stories, places and circumstances. In his humble reluctance to participate in a book about himself, it is therefore a product generated by many key players fortunate enough to be reflecting mirrors, as it were, of the brilliance of it all.

The mystique of The Phantom of Phu Bai was inspired by Eric's cunning skill as a Scout-Sniper and Tactical Weaponry Instructor in Vietnam. But the overall mystique was also a proliferation of his expertise on the part of his many students, admirers and colleagues in the field.

The result is that the accounts of his combat missions had to be gleaned from many people and reference sources. Thus some exploits depicted herein have been attributed to him on the basis of best-available accounts. In terms of inspiring the legend of The Phantom of Phu Bai, Eric was the prime integer. Yet he was more conversant on his days as a competition match-range shooter, as are all his sniper buddies.

As with any great historic legend, it is sometimes as difficult to pin any confirmation on them, as it would be to pin a badge onto a ghost. But whether any particular feats were those Eric actually carried out, or those executed by his proteges, all were an essential component of The Phantasm which came to be feared by the Communist enemy throughout I Corps.

Several absolutely qualified sources have confirmed Eric's superior combat statistics, which at his request are not quoted herein. Competition scores and personal career narratives are accurate, and were obtained from official files of the National Rifle Association, U.S.M.C. History Center, and qualified eye-witnesses.

The reader is admonished to bear in mind that Eric seeks no attention for his fabled achievements. Destiny has nonetheless thrust this upon him, spurred on by his many admiring folks and friends. But he is on record as being in strong opposition to the deed. Those who remember him best from his days as a Marine competition shooter and combat sniper, all attest to the same fact: That Eric was equally legendary for his honesty, modesty and team work. He personally gives all competition and combat credits to his team mates. Moreover, any discrepancy in technical or factual aspects of the text is the sole responsibility of the author or his informants. So don't hassle the hero.

~ Joseph Blair Turner ~

ROLL OF DISTINCTION

This book was influenced by many people. Tremendous gratitude is due them all. Anyone not given due credit herein will kindly overlook the unintentional oversight as just that. The entire book was influenced by the following persons or organizations, whether by first-hand interview, or in a few cases by second-hand reports from their admirers. (An asterisk indicates a personal interview or direct material contribution. Most are still among us. Some watch and wait for us from above...)

A. Adams Tom Arline Don Barker*
Col. "Red" Barron, USMC Don Bartlett*
Lon Berrong* Leon Berrong John Boitnott *
Jim Bowen * D. I. Boyd Steve Briggs* James M. Brown, Jr.* Ronald Cantey Clare Carlson* Richard Carroll* R.C. Cate Lt. Col. Norman Chandler*
Greg Connor* Neal Crane* Joe Creech Col. Jack Cully Dick Culver R. O. Culver Jesse Davenport*
Frank Deal Raymond Dinnan Steve Disco
Lawrence Dubia Bob Dudash Timothy Dunn
Tom Easley A. L. England* Mary Nix England*
Sue Berrong England* Edie England* Jim Ensley*
Kenneth Erdman W. E. Eubank Tom Ferran
David Fiehtner * George Filyaw Ron Fisher

George Fullwood   Fred Gabroske*   C. Galkowski
Jared *"Gunner"* Garfield*   "Gator Hide" (Anon.)*   N.
Goddard   Bob Goller*   T. Green   Ray Green
R.H. Green   Karl Grosshans   James Gularte
James Stanley Harkins*   Bill Elliott*
Claude Harris   Carlos Hathcock*   Jo Hathcock*
Sonny Hathcock*   Al Hauser   Clark Brule
L. L. Hausman   F. A. Higginson   History Center,
USMC   T. Hitchcock   Thomas Holcomb
Ted Hollabaugh*   T.N. Horner   George Hurt
F.A. Johnson   Walter K. Jones   Elmer Keith
Slingshot Kelly   Jerry Kozuch*   Greg Kraljev
Gen. Charles Krulak   Ed Kugler*   Gary Lakis*
Maj. Jim Land   Kernice Landry*   Marvin Lange
Col. Fred Lasher   C.E. Lauer   Sgt. Maj. L.G. Lee
Bobby J. Lee   Thomas Leonard   R. Lewis   William
Lucas   Ron MacAbee*   Earl Manning
Robert Martin   William B. Martin   Charles Mawhinney
Collin McGee   G. B. Merrill   Black Jack Mesko
Sen. Zell Miller*   Albert Miral   V. D. Mitchell
G. R. Murdock   Bill E. Nation   Nat. Rifle Assn.*
Otis Napper   Col. Roger Napper*   Maurice Nelson*
Dennis Ocier   Emmett Orr   Robert Partridge*
Dan Peltonen   Mike Pietreforte   Tony Reece*
Donald Reinke   Gary Reiter   M. Reith
Lt. Col. Craig Roberts*   James W. Rogers
Wess Rodgers   W.C. Rose   Hayden Russell
Bob Russell   Danny Sanchez   Billy Savell*
K. W. Schmidt   Lewis Scoggins   Dick "Max" Scully*
R. F. Seitzinger   Bobby Sherrill
Turk Smith   Don Smith   D. L. Smith

Wayne Souther*   Red Stamey
"Stone Face" (Anon.)*   Steve Suttles   John Swartz
Ron Szpond   Jerry Tamlin   Jack Tenerington
Edward M. Turner*   Dr. Harry Turner*   Randal
Turner*   Lonnie Turner*   William Price Turner*
USMC Staff* / Commandant & Sgt. Major of the Corps
Gen. George Van Orden   R.C.
J. R. Verhaal   Col. Walter Walsh*
Jack Ward*   Joseph Ward   Ray Westphal
Col. Lloyd Williams   Col. Dave Willis*   R.Yale
Lt. Gary Yee, SFPD*   Wallace York   Jim Zahm
Vernon Zuleger

ADDITIONS TO THE ROLL OF DISTINCTION:

*The Author And Publisher Will Be Pleased To Consider The
Addition Herein Of Any Person Who Deserves Credit For
Having Influenced This Book, Or Who Is An Officially
Designated Distinguished Shooter From Any Era.*

Please Submit Nominees To: NathanHouseBooks.com

CHAPTER ONE

THE HUNTER

SWEAT—salty and stinging—rolled into the tired eyes of The Hunter. Cautiously he blinked it away, avoiding any unnecessary motion. For the prey he sought was likewise predator. The victor in this savage jungle arena would be the warrior who counted trivia as increments of perfection. Scout Sniper protocol; just *routine flawlessness*. Perfecting this crucial shot—saving lives of fellow Marines—(and as a fringe benefit, possible personal survival)—would be a grand edifice built upon minute stones of adversity. It was the irony of sacrifice.

Six grueling hours soaked ounces of life from the bronze and wiry Hunter. As sentinel over the curve in the trail ahead, his vigil never wavered. One briefly exposed curve, amidst the prolific jungle canopies, would soon be center stage in its one flickering moment of fame. The kill zone. Range, 800 yards.

Morning ebbed into evening. The able eyes of The Hunter sifted every moving shadow; every variation in flora, fauna, cloud, and scent. Slowly he panned the 10-power scope to survey the exotic and treacherous vista, vigilant to sight the enemy before the prey spotted him.

He gripped the intelligence report firmly in his mind: aerial reconnaissance photos, enemy movement patterns, weather forecast. And standing out like a gallery portrait

1

was the snapshot of his intended target. The Colonel. A bloody criminal officer of the North Vietnamese Army, with the cunning and authority to execute a disruption of sensitive US Marine Corps operations, was in dress rehearsal to take his bow for fleeting fame.

Objective: Single out The Colonel from his battalion, his staff officers and NCO's, and send him a final curtain call—wrapped in a .30-06 cartridge. One old horror story ending with a new one. Go out with a bang.

The day wore on like sandpaper drawers. Man, for a chaw of deer jerky. A sip from a cool mountain spring. A good long nap.

But all creature comforts were filtered out and eliminated by the laser-like concentration of The Hunter.

Evening announced itself with chilled air flowing down from the Central Highlands. With it came faint traces of friendly sounds: distant artillery barrages, helicopter missions. But the Friendlies they represented were far from him now. Far from his private war. He tuned them out in favor of the task at hand.

The notoriously sinister night-cloak of Vietnam encroached. Daytime visual instincts gave way to auditory perception. The sensitive ears of The Hunter could discern a bug belch from a snake sneeze. Each blowing leaf, every snapping twig, could signal an approaching enemy. Or a wasted mission. Or the abrupt end of the life of a good Marine.

The intensity of the stealthy night was punctuated with the symphonic subtleties endemic to a rain forest, magnifying and expanding as night shrouded the senses. Occasional comic relief was produced by the infamous lizards whose croaking call was practically indistinguishable from a certain expression of English profanity.

"My sentiments exactly," thought the persevering Marine Hunter, dedicated to the somber and sobering task ahead. The awareness that the success of this difficult mission could result in the deliverance of countless lives of fellow Marines, firmed up his resolve.

To remain awake and fully alert within the unsettling electricity of nighttime Vietnam was not, in and of itself, so difficult. But to have cautiously humped and slithered through miles of dense foliage on an upgrade, from the point of helicopter insertion—then to have methodically crawled another quarter-mile through equally challenging conditions—would exact an inordinate degree of stamina from the toughest specimen.

Compounded by the choking heat and long receiving line of pests—and the weight of weaponry, ammo, canteens—and the burden of maintaining hyper-perceptual reconnaissance—the cumulative tools of the Scout Sniper trade could render the most vigorous warrior limp with fatigue.

Then there was the slow and cautious climbing of the tree, the constant vigil, the self-denial of water and rations, and the endless cycle of self-motivation. The Hunter was tired, though he would not let himself know it.

The stress of the mission was lightened somewhat by his many years of roosting in tree-stands, in the hunt for the white-tail deer indigenous to his native Appalachian domain. The self-discipline of his youth in Northeast Georgia had been practical, the parallel only slightly metaphorical, yet the inherent risks far more substantial. The Hunter in him knew he could abide and withstand the challenge, concurring with his warrior component.

For now, the hunt was not for trophy bucks, but aggressive two-legged badgers, trained by Soviet bears and Chinese dragons to carry man-killing guns. The North Vietnamese were invading South Vietnam like a horde of ants, poisonous ants stinging and devouring, that had grown up to be an army.

When the NVA battalion rounded that curve ahead, he would be outnumbered hundreds to one. The standing order for Communist forces in South Vietnam: *Execute American snipers at the scene of capture.*

And the outlook got even worse. For if they identified The Hunter as the mysterious high-skilled killer who had left his personal *stamp—signature—mystique* on so many of their comrades, he would be tortured, probably taken to North Vietnam for humiliation and further defilement, and again tortured slowly to death.

Unlike the common soldier, the Scout Sniper is privileged with a greater degree of command disclosure, vital revelations of the import and specifics of a combat mission. Each battle boils down to his own ultimate strategy, tactics, and personal sense of victory or defeat. As a matter of course, his mission is underscored as his own sanction and bidding. He becomes embued within the broader fabric of war, until the enemy fears him—hates him—blames him. He symbolizes all the agonies of the enemy to date.

Then he must punctuate their dread once again. One clear and effective shot. Once more terrorized and humbled, the great enemy would be abuzz over the far-reaching impact of one phantom-like warrior against many.

The night wore on heavily. The Hunter mentally rehearsed the smoothly honed techniques of his craft. He felt the bolt and safety of his Winchester Model 70 .30-06 repeatedly with his sensorial fingers. He took care to keep objects well away from the lenses of his scope. In the battle theater of memory, he rewound and replayed the tight skills of marksmanship as though he were his own range instructor. He reflected upon all he had learned in his sixteen years in the Corps; and all the wisdom he had imparted to trainees across the globe.

He allowed his mind to dart briefly back to the countless championship matches in which he had competed, but only for the additional discipline it afforded. And as a reminder of his duty to his marksman comrades, not to miss the mark. To a career Marine Shooter of notable repute, anything wide of the bull was utter disgrace.

He could not hold back a sudden grin, at the thought of old Sergeant "Slingshot" Kelly back at Quantico, Virginia. He would humiliate marksman trainees who missed their mark. Picking up an expended brass casing, he would load it into the slingshot he kept handy. Then tossing another spent casing into the air, he would shoot it with the shell in the slingshot. His point was always well made: know your mark, and hit it. Without fail.

The Hunter now wrestled with a budding laugh, at the memory of he and Slingshot seated in a club, when a mountain of an angry Marine came to their table to confront Kelly over some grievance. Kelly merely drew his loaded slingshot from beneath the table, and prepared to fire on the antagonist.

The bully recoiled in horror, spurting, "*Never* mind. *Just* never *mind!* I've *seen* you shoot that thing!" He scurried backward and hastily vacated the establishment.

No, a Marine match shooter could never miss the mark, even when alone. Shooting was the paramount topic of their conversation on and off duty. It was their life and their bond of allegiance. Among this elite coterie—grand notables such as Turner, Walsh, Kozuch, Bartlett, Hathcock, Bowen, Chandler, Goller, Boyd, Sanchez, Hurt, Merrill, Boitnot, Barker—even legendary old-timer Elmer Keith—camaraderie was sure as concrete. Even so, the slightest nonperformance among them was not soon forgotten.

The Hunter now tapped the essence of key moments on championship ranges: the Nationals Match, the Leech Cup, the Palma World Trophy, the Interservice Match, the Queen's Match. Recounting laurels was not for glory at the moment, but rather a drawing from the well of experience; crisp memories of rifle mastery that could pay off now, here, in his one-man war.

His accomplishments were already legendary. And if he survived this tour, he had it in him to go down on the books as the greatest long-range rifle marksman in world history. But to survive, here, today—would be recognition enough. For today, history would be written second by second. The outcome was riding on the accumulation of his shooting experience to date, funneling it all into one masterful crack. In effect, he was working his way into his "bubble."

The "bubble," that self-encapsulation into a state of maximal concentration, ensures the precision of the hit. Once into his bubble, nothing exists to The Hunter except the weapon, target, and trajectory; supplemented by a complete harmony of all body parts—muscles—nerves—thoughts—energies; aligned to make the hit true.

Once into his bubble, he cannot escape it until the deed is done, and the mark made absolute. He cannot enter it prematurely. He must ease into it, until timing and instinct confirm to him that the precise interval has arrived for sealing himself in completely. Only then does he begin to shatter the bubble, with rifle fire of uncompromising and deadly accuracy.

TURNER

On the competition range, the bubble dissolves slowly after all the match shots are fired. In combat, the Scout Sniper is allowed but one, sometimes two perfect bullseyes. Then he must shuck off the bubble stealthily, as a snake sheds its skin, and expeditiously vacate his "hide," or vantage point.

The enemy knew of him. Quite well, in fact. They had seen his calling card many times. But seldom did they know when or where he may call again. No Viet Cong or Bo Doi could admit having actually seen The Hunter, but his stamp was all too familiar and up-close. The sudden termination of a key comrade's mortal sojourn, usually stone dead before the sound of the rifle was even heard, was being effectuated from as far as 700 to 1200 yards. Always, the shot was clean and crisp, directly through the heart; or laterally, straight through the ears. Or centered exactly in the medulla. Or frontally, plumb and level between the eyes— in the middle of the belt buckle—or the center of the mid-shirt button. The shattering force: a 173-grain match-grade projectile from an American-made match-conditioned .30-06.

Surgical perfection was the hallmark of The Hunter's reputation, in his personal war with one *Charlie Cong, Esquire*, and his entourage.

Unlike the average ground combat soldier, (who must expend vast amounts of ammunition in a skirmish or battle, and still may never know whether he actually struck a foe,) The Hunter—the Scout Sniper—was compelled to rely upon his own singular fighting ability. Within this profile coexisted the facets of the gladiator and the infiltrator, in a harmonious determination to win one's own battle, to annihilate one's personal enemy, carry the entire burden of the mission, and win and withdraw unobserved.

Superhuman perception, steely nerves, endurance beyond any norm, and a goodly dose of Providence were his stock in trade. He lived one breath at a time, with each being perhaps his last.

Night abraded by, gnawing at his senses like a rusty chainsaw with an attitude, chaffing the bulwark of endurance. Near midnight the cursing lizards croaked in again, and muddied the air. The snap of a twig or rustle of a

6

leaf made him cringe, knowing the possibility of a forward enemy patrol approaching. He recalled the sniping mission in which he and his spotter were surprised "out of season" by a mostly unarmed squad of enemy, returning to duty from an underground VC malaria hospital—having to exchange fire with three of them while hoping the others would flee, and not pursue them.

How he had revelled in the brisk and effective conclusion to that sudden heart-seizing firefight, and how he had wanted to stand and finish them all, hand-to-hand if necessary—he was primed for it at the time. But his knowledge and skill had to be preserved. The two Marines had to escape, and hunt another day. They didn't even report the kills, in order to protect the secrecy of their scouting movements and operations.

For now, he shrugged and squelched out the memory-channel, and continued to grapple with tonight, and its long and widening queue of death-variables. Occasional clouds languidly passed beneath the bright moon, shadows lengthening and darting tauntingly, heavily taxing his senses in their absorbent analyses.

Night grew cooler in the high green country. The fanfare of subtle jungle noises paraded by. Fatigue surfaced, but was promptly put on hold, as the confidence of The Hunter's vigil relentlessly swept the ambiance—and gradually shrank with him into the bubble he knew must engulf him, before he could deactivate his forces and relax. He did not sleep.

CHAPTER TWO

KILL ZONE: SOVEREIGN JUSTICE

AS the sun peeked upon an earth refreshed, The Hunter scanned tenaciously through the scope, toward the down-range trail. Confronted by a tandem shift of *intensified immobility*, he was all the more determined to make good on this challenging shot. It was a matter of personal economics at this point—of justifying the expenditure. And time was still on his side.

He inwardly prayed that he would not spot a trophy buck, or a tiger on the prowl. The frustrated desire to shoot would be equaled only by the danger the disruptive noises such beasts could make. And any sizable creature plodding about in the bush would surely spur on an aggressive NVA patrol, eventuating in his own exclusive Waterloo.

To the excitable ears of many men on ambush or perimeter guard, the paddy-splashing hoofs of errant water buffalo had sounded like an enemy squad approaching, setting off a one-sided firefight ending in victorious defeat of the buffalo. The Hunter desired no outside help from jungle beasts, in sparking a hostile manhunt in this sector.

A brief bolt of dread shot through him as he observed various species of birds alighting in trees about him, but seldom in his own tree. An NVA scout with a keen eye would make inventory of such an oddity, figuring he had treed himself a Georgia coon hunter. Thankfully he had

8

selected a perch well above the visual field of NVA on the trail, askew of their vantage point.

Most NVA, though toughened by the hundreds of miles marched from Hanoi, were still not as adept at jungle concealment and stealth as were the local VC. To The Hunter, the nigh-invisible VC provided a frustration comparable to stalking small game birds back home, after they had run into the dense underbrush. But as for their NVA counterpart, he would know when the main body of the NVA battalion was coming. There would be signs aplenty.

But was Victor-Charlie also watching *him*? It always felt as though he were; as if Charlie's invisible, steamy, fermented-fish-sauce breath were scorching the back of his red Georgia neck. Today he had to beat Charlie *and* his Uncle Ho, and he felt them both, up close and sweaty.

He checked and rechecked his focus on the curve in the clearing ahead, surveying every detail of the kill zone, weighing his firing options. He estimated the range at 800 yards, but also at a sharp downgrade and oblique angle. His evacuation plan was already hashed out and set aside. His bubble was enveloping him. He was a piece in an unbalanced jigsaw puzzle, struggling to rearrange this odd picture without moving the other pieces. This could be a monumental task at a mere 800 feet. Today it felt like 800 miles.

So many times The Hunter had lain atop a ridge and nailed an NVA Bo Doi on the belt buckle or sternum button from 1,000 yards and more, though ideally with little visual obstacle, or target movement. Today a slight breeze was whipping up the steamy heat of the jungle floor, a factor which would drastically alter the trajectory of the bullet; laterally, by the force of the wind; vertically, by the rising heat waves. The high humidity could thicken the air like a series of wet blankets. The gentle but steady swaying of the foliage caused additional distraction. And any change in temperature altered the rate of gunpowder combustion, affecting the velocity of the bullet.

Like a classic *Field & Stream* photo, The Hunter was poised and prepared to nail this predator-prey. Not pheasant, nor duck. A wild turkey, maybe: this most malicious of all NVA senior officers, a varmint turned

9

poacher, out to ruin the game balance. The Colonel gloried in mutilating unarmed captives while photographing their agonies. He counted as great victories, his needless assaults on unarmed garrisons of support personnel. And now he was heading up a planned attack with strategic import: disrupt critical supply and communications lines. And like his mentor General Giap, he *would* do it, even if he lost men at a rate of 100 to 1. His reign of terror could not be allowed to survive the day.

By the time The Hunter expected his bubble to fully materialize, the intended target still had not shown. Already he had sat in the tree a day, a night, and half a day again. He had to postpone rations until after dark. He sipped water at the rate of a canteen-cap full per hour. And now he faced another night in his arboreal perch, stuck and restless like a tick on a lemon.

With the receiving volume set at the lowest level, he turned on his radio and whispered a commo back to the base: "Thunderspade 5... Bearclaw. Bearclaw hibernating at primary hide. No movement. Will maintain post. No further commo unless condition red. Will monitor transmissions for 15 seconds at established daily intervals. That is all."

He wouldn't, though. He was burroughed in and on his own. A one-man assault force, cut off and alone, he had not brought along the customary spotter companion. This he chose, to facilitate stealth. And to avoid risking the life of a fellow Marine on a mission facing almost certain capture, death, or "going native" on an extended outing.

As day broke again, he had held his position for over 48 hours. He wondered if the Intel report were wrong; or, more wrong than it usually was. And if so, within what correctable dimensions. Mentally rehearsing his briefing, recon photos, and grid-map coordinates, he knew he was in the right place. Buddies used to marvel over his detailed topographical maps of favorite deer hunting regions in Appalachia; every track, every deer dropping—marked, dated, conditions noted. He could track a deer by the color of its teeth. No, he was not lost. He waited.

Still, some new factor had to occur, to shift the scene. He needed to abandon his hide, gamble advancing along the ridge line; find good concealment in the bushes;

perhaps reconnoiter to pick up a trail. At least in the low bushes he could safely get a little sleep. No, he could not. His briefing was correct, all but for the variable of timing. His course was clear. Endure to the end.

His sensitive scanning ears were jolted by the unexpected firing of an enemy AK-47, followed by two others. They were rather distant at first, then coming closer before ceasing altogether.

"Recon-by-fire!" his mind shouted to itself. "They are spraying the ridge and the trees to flush out intruders!"

Soon the three shooters—an NVA advance patrol—appeared within the kill zone, tempting his trigger-finger reflexes. They were gone from view again as quickly, advancing along the obscured leg of trail some 300 yards beneath him. He regretted that he would now have enemy to the back of him as well as to the front. He counted the minutes, to maintain an estimate of how far past his hide they may be, by the time Colonel Cutthroat made his final curtain.

The Hunter was now in his bubble. It was time. The entirety of his conscious existence was relegated directly upon a scant few paces along a remote jungle trail. Nothing else mattered. He felt like his Great-Grandpappy Nix, a Civil War veteran by age 15, might have felt after trying out his latest homemade turkey call. All that carving, all the planning and perfecting and waiting—and now, here comes the turkey.

He wanted to listen for stalkers behind him, but he could not afford to expend the sensory resources. All that mattered was this shot; more important than all the national and international match trophies of his distinguished career. More than the championship medal once pinned on him by the fabled General Chesty Puller himself. Puller had pricked him with the medal back then, and he felt Ho Chi Minh prickling at him now. Focus. Regulate breathing. Control the sweat; keep face and fingers dry. Pace. Pace. Breath slower—slower...

Then, more to his professional discouragement than to his dread, came approaching footsteps! Here, atop the ridge! They couldn't be more than 40 yards from him. Another three sets of footsteps. Their most logical path would course them to within 5 yards of his tree. His strong, verdant tree. Would it betray him, or hold him safely concealed within its clutches?

How long would they torture him, before they killed him? How many could he kill, silently, before they killed him or alerted the battalion? Could he hit the primary target *first*—and *then* take out the intruders? He would give his life before he would blow the mission. And he would not be captured. He would fight like cats n' coons first, to the death.

He could go out in a blaze of glory, taking The Colonel and as many of his staff officers as this rude, interloping patrol might allow. He could fire on The Colonel, then fling himself down the ridge, tumbling toward the jungle—but in the wrong direction. He could hit his principal target, then continue to hail down on the 3-man patrol with his remaining 4 rounds, then empty his .45 at them as they scattered for cover. That might work.

And there was the old mountain man back in Georgia who once scared off two approaching bear by waiting until they were in his personal space, then letting out a blood-curdling shriek that bolted them back in horror. Yeah, the old Rebel Yell! Might work long enough to scamper a few yards back toward friendly lines. Marine Sniper Ron Szpond, working out of Phu Bai, once stumbled across a VC squad in a trench, shooting half of them while yelling and scaring the other half away—and lived to tell about it.

The Hunter had fought his way out of every category of conflict from ambushes to redneck rumbles. Fast thinking, faster action, swift conquest, and expeditious withdrawal were Hoyle's Rules of Raid, Riot, and Row. He felt himself gearing up to take on the three Commie meddlers. Just for principle. But a higher principle dictated a forbearance of personal interest, in favor of completing the mission for the common good. He was prepared to give his life, if it would save life. But there were also the feelings of the folks back home to consider.

Forget it; he was in his bubble. He hardly noticed as one NVA leaned against the massive tree trunk, to take a glance back toward the selfsame trail. He made a mental note of the sound of one *bo doi* leaning his rifle up against

12

the tree. Then another. Then the third sounded as though he were laying his weapon down on the ground.

Their chattering ceased for a moment. He accepted the likelihood that they were looking up at him by now, discovering him. Or were they planning to pitch camp here! Or worse, were they laying their weapons aside in order to climb the tree, to make it their own lookout!

Was there time? Would their Colonel's *sayonara slug* soon be an obsolete concept? There was total silence on the ground below for several moments. Concentrate. Concentrate. Watch for the shot. Make the window stay open. Make the mark. Was his figure as camouflaged as he assumed? When would they react to him—yell and grab their weapons—kill him? Were they climbing the tree? No, it was the wind. The wind, brushing a branch against another. Focus. Breathe. *Concentrate!*

A momentary memory tried to flash into the bubble, concerning the time he was avoiding the school teacher back in Appalachia, and had to hide atop the school's outhouse. The teacher came to patronize the arboreal amenity, and now Eric was trapped up there. What did he do then? The memory seeped in. Ah, now he remembered. Students were starting to giggle and point at him, and to call out to the teacher.

Hadn't he grabbed walnuts from the branches overhead, and hurled them down at the students—jumped down and locked the hasp on the door—then escaped down the deer trail that led back to his home in Choe Stoe? *Concentrate!* The kill-zone was near prime. *Concentrate!*

Why did this three-man patrol climb up to this unlikely perch? What did they know? Their silence was more unnerving than any impending attack could be. Why so quiet? Were they setting up an observation post? He could kill all three and escape, he was sure of it. One grenade. Or blaze the .45 Old Western style. But he had to get that Colonel first. Packed, primed, and powder dry, he was going to get that Evil Eagle. But why the bloody, mysterious quiet?

Then came the sound of the bo doi's chattering about some amusement or another, maybe some *minh oi* back home in the north. Or how they were hoping to kill many Americans. Their levity, whatever the source, provided

13

no comic relief for The Hunter. Yet he hung cool. Cooler nerves were never so evidenced as those The Hunter brought to bear that dedicated day. Duty reigned supreme. *Semper Fidelis.* Always faithful.

Then came true relief: for suddenly, thank Heavens, they picked up their weapons and sauntered away. Good riddance.

No matter. The bubble was set. And just in time, as the first few NVA came into the kill zone in the trail. Then a larger body of men and matériel surged forth. Some of the little soldiers were pushing bicycles laden down with mortars, machine guns, bags of rice. Men and gear were spaced at intervals, to minimize the impact of potential ambush, landmines, fire missions, or air strikes.

The Hunter visually absorbed and categorized each greenish-gray khaki silhouette, every pith helmet, each insignia and weapon and set of eyes. His senses, now weary, took on nurturance from within the sanctity of the bubble— sort of a *boom-womb* which held the exhausted Shooter in sync with the scenario. Just a moment more—hold on. But all those little men with their big guns. Which one. Which one.

Then he saw him. A slightly grayed officer flanked by younger ones, and encircled by staff NCO's. Stately in bearing and manner, yet bent on an ill objective—it was all over him—evil and energetic. His very expression was one of villainy and contempt. And it needed to be erased. Forever.

CHAPTER THREE

VANISHING ACT

FINGERING the match-conditioned trigger of the .30-06 methodically, The Hunter calculated windage while gauging the most effective tension-release point. Fully primed to lance the Communist boil, perhaps one second remained before the pustule left the kill zone. Then as his bubble pulsated with "all systems go," his concentration was challenged severely by the unexpected approach of a US spotter plane.

Fortunately the plane was at sufficient altitude not to scare the NVA into hiding. But why in the abysmal blazes it was overflying this sector, during the time frame of this mission, was the factor bearing down hardest on The Hunter's reflexive readiness. Had the US forces abandoned him already, his mission and return so overdue? How long since he had broken radio silence? Command probably wrote him off as dead.

Or had Intel detected the late movement of The Colonel's battalion, and called for a fire mission—or air strike—about to commence! The spotter overflew the sector and did not circle back. Perhaps just a VIP shuttle. Or recon mission. Or trainer.

The NVA did not duck wholesale into the trees nor begin a rapid advancement; several did drop out of sight by habit, although The Colonel and his staff stood their ground, turning to observe the plane. He reached for binoculars from a junior officer. The entire column held in place as The Colonel visually tracked the slow plane, turning to his left, then finally a full 180°. And now, his back was toward The Hunter. Full upper silhouette.

Being the true master of the trail and hunt he was, he seized the opportunity to work the interfering plane to his advantage, now that it had become part of the environment; an integer in the savage scene, filtering through his bubble.

As he calculated his shot toward either the medulla or brain stem, abruptly one of the NCO's scrambled up from the ground, standing directly behind The Colonel, watching the disappearing plane with him. The Hunter had already fixed the base of The Colonel's skull snugly into the crosshair sights of his scope, then lowering the muzzle to allow for a range less than the zero of 1,000 yards. He was initiating the trigger-squeeze phase with the utmost sensitivity and evenness, when his reflexes responded in time to avert premature firing.

No time. *No time!* He aligned the scope on the back of the NCO's neck, calculating that the recoil and trajectory would place the round at the NCO's upper occipital lobe, or course along the top of his brain at the corpus callosum. With the velocity and impact, it should pass through the NCO's skull and intercranial matter, instantaneously into the medulla of The Colonel, who stood slightly taller than the NCO.

It was now or never. The entire mission had boiled down to this precise split-second. The pressure valve was opening. The concentrated dynamism would now be animated like a laser!

The Hunter's keenly honed finger slowly retracted the trigger mechanism. Then for a moment the universe revolved briskly around the magnitude of the ominous blast of that .30-calibre canon.

At that precise juncture the NCO had artlessly turned one step aside, as if to give an order to a subordinate. The round missed him entirely, though its hissing, whirring breath compelled him to fall to the ground a second time. But by that time, The Colonel was already antiquated—*passé*—

liquidated. The round had struck him squarely in the occipital lobe, taking the face and a goodly portion of cerebellum with it, like an exploding watermelon.

Within that bloody, microcosmic moment before the report of the rifle arrived upon the ears of the NVA, those around The Colonel heard no more than a brief, solid *thud* coupled with a faint *squoosh.*

The initial reaction of the junior officer had been to reach for his 7mm pistol, shouting at the NCO as though *he* had just clobbered The Colonel's head somehow. Then came the slower-traveling sound of the rifle, by now faint, but audible enough to make the NVA hug the ground like a bear stuck to honey. One man—one precision arm of the US Marine Corps—had flexed forth and swatted down hundreds of combatants.

Next came the typical panic reaction as men jerked in horror at the blood and brain tissue that had spewed onto them, followed by yelling, waving, and gawking foolishly in every direction. There was a clear field of fire for taking out two more, thus pinning them all down as another few were hammered. But there was no time. No good-measure punches. Disappearing—leaving the NVA in astonished humility—their column numb as a hypnotized wino—this would immobilize them just long enough until he could call in the big guns. Now another window of opportunity had to be created: from his window of escape.

Startled soldiers began firing wildly in every direction, vaporizing their confusion in droplets of hot lead. The Hunter had already scurried down the blind side of his tree, a companion of necessity he must now abandon forever. He slithered like a scalded lizard, his leathery belly scooting down the far side of the ridge, in his pre-planned route of escape through the concealment of the bush. He had crawled over 75 yards before the firing began to subside. He could hear NVA superiors shouting orders at their mean little men.

At last, The Hunter broke radio silence. "Thunderspade 5, Bearclaw. Request fire mission, priority. Repeat, Top Priority. Major movement, imminent attack, Operation Stone Bird. Coordinates..."

TURNER

The Hunter waited just long enough to hear vocal reaction from Command, then shut off the radio, listening for watchers in the wood. Then he said to himself, "Aw, shucks, give 'em the works!" as he switched freq's to call in an air strike as well. He had authority to do so; there was no need to avoid Command on that basis. But knowing they would bog him down with frenzied requests for more info, he had flipped freq's on his little radio to reach the Navy flyers who would deliver some much-needed napalm and antipersonnel bombs.

Of course, Command and Intel followed him right onto the other channel, but dared not interrupt as he placed his express-lane order for hot bamboo barbecue.

He was tired and hungry, and in need of rations. Still, he delayed them in the interest of time, moving on and on, pausing but briefly for a good tug on his canteen. Once he was distant enough to move on foot, he crouched low and ran like a rogue from a revival.

Darting through heavy bush, he was soon a quarter-mile from his hide, yet continued to hear random shots fired by probing patrols. The ridge between them was no guarantee of security. Even now, he could hear the gunfire and voices coming closer. NVA were climbing the ridge!

They might spot him from their vantage point above. He could get pinned between the battalion and one of their recon patrols, or Viet Cong counterparts. He crouched low, and sprinted on through dense jungle, vanishing into its darkness.

His cammo facepaint oozed with stagnant sweat. His muscles cramped from loss of body salts. He hankered for a chaw or a morsel of beef jerky, with a covetous zeal. But two more hours of brisk, methodical humping were required before he could reach the designated extraction LZ.

Then he knew he had to pay attention to the detested radio, to guide in the fire mission—and if luck prevailed, a bonus air strike.

Soon the marker tagged the ridge: a white phosphorus round from a US 105mm howitzer, to test the accuracy of the artillery battery. "Correct your fire—correct your fire. Right, 100 yards, sweeping to 300. Forward 100 yards." The radio freq's were pulsating with the powers of warfare.

The airstrike was not far behind. The Navy A-4's were locked onto the trail and jungle beyond the ridge, needing no guidance. "*Dead on, Eagle Claw!*" he advised the winged warriors, as the napalm and antipersonnel bombs hammered at the stalled column with undeniable power and authority.

With all the distraction, he was able to hasten his pace back to his pick-up point; yet ever-wary of lurking enemy eyes. Charlie Cong coveted The Hunter's scalp like a dog wants a hambone. The entire 'Nam was Charlie, and Charlie was the 'Nam. That was an essential fact of life he could never neglect. A mission like this could turn into a submission without notice, like a badger hunt at a rattlesnake roundup.

Command had been angry yet relieved to hear his crackling Scotch-Irish Appalachian accent on the air waves after so much delay. Any misgivings were further mitigated by his reassuring announcement, "Mission complete—*target down.*"

CHAPTER FOUR

THE MOLDING OF A LEGEND

BACK at his fortified hooch at Phu Bai, The Hunter began to requisition the essential military resupply of shower, sustenance, and slumber. But not until debriefing: first at Company, then Battalion, then two separate contacts from Intel. For them he maintained the Spartan exterior, while within he longed for a can of C-rats and a cot—or to plunge headlong into the coldest river and swim over to a shore of beef jerky and fried rabbit, washed down with cold Appalachian spring water.

A privileged few Marines knew of The Hunter's exploit. But the enemy ranks were abuzz with the daring deed. The USMC Scout Snipers were blazing deep scars on the enemy mind, from the lowly Bo Doi privates and VC guerrillas, clear up their chain of command. Ho Chi Minh had personally offered a three-year salary bonus to anyone who could kill Marine hot-shot Carlos Hathcock, who was cutting too many notches, and send his head to Hanoi. And although the US dropped more bomb tonnage on Vietnam than in all of World War II without hitting Ho Chi Minh, Ho was ever mindful of a more personal fear: being surgically removed by a world-class Sniper.

Just who The Hunter was—where he was—"Uncle Ho" and his regime would purely covet to know. *"The scourge of our Struggle,"* Ho would call the USMC Scout Snipers. To their creed of *"One Shot - One Kill,"* one must add the far-reaching impact a single shot could make, in a war of politics and intelligence distractions and social disruption and deep-probing specialized operations.

A colleague of The Hunter, Gunnery Sergeant Carlos Hathcock had routinely found "wanted" posters of himself displayed in VC-infested villages. Intel had even uncovered a plot to have him captured or killed by an entire VC sniper platoon, while they were in the very act of infiltrating his camp. With every clandestine Marine operation, the pressure from Hanoi was tightened all the more. VC observers—even day laborers on US bases—were strictly instructed on what to watch for: Any US personnel bearing specialized weapons, scope-mounted rifles, cammo facepaint; attending briefings or debriefings where the term "Sniper" was overheard; any mention of marksmanship awards or competitions, no matter how long ago, regardless of where it took place; anyone seen leaving or returning with a reconnaissance patrol; or zeroing sniping rifles or teaching scope-mounted rifle technique. They were to be singled out, researched by Communist Intel, captured and tortured for facts about US Sniper operations (variably;) and killed (invariably.)

VC factions had zeroed in on a very important element of the Sniper profile. These were not blood-mongers or even revenge-seekers. They were the most psychologically stable, well disciplined, dedicated Marines who had gained distinction in the most prestigious rifle matches of the world. Based entirely upon their shooting skills and stable adjustment, they were called upon in time of war to fulfill a difficult yet vital need. And they complied, as good Marines would. Those who survived returned home to their first love: competition match shooting. They seldom discussed their Sniper roles after 'Nam. "*But when in 'Nam...*"

The Marine Snipers survived by staying a huge step ahead of Charlie. They honed their craft until it reached mythological proportions. They were tough and wise and deadly effective. Still, they needed an extra element—a Madison Avenue gimmick—to keep Charlie as unstrung as a bow-legged banjo.

The solution: The Phantom. Native informers had gleaned a priceless pearl of intelligence from a budding

21

tidbit of local lore: *there was a Phantom in their midst!* The image was being generated by The Hunter and his colleagues and protégés. The Hunter, by natural style, had in turn built the reputation to the point that many were coming to think of him as *The* Phantom, striking with a precision style yet showing up in so many places—winning and escaping against impossible odds—surely the USMC's Top Shot. The legend grew: Could this Phantom, this Hunter, be the lead-n-leather Gunny Sergeant Eric England?

The USMC wanted no one to know for certain. They protected The Phantom's identity like a goldmine. It was sufficient to leave the enemy chilled to the marrow at the mere mention of names such as *Awick-Ainlan, Cah-lo Hah-kah,* and others. For such Snipers—England, Hathcock, Bartlett, Kozuch, Barker, Bowen—all comprised the phantasm. They brought to bear many years of match-team camaraderie and gung-ho dedication, cemented with range house humor and Semper Fi honor. Neither they nor Minh's Minions could have foreseen the destiny being built all those years, upon the competition ranges, and within the shrine of honor embodied by these gifted Leatherneck buddies. But here and now, where blood was gold and life was more abstract than death, this elite coterie of US Marines began to see it. They worked it to precise advantage.

The ingenuity of the US Marine Snipers in Vietnam never faltered in its service-delivery. The willingness to work toward perfecting and modifying the approach to their deadly task provided a variety of tactics which Charlie could not predict nor hope to vanquish. The native Marine instinct is to rush to the forefront of challenge, meet it head-on with stony courage, and pierce the heart of the enemy with relentless terror. The Phantom of Phu Bai was a natural extension of that quality, honed to a fine edge by the coupling of genius and destiny.

The name of Eric England continued to surface, at important times and important places. The more humble he tried to be, the more admiration he seemed to gain. Fact is, Eric England is as entertaining as mere mortal can be, Georgia mountain coon hunter or no. His spirit is unsinkable and his dedication defies description. The Sniper program's demand for skill, endurance, creativity, and surprise was snugly packaged into his wiry frame, projected keenly by his jaunty persona.

The principal surprise Eric gave his own command figures was his bottomless barrel of surprises. Always a step ahead of Charlie and the Marine Corps as well, he was constantly aiming, forever scheming and drilling, looking for that extra ace that would trump Charlie every time—and circumvent the military bureaucracy just enough to get the job done.

Born and raised an Appalachian coon hunter, it was not at all unlike Eric to awaken in the Vietnam night with the scent of the hunt wafting beneath his nose, some scheme formulating in his on-guard mind for heading off Charlie at some strategic point in the field. Then, grab a buddy or go it alone, taking weapon and wits and reenacting the nocturnal coon hunt, minus the braying hounds and bellowing calls echoing through the coves. Except in the present case, the coons were VC—*Viet Coons.*

Like the intrepid frontier scouts of the Old West, he would play scoot-about with one to three enemy scouts, gathering observation data; planting misleads and diversions in their trails; ensnaring them. And when the info-gathering was done and Charlie had outstayed his usefulness, eliminate him; but only for the defense of decent fellowmen. The sport was in the survival.

A typical mission would be a precision daylight kill from at least 300 yards, though often occurring at 800 to 1100 yards. The hits were not always key enemy officers or Communist officials or spies. The scouting was as important as the shooting. Yet a good Scout Sniper could often distinguish an important VC courier or gun-runner; a weapons or strategy specialist; or a bearer of maps or sensitive equipment. And down he would go.

A bag-limit mission might involve luring several VC out of a cave or spider hole by plugging one, at such a great distance that his cohorts may have heard no more than the sound of their comrade thrashing in the leaves or rice paddy. Then others would emerge to assist him or see what odd calamity could have befallen him, only to join him in silent slumber.

TURNER

The shots were keen and clean. Seldom any WIA's left groveling in anguish. Even fewer survivors left to report on the deadly dealings of The Phantom and his technique of terror.

Many Snipers began to model after the style of Eric England, especially his students whom he often accompanied to the field for the "on-the-job" training segment of Sniper School. Every school approached this differently; some instructors did not go to the line with their fledglings. But Eric would never send a trainee to do an Old Salt's job. And the boys loved him for it. They were inspired to be hard-hitters like him. Hence the birth of the legend of The Phantom of Phu Bai; and the more Eric tried to share the credit, the more it formed itself around him. His phantasmic arms were extending all over I Corps.

Released for some rest at last, he fell asleep in his usual manner of rehashing the mission, analyzing its rights and wrongs, and scheming future "outings." He could now afford to flash back to home, the folks—memories of the paths that led him here to Phu Bai. He could not help recalling the image of the fabled General "Chesty" Puller, icon of the USMC, pinning a Nationals Match medal on him back in 1954. He served in Puller's last command at Camp Lejeune, and it was a momentous occasion in his own budding Marine career.

It was Eric England's first year in rifle competition. He took 5th in the Nationals, then 12 months later moved to 2nd. His bolt-gun scores were highest in the nation even his first year, and shooters were actually betting he would take overall National 1st Place. He had been satisfied with firing top expert in boot camp, back at Parris Island, a raw recruit of 17. Yet within his first year of match competition, his meteoric rise to the ranks of Distinguished Shooter had brought the attention of history's most acclaimed Marine: Chesty himself. From that moment forth, Eric England would never fade from the limelight. He would become the limelight.

In the solemnity of the occasion, Eric stood fast and fixed as he received his laureled leader's attention. But then at close quarters, Eric detected the distinct after-odor of spirits about the fabled Chesty. The gaunt face, the

24

sanguine eyes, and queasy demeanor of the great hero-general readily betrayed the apparent status of a hangover—and a heavy one.

A momentary lapse into this diversion of comical irony, then Eric was stimulated to return to the ominous occasion of decorum—as Chesty pricked him with the medal! Chesty seemed unaware of the injury he inflicted upon the stoic young buck. Both exercised the true spirit of the Spartan as they faced each other in their respective agonies.

"Felt like I'd swallered a hornet!" Eric would reflect in later years. "But the General looked like he'd took the whole hive!"

Eric had found his niche in the Marine Corps, following in 1950 the example of his cousin, then-Sergeant Harry Turner. Harry was 22 and already an Old Salt with three years in the Corps. Eric was 17, bucking without a bridle on his world. Harry had the world in rein by now. Eric jumped on the war wagon.

They were men of the hills. Their Grandpa Nix lived off the bounty of the woods. Growing up in his shadow, they could shoot small game with their great-Grandpa's old musket at great distances, as mere striplings. Tough young lads, they reveled in scooting up and down the mountains through miles of briar patches and over jagged bluffs, in storm or thick of night, with a fresh deer-kill in tow.

And shooting? Their entire life's arena—self esteem—very identity—was centered upon flawless, deadly accuracy with firearms. Forever in competition, relying on well-placed rounds for food, and growing up tougher than aggravated nails, the die was cast for molding the types of legendary Shooters their country would come to call on in time of great need.

Great-Grandpa Jasper Nix was mustered into the 23rd Georgia Infantry Regiment in the Civil War. He was only 15. Joining him were his twin brother, a younger brother aged 13, two older brothers, and their father who was 53. Jasper's woodland skills earned him the dubious honor of foraging and hunting for food, to help feed his ever-hungry comrades. Whether tracking bear or making a fish net of vines, or "commandeering" and running for miles with a honeybee hive, Jasper was a capable middleman in the struggle for essential commodities. And if survival meant consistently hitting small game with a single shot from a smoothbore muzzle-loader, then his battlefield marksmanship came to be a natural extension, where the game was hostile enemy.

Jasper's younger brother, at 13 a Confederate sharpshooter, died in the Battle of Antietam where 500 Rebel crack shots held off 10,000 charging Federals trying to take their stone bridge. But before losing his own unseasoned life, he laid low more enemy than did many Rebs much older than he.

Jasper's son, John Washington Nix, inherited this mountain machismo, and imparted of its essence to Harry and Eric. To them, life was a matter of three key essentials: living the Appalachian code of honor; always finding fresh game for the family; and never missing a shot at anything. Add the inherited ruggedness of Eric's father, the western cowboy; and Harry's father, the World War I veteran; and their constitution was everything the USMC could desire for the positioning of destiny.

Grandpa Nix, who when he wasn't hunting, was training hunting dogs or planning his next hunt, could never have foreseen the impact his woodcraft and superhuman target skills would have not only on these budding Marines, but on the deadly puppets of Communism half a world away: Minh's Minions. Nor could Ho Chi Minh have ever weighed the value of the wilderness skills, perseverance, ingenuity, and deadly individual firepower which the arms of Appalachia would bring to bear.

Eric gives Harry credit for inspiring him to be a Marine, even coming out to the Bootcamp range and teaching him to master the M-1, just in time to fire high expert—and to launch a career which would rank him in history as the world's all-time greatest long-range shooter—and to inspire men to become leaders, officers, even governors and men of great accomplishment. Harry shrugs off the acclaim, returning the credit to Eric, truly a self-made giant of a figure in American history.

As a Combat Scout Sniper Eric England would inspire good men to become better men, and would leave an indelible stamp upon the USMC sniping efforts in I-Corps, Vietnam. Often this meant solo excursions into the killing fields where entire companies of men were averse to go. He was everywhere. His long string of personal victories ran through the jungles and highlands like kudzu vines. But he was unseen. Thus Charlie never knew when this phantasmic death knell would strike, or where—but that strike he would. Or his comrades; or protégés; it was all the work of The Phantom. His reach was growing, grasping, upsetting Charlie's playground. And wherever Charlie's ears extended, the name *Awick Ainlan* was beginning to be whispered with fear.

The Phantom's evasiveness and astounding mobility made Charlie cringe, with a new respect for the American warmaking machine. Such a mystique of mounting magnitude compelled Charlie to dub him "*Ma-Quai Phu-Bai*"—*the Phantom of Phu Bai.*

CHAPTER FIVE

FIRE ON THE LINE

CHARLIE was in the hills and ravines. VC and NVA were fixed on the desolate US Marine base at Khe Sanh, near the Laotian border. They crawled forward and buried themselves, then unearthed and crawled some more. They tunneled. At times they attempted bold infiltration in squad or platoon strength. Their companies were continually moving around in the hill country, poising for any opportunity at savage and mortal confrontation. Their objective was clear: *Erase the Marines at Khe Sanh!*

The business of warfare demanded some fire on the line. Well-placed, withering fire. Charlie was sure to take advantage of the fact that many Marines at Khe Sanh were not hitting the mark. New replacements had lost considerable rifle skills since their training. Massive firepower alone could not infallibly underwrite a sufficient enemy body count, especially when the enemy was fortifying defenses against the pounding, and striking out in a challenging flow of small operations. All too many recon flights and patrols were being necessitated, and some decimated, by the efficiency of Charlie's encroachment. Even in open expanses of terrain his techniques of concealment and infiltration were simply too effective, proportionate to the American numbers and resources he faced.

Yet Charlie seemed to possess a self-image of being dispensable. Under the effects of his army's drugs and indoctrination, or threats made upon his loved ones, Charlie would simply sacrifice himself. The effect ranged from senseless self-slaughter, to sheer terror. After painstaking effort to stealthily advance to within attack proximity, Charlie would leap into a startling act of terrorism, or a poorly backed assault on the perimeter, or a brazen effort at sniping. He was stopped, but only after great expense of firepower.

More significantly, Charlie was probing, testing, gathering data for an all-out assault—a gushing flood of NVA. Chiseling away at the Marines' morale before an attempted bloodbath was another of Charlie's calling cards.

Marines would yell out from their perimeter posts, "Here they come!", and open up with so much firepower, that other enemy elements mobilized elsewhere, under cover of the distraction. Artillery would pound the hills. Air strikes would scorch and re-scorch the scarred terrain.

Or all would be quiet for a time, then a VC sniper would drop a single Marine, demoralizing all within the compound. Or tease and torture with mortars and rockets, amply supplied by China and Russia, pinning men within their bunkers for days and keeping them restless at night.

All the firepower in I Corps could neither foresee nor forestall Charlie's many venomous heads popping up. His insidious influx, stemmed for a moment, continued to eat its way into the free-fire zones like corrosive acid. Charlie needed to be spotted, fired upon accurately, and dispatched rapidly.

One well-placed rifle round could save a couple of A-4 jets a costly napalm run, preserve the lives of Marines to fight another day, and teach Charlie to keep his head down on a more consistent basis. A specialist was needed to get the men of the 3rd Battalion, 3rd Marines shooting Charlie in more significant numbers before he could advance to close quarters. Line Marines needed to be hitting him at average ranges of from 200 to 400 yards. Snipers would pick up the slack at 400 to 1,000.

The specialist selected by the US Marines was Staff Sergeant Eric R. England, promoted to Gunnery Sergeant and transferred directly from the ranges of Quantico, to the free-fire zones of Khe Sanh—to put some fire on the line—and retrain the Marines there to get some blood.

His reputation preceded him. The year before he had won the prestigious Leech Cup as the nation's top high-powered open-sight shooter at 1,000 yards; one of many top honors earned over his 15 years in the Corps. And all-time dominant world scores were still to be earned, if he survived this tour. For now, old match scores took on a new meaning: The time had come to run up the ammo-to-kill ratio.

The first order of business was to visit the perimeter posts. He set right to work with a few brief demonstrations on how to shoot sappers and observers with startling efficiency. Just routine heroics. No one would have suspected he was brand-new in-country. He had run up the body count even before receiving a formal orientation from Command.

"Whatcha gonna do about *that*-un, Mac?" he would churn in his Scots-Irish Appalachian tone. Before the perimeter guards could begin to pop off their usual rapid-fire fusillade, he would draw a bead and slam down a charging Charlie with one round through the sternum.

"Or *that*-un?

"Wh...*which* one, Gunny?" a guard would ask.

"Why, that-un, right up yonder. Got 'im a Soviet spotter scope, too."

"But *where*, Gunny?"

"Just watch that bush." A single rifle report later, and a well-placed round ended the career of an NVA observer. Range, 200 yards. Elevation, 20°. Cross wind, 5 mph. Open sight, service-issue M-14. "Take your time, make your target. If you miss on that first round, *then* you can go hawg-wild!"

"Uh, *yes* sir, Gunny. And—*thanks!* "

"Now, we duck a minute. Hunker down, Mac!"

"Sir?"

"We just flew our flag. Marked ourselves. It's Charlie's turn!"

As the men crouched low, sure enough, an enemy round whizzed over the bunker. Two more plowed into the sandbags. Eric took the field phone and called for directed fire against the far side of Hill 881.

"Your authority?" a voice came back.

"Authority? Why, *hayle*, they's a NVA sniper team advance of there, and a forward observer. A battalion or regiment probably ready to mount down on top of us!"

"Need aerial recon to confirm. No mass movement reported."

"Why, son, if you don't get them 105's hummin' up here, I'll mass-move somebody's..."

"Call sign?"

"England."

"Sir? Repeat?"

"*Gunny* England. Oh——*Hot Shot.* Yeah, that's it. Put some fire up there, double-time!"

"Arty's in the air , sir!"

A battalion runner finally found him, and summoned him to HQ. The Colonel was eager to meet their new celebrity.

"The essential question is this," the Colonel asked. "How do we *hit* better?" He emphasized by jabbing his finger at his palm.

Eric replied with confidence, "Zero 'em. Get 'em zeroed all over again. They've forgotten too much. And discipline them to stay off full-auto awhile."

"Granted. What approach?"

"I can quantify their assets and deficits as marksmen, immediately, if we can get them cracking at some standardized targets at, say, 200 to 300 yards."

"And how do we accomplish that, lacking sufficient space for a range?"

Eric grinned his famous, disarming grin; a catalyst to instant camaraderie. A look of budding doubt was easily erased from the Colonel's face, in deference to the much-needed trigger skills Eric could supply him. Then the hook of respect reeled the Colonel in, with Eric's continued confidence.

"I'll have a miniature range laid out here by 1600 today, and have the first training group assembled by 0700, Colonel!"

By now the Colonel was sharing grins with the NCO. Big-buddy grins. They walked about the base surveying the lay of the land, such as it was. Eric selected a site and excused himself to go muster a digging detail.

31

"Here's the roster, Gunny, if you prefer…"

"Oh, no thanks, Sir. Already got some prospects!"

Eric wanted to pick men by visual analysis, selecting some stout and compliant-looking Leathernecks. His personal and confident approach won the loyalty of the men, up-front. They deemed it an honor to dig a firing pit for him, then to level out the minuscule range and post the little targets; joking privately back and forth about it being custom-built for little Charlie, or for G.I. Joe.

Eric moved about ensuring his precise specifications. He made a few more calculations, nodded, grunted, and grinned.

Next he gathered materials for his little arcade-sized shooting gallery. With the sounds of war for a background, the need to expedite was constantly emphasizing itself. Eric quickly set about assembling little targets to scale, fashioned from C-ration sleeves mounted on bamboo sticks. Drawing black dots the size of a dime for bull's eyes, he inserted them into the ground at a distance of 900 inches, the scale equivalent of 200 yards.

Once a trainee was zeroed "on the dime," he could rotate his M-14's rear sight one or two clicks, and automatically be zeroed for 300 yards. It was all pat and ready. He posted a rotating watch, to protect his "Little Camp Perry."

The night was humming with sounds of gunfire, artillery, choppers, jets—some distant, some too close. The cacophony of combat only served to accelerate Eric's eagerness to get the men through his cram-course, and sic 'em out there, getting blood. He fell asleep running it all through his mind, and continued to play out the script in his sleep. By 0500 he was up and shining. By 0700 he had assembled the first firing relay.

His days as a D.I. rang through as he paraded up and down energetically, orienting the men to the range and imparting morsels of his legendary technique. They were soon in the pit plinking away at the targets, a scant 900 inches down-range.

Eric's natural ability to win loyalty, and hold it, and to dazzle with his wit and keen insight, soon coordinated the entire exercise into a substantial success. Morale soared like eagles. The men wanted to be part of his mystique; they wanted to be Little Hot Shots in their own right. And they began to shoot so.

The Colonel came out after two days to assess it all, joining Eric in the pit. Eric fired first: dead-center, every time. Then he coached the Colonel to a considerable score improvement. Every man got good hits except one. The Colonel asked why.

"He was on R&R until today, Colonel," Eric explained.

The Colonel said to his XO, "See that Gunny England is appropriately commended—a decoration, a promotion— or a choice assignment after his duty here. I'll approve whatever..."

"No, thanks, Sir. No need for that. Still got Final Rounds!" Eric nodded toward the hills above the perimeter. He and the Colonel grinned like they had just qualified for the Olympics.

CHAPTER SIX

THE SKY TRACKER

RIFLEMEN out on the perimeter posts were soon calling their shots with a deadly flair. Eric joined them regularly on the line, imparting priceless expertise and moral support. He frequently applied his own M-14, and .30-06 match-conditioned Winchester, to "show 'em how it's done at Camp Perry." He taught them, above all, to understand that flair comes from a mastery of the basics: to know their target, and know their weapon. Seasoned combat vets sought him out to thank him personally, for getting the Newbies in condition and out of their hair.

Eric then began to train Scout Sniper teams, taking them to the field. Able to weld a cohesive team under the most varied and trying circumstances, his men would follow him to Ho Chi Minh's front porch if he gave it the nod. If all else failed, he could move mighty boulders with a crack of his homespun wit. It held many a discouraged team together at the matches, spurring them on to victory. And it worked upon the mound of misery known as The 'Nam.

Though able to discipline the toughest Leatherneck with the convincing ferocity of a grumpy grizzly, he was just as likely to mow 'em down with that rapid-fire humor. Blended with his outrageous knack for adventure, he was unstoppable.

Consider a scenario: A young Marine private, already being hassled by fellow grunts for his poor attention and melancholy demeanor, appeared on the brink of depression. Up saunters Eric.

"Hey, Marine," he calls. The boy warrior does not look. He maintains a 1,000 yard stare through the perimeter wire. "Lookee here, boy. You hear me?"

Slowly he turns. "Sir—" is as far as his slurred speech gets. His weapon is poking into the mud.

"You got a constipated muzzle there, Mac Marine! How you gonna blow *Charlie's* stuff away, when yer a-stowin' yer *own?*"

Some say it was the first smile the boy had made in weeks of combat. His near-catatonic hand began to clean out the obstructed muzzle.

"Now lookee up yonder. Sky trails."

"Sss—sss—sir?" the withdrawn lad tried to groan out.

Eric looked through the scope of his .30-06 a moment, then said, "Try huntin' like this—by *sky trackin'!*"

"What, sir?" some of the other Marines asked.

"Like trackin' bear, 'cept this time, it's skunk. He leaves his tracks *in the air!* Lookee yonder. See the birds startin' to roost on them bushes?"

"That means Charlie's not there, right, Gunny?" one asked.

"Maybe. 'Cept *these* birds, they're *scavengers.* Charlie's left his odor up there, behind that little rise of sand. If it's a *dead* Charlie they smell, they'll eventually hop down onto him. But if he's *alive,* why, he's leavin' a skunk trail in the sky—his *fascist fertilizer*—and they'll wait for him to move, to check out the manure menu!"

Men were chortling by now. The depressed one grinned, lightly nodding.

"Bird's ain't a-movin'. He's buried his bait! Lob a M-79 tear-gas round up yonder."

"Fire in the hold," a Marine cried out, and a round was inserted and fired. A shattering explosion irked Eric.

"Dang it, boy! That was a frag round! We need to flush 'im out, not keep ourselves mystified! Now, you—"

Then with lightening speed Eric sighted in on a frantically-crawling NVA, trying in vain to escape the burning fragments in his legs. Leading him slightly, he slammed a lead sinker into the foundering carp, who after a few reflexive spasms went limp on the downslope. Then a young, panicky NVA bolted and ran to the opposite direction in a dead heat. Leading him like a two-legged antelope, he took him down in the waist with another precision-guided round, slamming down like an invisible linebacker had just nailed him.

"And that's whatcha call *sky trackin'!*" Eric nodded at the distraught teen-warrior on the shoulder in parting, adding, "And that's how you *shoot the crap!*" The boy's face began to beam. He looked back toward the free-fire zone with renewed spirit.

Word of Eric's latest *tour de force* at Khe Sanh spread like summer kudzu. The Colonel came to the line and asked him to come to HQ.

"Gunny England, a difference in overall battle effectiveness at Khe Sanh is being observed and logged. There is hardly an after-action report that does not mention you, or personnel you've overseen," he began, in his office hooch. He motioned for Eric to take a chair.

"Yes sir, there are some good Shooters in the ranks, and some good prospects," Eric replied in modesty.

"Other commanders in I Corps are beginning to see the greening of the grasses. Charlie is being knocked back. And he is being picked off on the ridges, on the slopes, in the bush and on open terrain. His concealment is seeming less effective, as are his infiltration efforts. What is your principle technique? In strictest confidence."

"Colonel, it's a matter of seeing what *really* needs done, minus the Fertilizer Factor—"

"*Ahem.* Uh, yes—"

"—and what you have to do it *with*. But most of all, seeing what individual men are *able* to do. Things they *don't* see, about *themselves*. And once you show 'em, and show confidence in 'em, why, they'll fight to their last born tooth! Sir."

"Well, you've avoided the limelight when we've tried to write you up for medals. But your reputation in the field—it's apparent that you're not only very good, but you are also very busy! Not that I mind, but—well, the rumor mill says you are, shall we say, an *entrepreneur* of sorts. Carrying out a lot of operations no one knows about!"

"Well, Colonel, if no one knows, then no one knows. Sir."

"Okay, you've got me there. But here's the downside—and it's rotten luck, really. It seems a lot of other commands are eager to have your services!"

"Special Operations, sir?"

"That, plus every unit that has ever heard the word Sniper."

"Most units don't know how to deploy a Sniper Team, let alone what they are actually trained to do."

"Yes. And yet they are wanting us to loan you out. It's that, or lose you altogether, to some other commander whose brother golfs with LBJ, or something."

"Yes sir, knowing when to stay on the move—it works against Charlie, and works—well, adapts to—"

"Bureaucrats?"

"Yes sir. I know for reason!"

"We won't explore *how* you know. But, it's good *that* you know."

"So, where's the first assignment, Colonel?"

"That is generally classified to all US personnel. But not to Charlie. He probably expects you already! Operations are overdue for a man of your abilities, all across I Corps. DMZ, Cam Lo, Dong Ha, Hue, The Rock Pile, Con Thien. Maybe Laos. Maybe North Vietnam. I never said that! You'll probably base out of Divisional Sniper School over at—ever heard of *Phu Bai?*"

The matter of an ordinary transfer could have been revealed to him by his NCOIC or OIC. But the Colonel considered Eric a prime asset, and losing him was a personal privation. Yet the Colonel's loss was Eric's good fortune.

He struggled to conceal his elation over getting out of the miserable dump of Khe Sanh for a while. Just an inescapable slaughter ground whose only diversion was heavy artillery or sapper or sniper attacks. Good men were seemingly placed there as bait by the chief US commander, Westmoreland. "An Army doggie, in charge of Marines!"

37

Eric would groan, wagging his head in disapproval. "Chesty Puller would never have done that, not even to th' Army!"

Yet Eric would never have shirked a post, or fellow Marines in need. In his mind, he was duty-bound to remain at Khe Sanh, Army mandate or no, until the USMC deemed his transfer was vital to the Corps. But to get out of this shooting-gallery-sewer for a while was a welcomed relief.

At first he was choppering out to various assignments, from the base at Khe Sanh. These extended over time, to the point that he had a hooch and circles of buddies at many bases and outposts stretching across the war grounds called I Corps. This was part of the strategy: keep Charlie from pinning him down, like they had almost done to his buddy Carlos Hathcock at Hill 155. And the missions were becoming more extensive; more long-range. It was a key factor in inaugurating the move-about military mystery that would come to be called the Phantom of Phu Bai.

The favored approach being developed was the recon-insertion method. The Scout Sniper or the Sniper Team would chopper out to the field with a reconnaissance patrol. The recon patrol would escort the Snipers to a selected point, leave them, then after a day or more the recon team would be extracted elsewhere, from their patrol.

The orchestrated image gave Charlie the illusion that all US personnel were then gone, which left the Snipers free to deploy their own tactical operations undetected. Days later, their mission done, they would link up again with a recon patrol and be extracted with them. Sort of like human camouflage.

As their Hueys plowed through the treacherous skies of Vietnam, Eric England was forever studying the terrain below. He may be above it for a moment, but was always bound to be a part of it again soon. Every grid as stored away in his mental computer for future reference.

And surpassing all, he was cognizant of unseen enemy eyes in the jungles and ravines and paddies below, a communications network comprised of a thousand pairs of them—following these big green American dragonflies with avid interest and killer instinct—for Charlie, to, was a Sky Tracker!

CHAPTER SEVEN

LACING THE BOOT

ERIC ENGLAND could be a hard man to track down. His love of the woods and natural call to the hunt kept him swapping shadows with the jungles—and Charlie Cong. But then his new orders finally caught up with him: Permanent assignment to the 3rd Marine Division Scout Sniper School at Phu Bai. Another major stepping stone in the Path of the Phantom was being laid. And here were the old shooting-buddies to help shape it all together.

The school was glad to receive him. They knew he was in-country and had made many requests for his transfer. His credentials and reputation caught the eye of the Division Commander, and history proceeded to fulfill itself. Eric was equally glad: for now he got to serve with his hero, G.B. Merrill.

"Sorry to say, the hunting is fine!" G.B. joked, welcoming Eric with a big grin and handshake. G.B. was a top Distinguished Shooter, and hero of the two previous wars. Two decades prior, he had been stabbed through the shoulder by a Jap officer's sword in hand-to-hand combat, before bayoneting the Jap to death. His shoulder still bothered him, but he took it like a Marine. It did not prevent him from competition matches, nor his present duties as a Scout Sniper. G.B. was *of the breed*; a rugged gentleman-Marine—the best kind—humane as well as hardy. And he had many good miles left in him.

Another great buddy, described by Eric as "the most squared-away Marine to ever join ranks," was MSGT George Hurt. George had been the NCOIC in establishing the school. He had written Eric regularly until his recent departure home, describing the action and their need for him there. In all likelihood, official requests for Eric to be transferred to their new program had begun long before he even received orders for 'Nam, and probably were initiated by George.

"Only reason you weren't over here a year ago," G.B. explained, "was they needed you in the Nationals and Interservice matches! Ever since the Nationals of '54, the Corps has had a keen eye on you!"

"Sha!" Eric wagged his head as if shaking the compliment off. "And if shootin' did keep me there, it still got me over *here!*"

Captain Bob Russell had been the school's first OIC. Jim Bowen and Don Barker, long-time Match Team buddies, helped get it started. They essentially designed it. They were told to start a Sniper School—they went to the field with match-conditioned rifles crafted by Billy Savell—and taught themselves the art of sniping, first-hand.

They were top talent: Don had won the National Individual Service Weapon Match the year before. A year later, Jim would win this same honor. All three were on hand the day the first VC kill was made by a USMC Sniper. Don "Boo-Boo" Barker is credited with that 1965 shot which established the presence of the Marine Scout Snipers in the Vietnam theatre of war.

Jim had almost gotten the first Marine Sniper VC kill, going to the field on a "learn-and-survive" Sniper mission, but suddenly found himself exchanging gunfire with a VC at a mere 50 yards. The VC squatted behind a small sand mound. Jim shot him dead through the mound with his Sniper rifle, but the hit did not go down as a Sniper kill. *"Just line of duty,"* Jim would tell Eric.

Distinguished Shooters, the leading shots of the nation and the world, were brought to bear by the Corps against the wiley VC. They were receiving international news and magazine coverage before their tours were half over, despite efforts by the USMC to protect their identities.

TURNER

The Marines had all the big guns: Carlos Hathcock, Jerry Kozuch, Don Bartlett, Norm Chandler, Danny Sanchez, Bob Goller, Greg Connor, Dale Barrett, Neal Crane, Jesse Davenport, Donald Reinke, D.I. Boyd, Jack Cuddy, Ron MacAbee, Dick Scully, John Mesco—the list included the best in history. They were formidable.

And now they had this humble genius of a team-player who would apply the necessary grit to cement this brotherhood of patriotic power—the founder of the Distinguished Shooters Association himself. They had Eric England.

Billy Savell, who would retire as a Master Sergeant to become a renowned armorer for the Federal Law Enforcement Training Center, had actually arrived with a Marine landing force offshore of Vietnam as early as 1964. Then with the coming of 1965, the lanky Corporal made his mark in history in the official photograph of the USMC beach head landing at Da Nang. His job: to create the 3rd Division's first Sniper weaponry.

No sooner than the Russell-Barker-Bowen team finished training themselves in the field as Snipers, than they were whipping into shape a highly professional Scout-Sniper school whose students were lethal units of warfare in their own right. Students were scoring important VC kills even before graduation from the two-week program. New graduates Richard Morrison and Charles Harris racked up 18 VC kills on a single mission. These were "quality" kills: enemy observers, couriers, weapon runners, spies, advisors, saboteurs, killers of Marines.

Never in history had so many talented Shooters come together at once, in such spirited harmony, launching such an orchestration of warring skill. It was destiny at its grandest imparting. And they kept coming: Bill Dunnam, Ted Hollabaugh, Marvin Lange; the best of the best. They whipped the lustre off Charlie's brazen bravado, and let him know the Marines were in the ring.

Phu Bai had long become a crossroads of many of Eric's lifelong pals. Now it was 1966. It was his turn.

CHAPTER EIGHT

CON THIEN TURKEY SHOOT

EVERY job has its "flanking maneuvers"—those otherwise unrelated jobs within a job that fall under the category of *"other duties as assigned."* Forget the official job description; that last line incorporates all other jobs. "This ain't my MOS" was never uttered by a career Marine NCO.

Just as a chemistry teacher may be loaned out to a research project on water pollution, Phu Bai's Sniper instructors were frequently tapped on the shoulder and asked, *"Will you please leave your class duties a moment and go into enemy territory and kill someone for us? We would be most obliged!"* No briefcase or textbooks. No guarantee of return fare. Just a rifle, and all the guts and wits you could carry.

But many an NCO and line officer were heard to grumble when the order came down from HQ-USMC, to get all Marines in Vietnam trained on the M-16 before 1FEB67. Sniper school instructors were not exempt from this duty. But what seemed like a massive interference with Sniper training made a perfect cover for getting top snipers such as Eric and G.B. out to where their eye-trigger coordination was often needed.

Con Thien was a little hilltop outpost just south of the DMZ, in easternmost I Corps. It had been a French fort in the days of fighting the Viet Minh; Charlie knew the site well. US

43

Marines had in recent months held off partial-division assaults across the DMZ, aimed at suffocating and spearheading Con Thien. It was a coveted spot; an otherwise desolate territory unfortunate enough to now hold priceless strategic value.

Artillery fired from within the DMZ and North Vietnam hit the base with accuracy. Tunnel networks full of enemy observers and sappers surrounded the zone. And there were hostile snipers out on the plains and ridges, armed prairie dogs with eyes like eagles and snakelike cunning.

Full-scale US air strikes and fire missions, accented with ghoulish ground combat, had brought a temporary false peace, now taunting the Marines with the shattering disturbance a single NVA sniper round could create. Perimeter guard, routine patrols, aerial or convoy resupply—even latrine maintenance—were often met with harassing or interdicting sniper fire. The Phantom was choppered in to assess the cure.

Eric and G.B. were ostensibly in camp to teach the M-16 to staff NCO's. Any furtherance of their mission was kept under tight wraps. No one must know that The Phantom walked in their midst. At least, not until the proper NVA tickets were all punched and these top Marine Shooters had spurred away into the sunset. Then the rumor wheels could rattle.

Endowed with an eagle eye which had served him well since early youth, when he reliably produced fresh game for the family table, Eric had learned the value of making a good first shot. Any rounds fired subsequent to the first were guesswork. They set up failure and fostered hazard. No, blood must be drawn on that first shot. Make it count. The results paid well.

Eric England was a product of the great outdoors: he literally spent more time in the woods and streams growing up, than under a roof. Hunting on the ridges and slopes, in the vales and coves of the Appalachians, Eric's eagle eyes sifted colors, shades, movement, situations. He could bring down a squirrel with a small-bore rifle hundreds of feet away, through dense forest—or slam down a running rabbit from 100 yards in a field of corn stubble. By his teens, he could visually detect the mere shadow of a deer at 200 yards across open terrain. It has long been said that he could distinguish a bear cub from a black dog at over 600 yards with the naked eye.

Choppering in from Phu Bai gave a good eagle-eye view of several areas posing deadly threat. He looked not at the terrain as a bear or deer would traverse it—bounding over slopes and depressions at a careless gallop—but as a cow or a dog would do, in following the path of least resistance. For this is how most men would also do. In the open terrain between Con Thien and the DMZ were many visible trails. Some were obviously false, diversionary ones. Some were faint and followed gradual slopes;
these were hot-scented trails. But they kept fading from view.

Even with decreased foliage in many local sectors, Charlie was a master of hide-and-seek warfare. Many of the NVA's heavy and light artillery pieces were moved into the DMZ by night, then craftily concealed as artificial pieces were deployed as decoys. Pounding away at these artifices often gave the NVA time to move in a steady stream of resupply, ammo, and snipers. Eradication of the enemy's fire capabilities depended heavily upon the USMC Scout-Sniper on Charlie's turf, up close and sweaty.

At least a dozen rounds of small arms fire struck the Huey as they choppered in. NVA artillery also began to strike the base, only moments after hunkering down beneath the Huey's batting blades as it peppered them with sand and pebbles in its departure. Ducking into a nearby bunker, Eric and G.B. made the impromptu acquaintance of some of the local Marines they were sent to safeguard. The Marines were mostly teens, battle-worn but cool.

"Just daily fare," the security duty officer explained. "They pound us like clockwork everyday, then try to shift before we zero our big guns on 'em. We serve 'em right back, pay the check with a big tip."

"And their—*snipers*—they add a bit of daily flavor too, Captain?" G.B. replied, struggling with the idea of gracing Charlie with the high title of Sniper.

"Affirmative, Master Sergeant. You're work is cut out for you."

"Sounds like a full match relay, all ricochets, all up-range," Eric churned out through a tight grin.

The three men emerged from the bunker and darted toward a guard tower, hunkering down at its base for a moment. Sure enough, follow-up VC snipers popped a few wild rounds into the compound, in anticipation of Marines coming our of the bunkers to survey the damage. A newbie was hit in the top of the helmet by one of the more target-bubbled enemy snipers. He was stunned and could expect a colossal neck ache from the whiplash, but was otherwise unhurt.

After a few minutes the Captain and his Sniper Consultants scurried up the ladder and into the fortified tower. The sandbags covering the tin roof, and surrounding the walls, were ripped by untold numbers of bullets over the years.

As G.B. peered out toward the DMZ with a 20x spotter scope, a hostile round hit the sandbag on which he rested his elbows. The sudden "foof" sent they and a tower guard sprawling onto the floor of the minaret. Slowly Eric raised his eyes to the top ledge of the sandbags and briefly eyeballed the possible trajectory. Then he ducked back down before the shooter could rock another round.

"Just as I thought," old Salt Shooter England remarked.

"Um-hmm," G.B. validated, nodding.

"What's that, Gunny?" the Captain asked.

"Came from over yonder-way," Eric gestured with his thumb, as he rose to a seated position. "I thought I saw a bush a-movin', down yonder in the scrub, atop that little knoll yonder. Through my 'nocs. Nearly 1100 yards." He patted the 50x binoculars hanging around his neck. He prized them almost as much as the old US Army 'nocs passed down in his family since the Civil War. No one was sure when or where they were "captured" from the Yanks, but he was still making good use of them back home a century later.

"What?" the Captain gasped.

"Sir?" the guard echoed.

"Now, Gunny—your rep is bigger than a Howitzer in a spitball fight, but surely you're not expecting me to believe that you..."

"You've seen the little knoll, up yonder 'tween the two higher ridges, Corporal?" Eric asked.

"Yessir, but..." the guard reflexed.

"But what?"

"Well-sir, Gunny, I've pulled guard up here plenty of times, and I've never paid it any attention. It being so little and far-off, and all."

"Precisely my point, Corporal. *He* has paid attention to *you*. Not your fault, though. Just your problem."

G.B. nodded, supplementing with, "That's right, son. The Marines take care of their own! We'll cure your little infestation."

"Whatcha gonna do, Sir?" The guard was all eyes and ears.

Eric imparted more confidence. "Gonna have us a little turkey shoot! No need to crawl after this feller. He'll pop up, and we'll pop him. From right here, on the perimeter."

The Captain and Corporal smirked with contagious courage.

"We're still in Charlie's sights. 1090 yards. Take 'im out, Eric," G.B. spoke with cool professionalism, peering over the sandbags with the 20x spotter scope. Eric readied his rifle like a pool hustler would uncase his custom-made cue.

"That far, huh?" the Captain remarked. "Well, let's see it!"

"I'm gonna rise up to draw his fire again. He thinks we still don't know where he is. He'll clock out for the day, or else move to a different hide, after another two shots or so. We gotta make this a *reverse turkey shoot*."

Eric poked his head up, then stood and shifted nonchalantly about for five seconds, spewed a stream of 'backa juice over the side, then ducked down fast. As expected, another enemy round passed directly overhead, where Eric's silhouette had been briefly but gravely exposed.

"Just as I figgered!" Eric gleefully announced, squatting back down by the men after peering over the sandbags with the 'nocs. "Saw 'im, wigglin' 'round up

47

yonder. Now, we'll just register the site for our good friend, Arty—get a white phosphorous round dropped on that spot, or onto that rock overhang just above him—and let Willie Pete flush the little teaser out like a turkey!"

The Captain got on his field phone and called his commander. A "spotter" fire mission was requested, and within moments the deadly fireball would be enroute. "Arty's party," the Captain grinned as he clicked off.

They stayed low as Eric readied his scoped .30-06. Peeking over the sandbags through his 'nocs again, he did not detect any further movement. Then the WP shell hurtled in, striking within reasonable proximity to the rock overhang to the left of the slight knoll. Soon the burning white phosphorous was slinging down onto the suspected hideout of the taunting turkey.

The NVA shooter leapt screaming from the assumed security of his lair, in a futile struggle to remove the sizzling substance from his body. It spread to his hands by touch, as he ran wildly about the knoll, thrashing in agony.

Eric stood up quickly, got him fixed several times in his crosshairs as he moved erratically, then led him as he lunged to the left. The scope being zeroed at 1000 yards, Eric had to aim at head height to strike the chest, but the turkey kept gyrating.

Following the target's movements for a clean shot, he noticed another NVA rushing up to aid the sizzler. As the sizzler lunged toward the right, Eric engaged the trigger mechanism to slam a .30-06 round precisely through the mid-chest. As the new NVA stopped in his tracks in horror, another Winchester round made true its mark as well.

Then by surprise three other NVA popped up through the scrub brush, apparently attempting to evade the flaming fury of the WP now tormenting their own arms and backs. Running wildly down the slight incline, no perfect head or heart shots could be expected. Yet Eric's "miniature artillery" rounds halted the tide, as two of the NVA went down hard and fast, their chests and backs erupting with a red spew, leaving thoracic cavities where none had been before.

Eric rapidly ejected his brass and chambered a fifth round. By now G.B. was scoped in on the action, taking out the last NVA as he fell forward, drilling a round precisely through the crown of his head. He kicked in a spasmodic, neurological revolt.

As Eric reloaded, he wheeled 20 degrees left and squeezed off another round into the back of yet another NVA who was trying desperately to roll off the hill. He jerked, then slid a few feet downward, leaving a short bloody trail in the sands of Con Thien— *"The Hill of Angels."*

When it appeared the shooting match would be over, and with Marines down below emerging from cover they had just thrown themselves under, G.B. spotted and plugged another, who fell in a one-man wrestling match with terra firma. The round seared through the shoulder near the neck, and the little terrorist went limp, to thrash no more.

Eric pivoted thirty degrees right, as he noticed now a ninth NVA hopping across the hill, Willie Pete burning into his back. With the experience of guided lightening, a well-placed round ripped through his back and chest like a red-hot rivet, squarely between the shoulder blades. He slammed face-down onto the ground, which only moments before had been his unwavering domain. "The Hill of Angels" had been stormed by the Angels of Death.

The men plopped down again onto the safety of the tower floor, awaiting possible reprisals from any turkeys yet unseen.

"Not nice to turn down presents. Especially *monogrammed* presents!" G.B. joked.

The Captain and the Corporal betrayed their utter lack of comprehension at the Master Sergeant's levity, though the humor was obviously appreciated by Eric as reflected in his sly grin.

"A bullet with your *name* on it," Eric explained. They all had a good laugh, though a jittery one for the Corporal, now realizing that Charlie had him in his surveillance so long.

The Marine Corps' top gunslingers had nailed an over-confident NVA sniper, as well as eight comrades who may have been snipers as well, at a range nearing 1100 yards. Marine lives had been saved.

And the enemy trembled at witnessing this deadly power. The Phantom was in their midst—in their camps—in their daily dialogue. *Ma-Quai Phu-Bai,* the Phantom of Phu Bai, was in their quaking hearts.

CHAPTER NINE

THE ROCKET BELT RAID

FIRE POWER unequaled in history kept the NVA hordes in check along the DMZ. But massive air strikes and fire missions, withering machine gun fire and rockets from helicopter gunships, countless recon patrols, surveillance with starlight scopes and electronic tracking devices, even defoliation, could not stem the steady flow of hostile ordinance floating down the Perfume River and its tributaries.

Enemy arms and munitions, especially the deadly 122mm rocket, were being loaded, toted, and floated by night, then disappearing with their couriers by day. In the rolling hills west of Phu Bai was an area called The Rocket Belt. From mountain tops there, the enemy could rain down rockets upon Phu Bai, Hue, and many other US bases with surprise and near-impunity.

Eric and his colleagues researched the problem intensively. They studied suspected trails from the DMZ, and Laos, into The Belt. Eric would seek out every returning Sniper team and reconnaissance patrol for an informal debriefing; quizzed every chopper crewman; pored over every scrap of map he could lay hands on. He made himself as familiar with the lay of the land, as he would have done with strategizing his masterful deer hunts back home, utilizing military maps and plotting every deer track or dropping or tuft of fur reported by anyone within 30 miles. On a typical morning in Georgia, he could give anyone a detailed report on any significant hunting or fishing results within the county the afternoon before.

Now in this exotic death-cloaked dreamland, every bent twig or misfallen leaf could signify going home upright, or feet first. Eric honed his hunting skill to maximize insight and foresight. What was the carrying capacity of the average Charlie? Where would his rest stops be? Or his pickup points in relation to destination? Was he nourished, or straggling? Did he use recon?

Caves, crevasses, tributaries—currents, watermarks, fords—slopes, foliage variation, evidence of belly-trails— these were crucial factors often overlooked by those inexperienced in tracking their next meal. He began to know the Rocket Belt like his own turf. His officers looked on him as a leader in his own domain. More accurately, he created his domain.

"Only way to own the territory, is to know what it can do to you—then do it yourself, first," Eric was known to say. "Know how it can help you, and how it can hurt the enemy. And think like a hunted animal."

It was time to get down to the ground for the hunt. Sniff out the hot trails. Eric selected as his spotter a rugged young Corporal; for the sake of anonimity called "Stone Face." He had been retained for further Sniper service while training in the Sniper School at Phu Bai. He was a Shooter extraodinaire, but most importantly he was at home in the woods, as native as a pine cone, and could tote the load.

Gearing up with light rations of cracker packs and "imported" beef jerky for the combined carbohydrates and protein; binoculars, two canteens apiece, water purification tabs, compass and map, Ka-Bar knives, a .45 pistol each, and a radio, they were ready to pass off another merit badge.

They applied their cammo face paint ritualistically. The Corporal toted an M-14 for back-up insurance. Eric slung his .30-06 nonchalantly and said, nodding toward the awaiting Huey, "Let's saddle up and ride."

They flew with a tight, seasoned recon team, divided into two separate Hueys. Flying inland along the Perfume

River, they surveyed diligently for any sign of VC. Then the Hueys veered off in an illogical course, zigging and zagging at times to become less predictable. In minutes they set down at an improvised LZ, created at some earlier point in the war by a B-52 strike.

The cammo-clad men all slinked off into the dense foliage and inched their way through a valley covered with triple-canopy rain forest. On first entering the bush, the Snipers set up defensive positions to the rear of the patrol to nail any VC trackers. Once they were well into the woods, the patrol took over the defensive role and rear guard, to advance the Snipers into the waiting backwoods.

The patrol skulked about 100 yards at a time, stopping to position themselves for a few minutes, then moved on until some 3 miles had been traversed. A site was chosen for setting up an invisible perimeter, and to crash out for the night. The patrol leader set up a rotating watch. But none of the men were ever more than half asleep, their senses filtering out the haunting sounds and smells of lurking death.

Before sunrise the Sniper Team were left to their own devices, until such a time as they would rendezvous with the recon patrol, who would then escort them to the extraction point. Meanwhile, the patrol moved out to another area to wait and observe, then would radio for their own temporary extraction. The decoy effect gave the Snipers the extra invisibility they needed to advance and hit hard.

The Snipers angled their way cautiously up the slopes as they neared the river. The meticulous vigil for ambushes and boobytraps alone would delete the nerves and energies of the average man. Yet self-disciplined to thrive upon adversity, onward they wormed like turtles with a belly itch. Occasionally Eric would pause to glance silently at his underling, the much younger Corporal, always pleased to see him staying up with him fairly well. A West Virginian, Stone Face was born a mountain man like Eric, and was a real hunker-downer.

They avoided areas of low foliage, sunspots, or heavy layers of dried leaves. Eric selected a temporary hide in the concealment of thick scrub. Skillful use of natural camouflage was among the foremost tactics brought to

53

bear in their singular battle strategy. They manually cleared back some petiole with utmost sensitivity, to create a spotting zone and field of fire.

Scanning the river some 1200 yards out and gradually downward, they began to soak in the picture of such vast hunting grounds, much like Daniel Boone on first sighting the Ohio River and Kentucky. So much turf, so little time. It was like looking for a grain of salt in a sugar bowl. As night approached, the vista seemed to fall like a stage curtain in slow motion—the final curtain, yet in the middle of the first act.

Then within the hour, they heard low Asian voices, behind and to the lower left of their perch. The sound of accompanying foot traffic suggested there were four of them.

"Probably don't suspect we're here," Stone Face whispered. "Do they, Gunny?"

Eric felt he had to break silence, after two days of restraint. He whispered close to the Corporal's ear, "Still, I wish Bob Goller was here. He's trained in Gooknamese. Durn-near fluent, too."

"What I'd give, to know what them little slopes is saying."

"Basically, they're talking deployment of rockets, and how surprised they *think* the *Americans* are gonna be. We'll sell 'em on the counter-surprise business. Bust up their little party before the fireworks start!"

"Su-*prise*, su-*prise*! Who's the Gomer *now?*"

"Shh. Listen. Headin' toward th' river."

They tuned their ears toward the intruders below. They could almost hear their own heartbeats as the intensified minutes—those year-long moments—struggled by. Finally the intrusive sounds diminished, disappearing around the west slope and down toward the river.

With the enemy spotted and moving toward their own kill zone, and remembering the boxed-in feeling of NVA all about him the day he waited to plug The Colonel, Eric knew it was time to advance their position.

"Can't spend another day on this crag," Eric whispered, as calmly as he would advise a fisherman on his choice of bait. "Overexposed. No water, no exit. And a bad place to die."

Stone Face listened compliantly to his esteemed mentor, who continued, "We need to shuttle on down to river level awhile, before sun-up. Let's start working down the east slopes—let Charlie go on through the valley. We might could lay around here and pick off a few of them wild turkeys down in that hollow yonder, come mornin', but we'd miss the prize and we'd get cut off and killed. The game-hens will all be a-swarmin' down at the river. And we'll meet 'em there!"

"I thought the rockets were supplied down from the north. These Charlies are trekkin' up from the south trails," Stone Face quietly noted.

"They've crossed at a bend upstream; I'll show you on the map later. They're avoiding fly-by's and recons. But they'll all be gathering faithfully at the river, Reverend."

As they began their gradual prone descent of the east slope, moving away from the hollow to the left, they could again hear the intruders clamoring up a low, round peak not far ahead of them. To the north, between them and the river, Charlie was setting up his rocket launchers!

The Snipers lay and listened, staring into the dark of night, straining to discern any of Charlie's audible misdeeds.

Then with a startling *whoosh*, fiery 122mm rockets began to be launched from atop the little enemy outpost, some 300 yards from their hide. There was a bounteous supply of rockets, no doubt imperiling many Marines to the east. Eric's desire to do something burned through him like a brush fire. Yet he converted futile trepidation into laser-like concentration, determined to snuff their Commie candles. He needed illumination. Yet from the brief flashes of the rockets, being fired two at a time, he quickly gauged the positions of the VC. There were two loaders, two handlers. To fire on them would be a major gamble, and would expose them for a fight to the death.

Eric decided to break radio silence. He had Stone Face call in as he calculated exact grid coordinates. He knew the peak and had studied it on maps and fly-by's. He demanded an immediate fire mission, air strike, heavy explosive—napalm—white phosphorous—anything. Just get it in the air, and double-time!

"Ranger Red-Eye, this is Smoky Bear Two-Six, spotted live-fire enemy arty in progress. Priority—priority—request immediate string of zippos at coordinates..."

"Negatory, Smoky. Too slow. Arty can get there faster, over," came the response from mission control.

"Just do it! Do something, fast! Compromising position with interdicting fire. Mission lost. Need fire now! NOW! OVER!"

"Smoky Bear, arty will be on-target in seconds. Repeat, arty is in the air. Now get yer tails outta there! Over!"

"They'll get a lap full of them rockets, and *then* they'll think double-time!" Eric groaned out, trying to fix his sights on the firefly-flashes atop the opposing hill.

Stone Face seemed to be praying as he anticipated Eric's first shot. Then he softly clicked off the safety on his M-14, and waited to dispense death in the darkness—and to receive it.

CHAPTER TEN

HELL IN HAND

DEATH wanted its way tonight. For Eric England would take death's ticket before listening to another rocket pierce the night, knowing from the enemy's own viewpoint that in moments, fellow Americans would be slaughtered. Fully prepared to risk exposure, he was further committed to a fight-to-the-finish, rather than surrender to onrushing VC. No time to think about it. Maybe just enough time to shoot some of them.

Stone Face was back on the radio, "Roger on th' arty. But doncha have any napes in the area, now?"

After a pause came the words, "Roger that, Smokey. A returning air mission will also expend any remaining zippos on coordinates. Repeat, fire is in the air. Over."

But it would not come soon enough. The rockets would all be launched, their damage done. Eric scoped in on the flash of the rockets, then moved the muzzle a slight distance to the left—or just behind—the launchers. He methodically executed the trigger-squeeze, ejected, rechambered, and fired again. Two precisely placed .30-06 rounds, directly toward the unseen culprits, had the desired effect.

His fire had to be quick and sure; so far as the cloak of night would allow. He had no "Hollywood silencer." The only silencer a Sniper with a large-bore rifle gets is daylight-distance. A shot from several hundred yards, and the two-eared target never has an audible clue.

But tonight was up close and personal; their position could be compromised. Just two quick shots followed by silent observation would be Sniper protocol. Use of Stone Face's M-14 on rapid-fire or full-auto may have cleaned out the commie cannonade, but would have the Marines in a net within the hour. A Phantom's legend does not live on in captivity.

The launching ceased momentarily, but then another unseen VC took up the battle, and resumed the firing of the 122's. Having drawn no return-fire from enemy positions, Stone Face supplied the launch site with half a dozen rounds of semi-auto fire from his M-14. Then the Snipers laid low for a time. In renewed silence, even at 300 yards, they could hear a VC body tumbling down the steep, wooded peak.

"Sha, first time we've ever been night-coon huntin', and bagged us a bear!" Stone Face marveled.

"Dang sure sounded like something heavier than a coon!" Eric hissed with amusement. "Musta been a *Viet-Coon!*"

The rocket firing had ceased altogether. Surprisingly there were no enemy voices or gunshots heard. Then an explosion of impressive magnitude illuminated the peak. Fire erupted as though a volcano had become acutely active. The massive flames served as a guiding beacon for the approaching A-4's, which dropped a couple of leftover napes to finish off the crest.

The balls of fire outlined the silhouettes of the Sniper Team, clearly profiling their hide. Atop another peak 200 yards to the northwest, heavy machine-gun fire could be heard, making a futile attempt at hitting the low-flying jets. But they were long-gone within a heartbeat.

Hugging the ground until the tell-tale flames abated somewhat, Eric grunted, "Okay—*now!*" The two scurried on their bellies toward the east, moving head-first down the slopes. Halfway down the finger ridge, they paused to observe. No sound or movement on this side. Checking their gear, especially their rifle muzzles and Eric's scope, they continued like suped-up snails, traversing the side of the mountain, edging toward the river below.

Reaching a sharp ridge overlooking the stream, sunrise greeted their low panting, urging their need to harbor up and rest. As Eric took the first watch, all seemed so tranquil along the deceptively pastoral scene. The river was browner and moderately swifter than usual, due to the monsoon runoffs. The murky mysteries of the accelerated flow taunted the overworked senses of The Phantom. It was like a near-dream state, the serenity of the landscape bemired with hostility, hinting at dangers yet unseen. It was always like that, the Nam. Always.

The monsoons were barely over, but left behind a chilling mist in the highlands. The men coveted the warmth of the fireworks the night before. The new dawn lapped at Eric's tired and crusty eyes like a deer at a salt lick. Still, he knew he was good for days yet, if necessary. He keenly observed for variations in shadows, with each progressive stage of daybreak. What other creatures were on the early-morning prowl? Were they refreshed enemies responding to the aurora—or perhaps adrenaline-driven executioners carrying over from the night, as was he?

One thing remained certain: the game was still afoot. Eric knew they were now the hunted, as well as the hunters.

Down along the shore, now only 600 yards distant, at a downward angle of 30°, something odd caught his eye. One of the many clumps of bushes in a segment of rocks seemed thicker than the other native flora. They also gave an unhealthy appearance, as though on the verge of wilting. Closer inspection through the spotting scope revealed that the thicker bushes were not even of the same species as others along the bank.

Eric wakened his partner by the prearranged method: poking at the elbow. This gave the sensation of naturally bumping one's elbow on twigs or stones, resulting in a calm awakening, as often occurs to anyone sleeping under the stars. Having a predetermined tapping-zone also reduced the chance of a partner bolting up startled.

As Stone Face was "lulled awake," Eric was scoping up and down the river. In time, a small fishing craft drifted along the slower waters. Eric kept it under close surveillance through his rifle scope. One old papasan gave the innocent appearance of dragnetting for his next meal. How long would he have to wait for the papasan to show his intent? And if he were VC, he might not afford Eric the luxury of so long a wait; he would simply kill him. Yet until the papasan was a proven VC, Eric had the frustrating duty of defending the old man's freedom—right up to the moment papasan shot him or hurled explosives at him. Then a fat log floated downstream, somehow steering clear of a sandbar while also avoiding the small craft. Eric grinned. One look at Stone Face, and he knew they were both in sync. Nothing brash would serve here. They had to work smoothly on this one.

Stone Face kept his M-14 trained on the fishing papasan. He had hit harder targets with an open sight service weapon. Still, the situation was uncanny. Eric remained focused on the log, which predictably drifted out of the current, and over toward the clump. Then a Vietnamese man clad only in black shorts appeared from beneath it, breathing through a bamboo tube. Another VC emerged from the clump and pulled him ashore. Tied to the blind side were plastic-wrapped bundles, which they began to offload. They seemed heavy. Two more VC emerged from the shrubs, silently assisting as if by script.

Pulling back the phony bushes, one VC revealed a small cave in the bank. Bundle after bundle was being handed up to him. He opened one to examine its evil goods. Eric could see plainly the contents: *122mm rockets.*

"It's now or never," The Phantom whispered with a grin.

"Roger that, Gunny! Hammer-down!" Stone Face replied.

"They're VC, aw-right. Ordnance confirmed. Watch the effect the risin' humidity makes—okay—stand by..."

"*BOOM,*" the .30-06 announced itself, as Eric rechambered, dispelling all doubt with another crack of, "*BOOM.*" Within two seconds he had dropped two VC, whose bodies strategically blocked the entrance to the little cave. They were dead, square through the heart, before the others perceived any disorder.

"*BOOM,*" then another "*BOOM,*" and the other two were dead, one between the shoulder blades and the other through the parietal lobe.

"Dang it, man! That last one was a Maggie-miss!" (A "Maggie" is the universal term on USMC ranges for a total miss of the target.)

"But ya got 'im, Gunny! Clean through the cocoanut!"

"But I was *aimin'* fer the *ear canal!* "

"Well, he *was* slippin' down the bank at the time! Wait—look, Gunny. Another-un, escaping, range six, zone..."

"Got 'im."

The little terrorist tore out along the bank like a buck with his tail afire. Eric led him, but could not hold him for the shot.

As Stoney watched to see if they had drawn the attention of VC trackers, Eric kept scoping for the runaway. The fleeing bandit must be stopped. He might point out the Snipers' hide; he would certainly alert others and salvage the deadly cargo. And he must not be allowed to warn his pals to avoid the hot-spot of the strategic zone around the cave, now that it would be reported by the Snipers as a likely hunting ground.

Eric took his binoculars in hand, and gave the sniping rifle to Stoney. "Here," he whispered. "I'll spot the scamperin' critter. You get to bag this'un."

Each time the VC appeared from behind rocks or foliage, he vanished again as quickly, popping in and out of Eric's view. Working his way along the bank more furtively now, the VC was about to get a go-to-sleep wake-up call. Finally he flopped over a fallen tree trunk to catch his breath, then sat up to wipe his brow. Eric caught him in his binoc's. He motioned to Stoney. For the tenth time, Stoney was initiating the trigger-squeeze sequence. This time he did not have to halt, resuming the finger pressure action in minuscule sequences.

The scope's crosshairs were centered right between the VC's eyes. As the firing pin was about to kick into the primer, the VC removed his boonie hat, his hair falling long and low, below shoulder length. As the deadly projectile arced into the VC's face, his features now came briefly into clearer perspective. This was not a man, but—*a woman!*

Her evil head disintegrated, carrying any Commie indoctrination with it, as the Snipers winced with regret. But as her body jerked grotesquely, their contrition waned sharply to see the Chi-Com pistol and grenades hanging from her belt. As a pistol-toter, she was likely an officer, and the one who shot wounded Americans in the head as they lay helplessly deserving mercy. And they were once again mindful of the many rockets she had helped to rain down upon good men—Marines—eastward of her lair deep within the Rocket Belt.

She was an integer in the VC cult of death, whose humble origins now reached with menacing arms all the way to the innocent families—the lovers of liberty—in America. She was as VC as VC come. Now, she was gone. Bye-bye, Charlie. The Nam made no delineation between the *Charlies* and the *Charlenes*.

"Just a female tiger," Stone Face reasoned. "Mama cobra."

A VC sentry began to randomly fire toward their ridge, from farther down the slope. He was of the breed that liked to call themselves "Sniper," but was nothing more than a green solitary rifle bearer filled with the illusory whims of the "wanna-be." He merely lay in concealment, plinking at imaginary targets all along the ridge. But the true Snipers were already plotting his sudden discharge as they stealthily vacated their hide.

"Do we return fire, Gunny?" Stone Face asked, ending abruptly with obvious embarrassment at his error.

"No, not yet. He'll note our position. Lay still and watch."

Soon Charlie was clumsily wiggling to retrieve a fresh clip, and signaled his own death when he dropped the empty one from his tree-top perch, 70 yards below them. Stone Face cast a visual inquiry toward Eric, who faintly nodded with a grin. Taking Eric's .30-06 and scoping in, L'il Charlie now appeared shockingly up-close and personal. Waiting for the sound-cover of Charlie's indiscreet fire, he lanced the annoying little boil.

They spent the next three days scouting and evading their way down river, forging an illogical route in order to mystify the enemy. They detected two additional places of concealment along the banks, shooting a lone VC at the first one from a distance of 600 yards. Risking discovery, they called the locations due to the probability of caches of arms, and guerilla gathering points. They also mapped VC trails to pass along to Intel.

They were essentially cut off, and on the run. They could not retrace their steps, being committed to advance ever-onward through the unknown bush. But they were always on top and in charge. They played the cards they dealt.

Still, they must find an area secure enough to rendezvous with a recon, or for a chopper to extract them. But to radio in for pickup at new coordinates would bring Charlie down on them like braves on a buffalo.

Thus they brushed on in search of the recon rendezvous point originally agreed upon. This delay they could radio in, using ambiguous terms. But it required an extra two days, on tightly restricted rations and tighter nerves. Sleepless nerves. communicating between themselves with subtle signals and expressions, augmented with a twinge of near-telepathic understanding, this was teamwork at its best.

By the time of recon reunion, their demeanor ceased to reflect "standard-issue." Their faces spoke silently but sternly of much hardship and conquered horror. But victory was theirs. Their eyes penetrated the jungle elements like slim daggers. They had become the Nam.

CHAPTER ELEVEN

THE MATCHLESS MARVEL

DESTINY and Chance present a balancing act in the arena of history. History foresaw Eric England's place within its unfolding scheme. Destiny provided the pages on which he would leave his mark. Within the hallowed Halls of Montezuma, the leaves of time would be festooned with his accomplishments, particularly upon the match ranges of the world; records and standards savored with the salt of personality.

In the words of Sergeant Major of the Corps L.G. Lee, "Master Sergeant Eric England's accomplishments set the standard for others to strive toward. Today's young Marines are continuing to follow in the footsteps carved throughout history by Marines such as Eric England." This comes a quarter century after Eric's retirement from the Corps.

In 1953 the gyroscope of fate had already spun in Eric's favor. He accepted an invitation from HQ-USMC, as one of the highest-scoring rifle and pistol experts during boot camp, to join the Marine Match Team. Though he already had three years in the Corps, at age 20 he was the youngest shooter in the Nationals that year. He placed, and won a

64

silver medal and instant acclaim. Yet his bolt-gun averages were the highest nationally, and several admirers were wagering he would take 1st overall.

Fate was finally dealing him aces. He had fallen into permanent company with the world's premier shooters, and was catching the attention of many important figures who would come to help mold fate's direction.

1954 launched him into celebrity status, taking 2nd Silver in the Nationals, and the coveted title of Distinguished Shooter. Yet this was only the keyhole; doors would open leading to his eventually *founding* the Distinguished Shooters Association.

With his 2nd Silver and gold Distinguished Shooter medals, he returned to Camp Lejeune with a sense of belonging and direction. To add the full seasoning, Gen. Puller took occasion to decorate him personally, acknowledging his welcomed place within the fabled General's last USMC command. Eric had only been in the match circles for one year.

He found his niche; shooting was his world. He was in center ring, and it was in him. While stationed in California a short time later, this aficionado would drive 400 miles over to Arizona just to watch Elmer Keith, last of the Old West shooting legends, compete in an open match. He arrived the night before and was at a local club. He asked the proprietor, "Who is that runty little spike over yonder, with the ten gallon hat and ten ton voice?"

"Why, that is Elmer Keith, the one and only!" he replied. "Don't tell me you never heard of Elmer Keith."

"Heard of him, *and* heard him. He must be range-deaf!"

With Eric's natural magnetism to greatness, he was soon acquainted with this rough-and-tumble anachronism from Montana, the cowboy said to have rocked on his cabin porch while casually shooting tails off cougars and wildcats with a revolver. Elmer was a holdover from the latter waning era of Wild Bill Hickock and Buffalo Bill Cody. He had also inspired Smith and Wesson to create the .44 Magnum. Elmer and Eric formed an immediate friendship and mutual admiration, which lasted all the remaining days of this last old tumbleweed from the trails of the Wild West. They shared the torch of greatness, lighting the path from history to futurity.

For Eric's ongoing career to hold the interest of great figures from the statuesque General Puller, down to the saddle-shooting Elmer Keith, was surely a jewel in his crown. But his motivation was his own, as he pursued his entire career with the gusto of a matador, to the highest heights. He would fire a record Grand Aggregate of .998-45X in the 1968 US Open, a near-perfect and still unbeaten score three decades later. Interservice Match championship teams kept him on as a regular for as many years as he chose to remain in the Marine Corps. He took Individual Interservice Champion. He qualified four times for the Internationals, taking Top International Score in 1969, the year he also won The Canadian Nationals, qualifying for the prestigious Queen's Match which he lost by a single shot, due to gastric interference from a strange folk-food eating contest in which the Canadians involved him the night before. In the 1976 Palma Match, the Centennial of the Internationals coinciding with the US Bicentennial, his firing was of such importance that souvenir-hunters grabbed up his expended shells.

NRA and Olympics officials have initiated an assessment of his cumulative lifetime scores, with present data indicating he is the highest-scoring long-range shooter in the history of the world.

Of twenty-four years in the Marine Corps, Eric spent twenty-one involved in competition matches, winning most of them—the Elliott Trophy, Leech Cup, countless Regionals, Divisionals, etc. He was consulted by top brass and celebrities for shooting skills and strategic input. As a top weapons instructor at Parris Island, Quantico, Lejeune, Pendleton, and Hansen. To him the highest achievements were to promote team unity and equality, and to train young Marines how to shoot to get blood—and to get home alive.

In his appraisal, his 200-plus trophies and medals diminish drastically in value, when compared to the

American families he enabled to receive their sons home again after war's haughty embrace.

Fellow shooters like to remember Eric England as the pal who stayed off fame's pedestal in order to bolster his teammates. Or as the man of honor who insisted on forfeiting an all-time record for the 200-Yard Rapid Fire. He fired 20 X's, or dead-center bullseyes, in swift sequence. It was scored automatically as a 20X since apparently all bullets had gone nearly through the same hole. But on clearing his M-14 he saw a round drop from the chamber—the twentieth round!

As the acclaim rolled in, he took the judges to task, formally demanding a 19X. The panel refused, insisting on making the perfect score stick in the history books. Finally a Colonel walked over and joined in the fracas, bellowing out, "If Eric England says it was a 19X, you can take that to church! Give him a 19X!" He got 19X, but won a higher personal honor. Thus is he truly a Matchless Marvel!

CHAPTER TWELVE

THE SHOW DOWN

DRIZZLY, damp and dreary. The winter monsoons of 1966-67 had arrived on time in I Corps. Unlike the unpredictable torrents of summer, the lighter winter monsoon hung around most of the time, dispensing an almost permanent wetness. Fog could form so thick and far as to stifle strategists and tacticians for days. Charlie took advantage of this natural cover, to infiltrate, shift equipment, or commit general sabotage. The restricted visibility was more of a hindrance to the US forces relying on aircraft, convoys, helicopters. Charlie Cong, and even large elements of the NVA, could strike and run; when one has little, one has to manage little. Even the USMC's ace-card snipers were trumped.

Eric was still with the 1st Battalion, 1st Marines at Phu Bai. Orders came down to move with a large operation up to Dong Ha, smack on the DMZ. They had to move fast to beat the unpredictable fog. Immobilizing fog could provide the perfect set-up for an ambush if Charlie knew they were coming. The VC expected any fog would work to their own advantage, as an ethereal shield. "Like a skunk in the outhouse," Eric would say.

After a mere 15 miles, fog began to form. The shotgun riders on the trucks and jeeps, and gunners on the escorting armored vehicles, felt their nerves jump-start over the already invisible Charlie now masked in a blanket of opaque atmosphere. Soon the road was not perceptible and precious time was lost in guiding trucks back onto the route. About half way to Dong Ha, the convoy was completely socked in. NVA light-infantry regulars assisted by Main Force VC guerillas seized the opportunity to whoop down on them like Indians besieging a stranded wagon train. Slipping through the mask of fog, they observed the stalled Marines and sent word back to their mortarmen. Their riflemen prepared to dispense fire.

The Marines, bearing limited rations and moderate supplies of ammo, pondered their plight. Choppers, even medevacs, could not possibly assist them now. The men were unfamiliar with this stretch of terrain. Visibility was limited to 6 or 8 feet at times. The sensation of having stepped into a slowly closing bear trap clung like a sticky slug.

Uncertainty ruled the day. Sentries were posted, and a watch assigned through the night. Sleep did not come easily, due to a lack of bivouac gear, and the deeply chilling nights of the highland monsoon. Troubled sleep can tug down on a fighting man's spirits like lead weights.

The men, mostly teens, made courageous attempts at morale-bolstering humor. *"They don't guarantee days like this in training,"* one would quip. Or, *"Marine weather, sir!"*

Yet no heartening device served quite so well as to see a salty leatherneck the likes of Eric England, striding with confidence up and down the convoy in a show of good faith. His keen perception and warring skills were razor-sharp, balanced by his cool courage and ability to find levity in the gravest circumstance. His spirit was medicinal.

The heavy rains began to pour in. Eric grinned as he sat in his jeep, reflecting on the many similar nights he had spent in a hastily-crafted lean-to, trapped alone in the Appalachians during a hunt. As young as 12, he had mastered any trick Boone or Crockett might encounter. He was never outsmarted by Mother Nature. He considered her his docile old aunt.

"...and I come outta the woods after four days, a-draggin' that big buck, and him not more than 6 hours dead," he chortled to another NCO. "And the folks marveled, 'Thay-law, you gone four days, and just today shot this buck?' And I told em, 'Why, he's the second-un! Got anuther-un the first day! A little spiker."

"And you were how old, Gunny?" the NCO queried, politely shaking his head when offered a chaw of tobacco. "Why, a shade shy of 14! And they asked real-serious, 'Bear take him from ye?' And I said, 'Naw, I ate him!' And I did, too!" Eric was accustomed to coming out of any storm with an honorable kill. Now the hunt was along the road to Dong Ha.

"A predator's not a-skeered to stalk about in the pouring rain. Game's gonna harbor up, burrow in. But a killing animal's gonna tromp around in the wet, if he's half-hungry," he went on.

He had his buddy's full attention.

"Charlie figgers us for game. He's out tonight, too." He spewed tobacco juice onto the road.

"Really think so, Gunny?" the Marine asked.

"Better reckon on it." Eric shook his head for emphasis. "I know for reason he is. Come sunrise, I'll not be perched in this-here jeep! We're gonna have what bootleg-runners call a slow-down show-down."

Early the next morning two Marine sentries were nearly knifed in their tracks by two VC. One Marine slammed his rifle butt into one VC's head, then ripped him with the M-14, stopping the advance sapper from escaping into the fog. The other Marine gunned his VC as he flung a satchel charge, exploding just short of a truck. The skirnish was on. M-60 machine guns joined in spraying the roadside jungle. Several M-14's and a few of the new M-16's were humming like sawmills. Occasional spurts of enemy 7.62mm fire, mostly semi with some pulsating auto, taunted the trapped men, then alternated and shifted, giving the illusion of many attackers. Marine fire would turn toward the sound, lobbing intermittent M-79 frags toward the commotion.

Then in a hail of enemy automatic fire, two squads of VC and possible NVA managed to traverse the road and close in behind them. Some Marines mistook this new angle of fire to be a separate unit—perhaps an entire company—or a battalion's forward skirmishers—closing them in for the kill. It was impossible to gauge their numbers and tactical strength.

The only certainty was that until now, the attacking force had been principally riflemen. Though Charlie's withering fire perforated the air about them, no mortar barrage or artillery had been directed upon them. No enemy machine guns flared. The Marines began to deduce that this was a VC Main Force operation, only company size, but could keep them pinned down until larger enemy units and heavier weaponry could be brought up. Yet the Marines were rendered unable to call in their big aces: the air strikes and fire missions. Not even reinforcements, by air or land, could be invited. This fight would be a private party.

Time was against the Marines, as distant shouts in Vietnamese indicated other units advancing. Then a .51 calibre machine gun was heard to crank out its first cycles of fire, as its heavy rounds punched into the vehicles. Then for reasons unknown, it stopped. More shouting was heard. The .51 was being brought forward!

"Concentrate fire on the west side of the road," an order was being shouted down the Marine column. "M-16's, fire full auto to the east. Mad Minute—commence—*fire!*"

For a full minute, withering Marine fire suppressed the prelude to an enemy charge. A young Marine lying next to Eric took a round through his foot. The call went out for a Corpsman. Eric muffled the boy's screams somewhat by covering his mouth and whispering words of encouragement, as the Corpsman injected a morphine syrette into his thigh. The young man quietened on his own, before the morphine set in, nodding his head as his anguished look signaled, "Okay, *Semper Fi*, I can do it."

Marines turned about, returning fire in many directions, some shouting, "This way," or "That way!" They faced both sides of the road, mostly from beneath the vehicles, firing heavily and blindly for the most part.

Defensive rounds filled the air with wasted lead. VC would stand and fire in the fog, then fall back to the ground, confusing Marines on the elevation of their positions.

"Aim low," Eric called out. "Low rate of fire! Charlie can't see us no more'n we can see him!" His admonition was reinforced when the call went down the column, "Conserve ammo!" Men near him watched him as he squinted, tuned his ears toward rifle reports, then squeezed off a round or two with confidence. It seemed to be working; at least a few VC rifles were silenced.

"If they ain't advancin', they're either poppin' up and down, or shifting laterally on the little bank-rise. Got good tree cover, too," Eric mentioned to a young Lieutenant. "We got to shift some before they mortar us to death, or surround us."

The LT was listening to Eric, his head making a circular motion—partly nodding, yet partly noncommittal, as though to mask his youthful lack of field savvy. But he kept listening.

"Charlie can't see us, and we got a little time-ration. Just time and cover enough to shift and dig in now. He might remain stationary, but not for long. He'll either charge, or mortar us. Or cut us off when his reinforcements arrive."

"*Charlie's* reinforcements?"

"We can't risk air strikes at close quarters. We'd be sure to lose men. Uh—Colonel knows that, let's hope anyway. Too precise of a shot. And it would only hasten Charlie chargin' in amongst us."

"Y-y-you've actually *called in* air strikes, Gunny?"

"Sha, part of my job! Fire missions, too. Scout Sniper."

"Numbah-wan! Well we gotta do something, Gunny. Colonel must be caught up in a bridge party. I didn't *say* that!"

Eric nodded stoically.

The LT went on, "Can't even get to the radio to talk to the OIC. Can't even crawl to him for a patio chat!"

Eric took his cue. "We need to use Charlie's fog-cammo to our own advantage," he offered. "Evacuate ourselves from the roadway—move the line forward and dig in—maybe in the gullies on the west bank, and behind some of those trees up yonder atop the bank. Take the wounded with us. But we gotta move. Can't wait for orders. Or we'll be a locked-in target."

"Move *toward* the line of attack, and not away from it?"

"Retreat to the east will slang us in a trap, Lieutenant. Charlie's trying to set up flanks there now, according to his shifts in fire. On the west bank we can entrench facing both ways, and still confuse 'em on where we're a-hunkerin'!"

"Think so?"

"Like ducks on a June bug! They'll have a thin line of small arms posted on the west. They may not even notice us move."

"G-g-good plan, Gunny." Eric grinned as the LT ducked a ricochet. "I'll pass word down the column, and you go pass it up. Uh—that okay? And pass it as orders from Battalion, move west, up and along the bank, and dig in. Yeah? Okay?"

"Roger that-un," Eric grunted. "And tell 'em to maintain radio silence about it. *Sir.*"

"Command sign?"

"*Foggy Mountain Breakdown!*"

CHAPTER THIRTEEN

WESTMORELAND WADES IN

"**FOGGY** Mountain Breakdown" had been Eric's theme song as a moonshine-freighting Appalachian Marine, cruising the Blue Ridge roads between Georgia and Camp Legeune. He and Shooter-sidekick Jerry "Kazootch" would stop anywhere, anytime they heard it, as though the National Anthem were being played, and do a little yee-haw knee-slappin' buck dance—once stopping in the middle of a mountain highway to dance around Eric's car like renegade rabbits off their reservation.

Today, Eric's theme song would be a bluegrass battle cry. A grin forming within his memory cells was forced into retreat as he focused on the grave task at hand. Impersonating the Colonel, assuming his authority, was serious enough—unless the maneuver worked out in the Colonel's favor. "They threw *this* bone to the *Lieutenant*," he would remind himself.

They both began to low-crawl along the line as far as they dared to go, passing the order to move. At the shout of "Foggy Mountain Breakdown," some men clung to their roots and then began to crawl cautiously. Others crouched and ran. The screams of men taking rounds had diminished, as apparently Charlie was unaware of the evacuation which had rearranged their sitting-duck gallery. All along the new defensive lines, men were digging in rapidly yet maintaining a silent, low profile.

The encroaching enemy lobbed a few more grenades at the convoy, though causing no further casualties. A VC mortar tube was brought up, but fired only sporadically, then shifted and fired again in order to appear more numerous.

The sudden absence of Marines shouting orders or groaning in pain evidently suggested to Charlie that most of the Marines had been wiped out, knowing they would not desert; and that it was a safe time to charge in among the remaining survivors.

The Marines were prudently holding their fire. At least two squads of emboldened NVA reinforcements ran into the road with bravado, prepared to make their final assault on the stranded convoy. But they could not see any, except for the two dead, into whose heads they fired "cancellation rounds" to negate any chance of their survival. This action resulted in a fierce wall of fire from the Marines, who mowed down anything standing near their two dead buddies.

The two NVA squads now in check, another crept in quietly, but equally bent upon carrying out a full and final erasure of the convoy, and a confiscation of its priceless supplies.

Suddenly all fury broke loose, as the Marines sawed the roadway and low rising bank across from them, with heavy suppressive fire. The fog allowed them to move into more protective concealment, while causing disorientation to anyone attempting to maneuver about within its clinging cloak. Once again, Charlie's reliance upon interdicting properties of nature was reversed by an adaptive turning of the tables—Marine style.

Then two or more squads from the first NVA assault elements charged from close quarters, from behind them, on the Marines' side of the road. Those Marines who could, spun about and returned fire. Some tossed frags. Many rounds were thudding into the trees and rippling the dense foliage.

Hundreds of rounds ricocheted off the vehicles of the convoy. Enemy charges now drifted from the middle, to the front and rear of the convoy, in a flanking move. Orders were being freely shouted in Vietnamese, as enemy began to run amuck within the entire skirmish zone, firing blindly. Marine fire could only be directed by dead reckoning in response to enemy clamor; or in sudden, blood-chilling response to surprise appearances of wild, screaming enemy charging right upon individual Marine positions.

Use of M-79 grenade launchers was generally ill-advised under current conditions, though a few Marines had had time to set up a limited number of Claymore mines. There were Claymores mounted on the sides of some of the trucks, and crates of them lay in many of the vehicles. Eric was especially attentive for Charlie pilfering Claymores and other munitions.

The Marines fired off their Claymores whenever movement was heard or suspected. Such awesome individual firepower helped quench the enemy's passion for the game, as the fighting soon subsided. The fog began to lift somewhat, as day wore on toward noon. Most Marines remained within their places of concealment; there was no real rest among them, despite there being no further Marine casualties. A few NCO's braved potential enemy fire to mozey over and conduct initial damage assessments.

No living could be found among the many NVA casualties. Evidence of several enemy bodies being dragged off was seen in the sand. There were also some dead VC Main Force. It seemed in all likelihood that Charlie had withdrawn, but the Marines kept their guard up. So long as the convoy was stranded, Charlie would probably return. The Marines would have to reposition again. And ammo was sure to run out.

Amazingly, only a few vehicles' tires were shot out, due in part to the Marines having stacked or leaned heavy gear of any sort beside the tires: sandbags from floorboards or hoods, empty ammo cans, even large mess pots. The APC, whose giant tires were filled with foam rather than air, had taken many hits but its tires were fully operational. But enough vehicles were damaged to further ensnare the entire convoy, which sat beached a mere 20 miles from its destination of Dong Ha.

Finally word came down to rearrange the fixed target they had again become: spread out more, advance farther from the road on both sides, and dig in deeply. Each position was alternated in opposite views, forming double lines of defense.

Active radio communication had alerted a number of key command centers, ranging from USMC Divisional HQ to offshore elements, and by priority all the way down to US Army General Westmoreland, supreme commander of all US forces in-country.

The situation was beng constantly monitored, but little could be relayed to the command entities in terms of newly developing insights. The need to suppress the situation from the equally eager ears of the press and enemy command figures was horrendous. The press could spark a propaganda campaign while Hanoi could send entire divisions of NVA onto the site for a claim of victory.

At the convoy, the future was etched out second by second. There were smoldering fires aplenty, and the presence of Charlie lingered like stale breath. There were a few light sporadic light skirmishes, and blind harassing shots from Charlie. Some two dozen NVA mortar rounds were fired, but fell on phantom targets as the Marines had already shifted. Some of the mortars fell in the treetops 40 to 50 yards beyond the west side of the road, suggesting Charlie's erroneous assumption that the Marines were withdrawing even farther west. This gave encouragement, as did the enemy's being strangely low on mortar rounds. But the Marines remained dug in. Some dug even deeper.

The Battalion Commander, a Colonel, conferred endlessly with his staff officers and senior NCO's, in monitoring status and implementing the narrow range of strategies available to them. By now the word was out to Charlie's constituents near and far: "The hunting is good. Come join the kill."

Continual plans for evacuation or reinforcement were devised, revised, discarded. Without flight possibility or a navigable roadway, they could not be reached in the pelting rains and enshrouding effluvium of fog.

"Ultimately," the Colonel confided, "the finest tradition of the Marine Corps will have to be thrown against the enemy. We will have to take a last stand, hold to the end—and fight to the death if need be. Perhaps some can break out, but not until such an order is given. We hold, we fight. If we die, it is for each other."

Matters being thus resolved, the wet and cold and tired Marines were apprised of the limited strategies available, which was really only a confirmation of their own foreknowledge. Still they continued to privately firm up their resolve to make the most of the outlook. The Chaplain kept himself busy as well, by way of priority communications.

On the fifth day, a miracle occurred. A clear patch of sky appeared, accentuated by the sudden arrival of General Westmoreland. In his private chopper, he had seized the brief opening in the damp cottonball atmosphere to assess the battalion's plight first hand. They were down to only one more day's ration of food and ammunition.

"No thank you, General," came the proud Colonel's surprise reply. "We don't need a thing. Our lines of command and commo are working everything out." The Colonel's staff stood stunned at his remark. In the face of death, visited by the most powerful man in the country who could rush in men and supplies in waves, he had simply turned up his proud Marine nose at him.

Westmoreland, satisfied by the Colonel's façade of self-sufficiency, left almost as quickly as he had come, needing to exploit the brief exit slot in the opaque stratosphere.

That night, the order was issued for half-rations and semi-auto fire. The Colonel and his entire command could not have cared less for Westmoreland's magnanimous gesture. To the USMC in I Corps, Westmoreland was said to be a political meddler who used the Marines as bait to draw out the enemy along the DMZ.

The convoy persevered. On the sixth day, the NVA threat subsided as the skies cleared sufficiently for the application of air strikes and artillery fire missions. On the seventh day, they were reached by relief choppers and Seabee convoys, tow trucks, armor, and a security force. Reparations were soon underway to relieve and sustain the men onward to Dong Ha. By evening, nothing remained but empty cartridges and blood.

Intel later estimated enemy dead at forty to sixty, though all but two dozen were dragged off by comrades during the fight. Lack of visible enemy dead may have dampened the Marines' spirits, were it not for the jubilance of not being entirely overrun during six days under siege. In addition to the two Marines killed outright, there was only one other death, due to lack of timely medevac. But one is far too many.

Absent the Marines' intelligent maneuvers and tenacious fighting spirit, the enemy might have pounced upon them as choice morsels in the banquet of battle spoils. The Colonel was never chastised by the Corps for his resistance to Westmoreland, their "Army Overlord." In fact, he rose to the rank of Brigadier General. But he could never find out which brave and savvy NCO had set their saving strategy in motion. Typically, Eric deferred credit to the collective Corps. Whenever asked about his role, he would simply grin, shrug, and deny himself utterance.

CHAPTER FOURTEEN

DOUBLE TAKES

FLAMES from the flickering fire cast a dancing glow upon all the faces about the camp. The profiles and countenances of half a dozen US Marines reflected a canny confidence. Faces bronzed within the amber rays shone with a sense of purpose and secure identity. They were "squared-away" sentinels of military bearing and propriety. Yet they exuded a deep-seated warmth of humor and zest for living which rivaled the thermal comforts of the fire.

Five of the men were clad in olive drab fatigues, shooting jackets, and red USMC caps with a gold "M" on the front. They were the Marine Corps Rifle Team champs of 1962. They came to the Appalachians of northeast Georgia—Eric England's native playground—to camp in serious style. They had brought an enviable supply of military bivouac gear, tents, cots, jeep, guns, ammo cans, rations, everything. To the young boys half-asleep on the ground by the fire, these men were lucky big boys having a big time, the way the littler boys would covet to do.

The sixth man, in civilian clothing and hat, was being hosted as a guest of honor. He was not a Marine, yet he had the bearing of a Marine. Then the boys recalled the saying, "Once a Marine, always..." —for the sixth man was their father. He was Harry Turner.

80

James Harry Turner was an ex-Marine. His boys were proud of that. Eric England was proud of it, for both their sakes. For Harry was his older cousin whose striking image as a US Marine had once inspired him to enlist also. Harry also influenced him to get back in and stay in, after his first stint was up. It made Eric's life. But Eric also made the whole spectrum of the Marine Corps—from the grind to the shine—a bit better for the time shared. These cousins had a long family and mountain heritage which generated a bond of brotherhood and gusto. The cement was strengthened by love of outdoors, sport shooting, and good-natured tales around countless campfires they had shared through the years. To the boys on the ground, these men had it all.

Eric and Harry looked to be brothers. Harry's boys often did a double take as they marveled at the two men's similarities. Eric was a reminder to the boys that their Dad had been an Old Salt. Harry was Eric's anchor line to his home-harbor. Eric was Harry's link to the Marine Corps world he had relished. Their tales—a mix of mountain wilderness adventure and Marine Corps grit—filled the boys' imagination like great gallant floods. And at every outing, shooting was involved: Quality shooting, which inspired.

Tonight was a special treat. The boys got to not only see their Dad and his cousin honor each other and display their good-hearted mirth, but they were also spellbound by these dashing young men of the Rifle Team. They were a team indeed. For their degree of Marine-like bearing, mutual understanding, and dedication, they could not have been more solid or delineated if they had been sculpted from stone.

Eric related with unearthly calm the events the Team had encountered that day. They had tracked a bear and killed it and cooked it on their fire, killed a snake by stomping on it, climbed down blindsided bluffs known to host slipping boulders and stinging scorpions among other perils, spooked a bobcat, and dashed down a treacherous rapid stream to save a runaway jug of something or another. Everything was either done with majestic machismo, or at least recounted with same. Or so it all seemed to the looming imaginations of the entranced young boys.

Then the humor. Eric grinned and cranked out an account of how he had stopped by Harry's folks' for a visit, and on entering noticed strangers singing what sounded like sacred songs. Assuming he had interrupted a wake, he snatched off his hat and slid silently into a seat. Looking about wondering who had passed, and how to react, his reverie was awakened at the realization these were merely Christmas carolers in the parlor!

Eric was hitchhiking back to Camp Lejeune once, with a fresh jug of moon in his satchel. A couple of ministers picked him up and gave him the longest free ride of his hitchhiking career. Unable to open the *corn cache* in their company, he fretted in the backseat, wondering if he was being tormented for drinking, or tormented into quitting. After all those hours, the ministers had to turn off at their parish. Eric was getting out to hail his next ride. He took a double take when one of the ministers asked if he couldn't come in for a "cordial" before continuing his trip!

He told of the famed mountain race driver, Jim Ensley, who despite his sincere good nature was not at all averse to shooting out all the street lights in town prior to leaving for World War II; or for riding his horse into the post office afterward, to collect his "rocking-chair money."

Jim had told him of a time when he was a boy, and was among a gathering by the bedside of a dying elderly lady. The very second she expired, her bed fell! One man grabbed a bottle of rubbing alcohol and downed a huge swig for his nerves, but Jim saw no more as he jumped through the open window and ran like a rabbit. Jim was so scared he hid in the outhouse. He couldn't get out because the door was stuck. He was small enough to exit through the "plumbing chamber," but got stuck there too just as patron traffic increased. Jim would maintain a poker face throughout hours of such hilarious tales. Eric can pose as stoically as any, but always succumbed to hysterical fits of cackling laughter whenever around Jim.

Jim Ensley's passion for Fords was so strong, he was once ejected from a racetrack for an altercation with a Chevy fan. He had to disguise himself to regain admittance. Eric certainly shared this fiery fixation for the Ford.

Harry is perfectly at home with any good-natured folk. Though an educated, distinguished gentleman, he has a manly balance of ruggedness, and a virile skill with shooting and woodcraft, known to few. The drop of Cherokee blood that flows through the veins of he and Eric is a vestige left behind by the very natives of the mighty mountains, whisked away on the Trail of Tears. That a part of the noble Cherokee remains within them to blend with the harmony of their ancient homeland, is yet another double take of the old grand life of those hills.

And on a crisp, cool night by a revealing fire, the torch was passed, witnessed by double partakers of the double take.

[UPDATE: Harry answered "Taps" on January 23, 2002.]

CHAPTER FIFTEEN

THE SNAKE EATER

KILLING a bloody, ruthless foe in the menacing jungles is never a singular act of skirmish. Overt victory is never achieved without dodging the more cunning and covert darts of death. In reserve to the fiery projectiles and the crushing machinations of war, maneuver parasites—malnutrition—creatures of prey and poison—dimensions of contagion and biohazard—these are the unseen armies which reinforce the invisible enemy.

In order to defeat the human enemy, Eric England knew he at times must creep after them like a bug. Living and slithering in the enemy's native sod was hardship enough. Confrontive combat was occasional; yet dealing with environmental barriers was a perpetual military mini-hell. Many a soldier, and battle, have been lost to disease, malnutrition, and a wearing away of spirit by living at a squalid level less than human.

Were it not for the stop-and-go base at Phu Bai, countless heroes would have fallen to the withering fire of hardship. Phu Bai was a large if crude base, offering a few rudimentary amenities to refresh body and soul. A shower and meal were priceless commodities not often enjoyed by those who must work the exterior of the perimeters, who only accessed Phu Bai as a sort of personal filling station.

Operating between the Loi Nong and Dai Giang rivers, Eric had a chance rendezvous with a salty Shooter, a former Rifle and Pistol Team member who was fighting both fronts.

Captain Roger Knapper, who would survive innumerable fiery pits of Nam'ish hell to attain—and well earn—the lofty degree of Colonel, had been surviving in the low-life existence of a peasant soldier. As an advisor to a battalion of the Army of the Republic of Vietnam (ARVN,) his prolonged ordeal of habitat survival rivaled the boundless battles and horrors over which he had triumphed. Eric did not recognize the emaciated figure of walking death who called his name.

"Eric! Hey, England! It's me, Knapper!" he called out.

Eric was accompanying a group of Sniper trainees, weighted down with observational officers on a "field tip," to confirm to the Brass that the school carried its weight—and undoubtedly to give some of the "desk pilots" and "wall-locker-warriors" some field time to call their own. Some Brass would order up such an excursion, and would later write each other up for medals and citations regardless of outcome. And of course many sought the sheer experience of being in a combat profile with a legend like Eric England.

Roger was returning to the bush with a protracted ARVN patrol, leaving Phu Bai after stopping in for long-overdue medical attention. He and his men looked like a remnant of a lost civilization. Ragged, bony, and war-worn, they reeked of it.

Eric was taken aback. He peered into the weathered face of this lone white American among a gang of ARVN grunts, and with much effort finally recognized the vestiges of his old buddy and team mate from 1959 to 1964. Roger was a crack shot so skilled and disciplined, he was once sent by the Marine Corps to Ft. Benning to train *Army* marksmen for the Olympics. His students took away many of the Soviets' traditional wins. It was a moment of professional glory. Now he was an ARVN grunt commander, and looked every bit the part.

"You haven't been out there with the Dog Eaters, have you, *Dai Uy?*" Eric asked, his grin wavering with curiosity. Roger made no reaction to the Vietnamese term for Captain, or *Dai Uy*. He was surely quite accustomed to it.

"Worse than *that*, Eric," Roger confided. "A steady diet of parasites, leeches—and *snakes*. The leeches bite me, I bite the snakes."

"You mean—you been *eatin'* snakes?"

"Oh, never without rice. Just a little, for supplemental protein. Mystery Meat menu. We never know *what* we'll get. Scroungin' for supper, in the most literal sense."

Eric made a radio call and pulled some strings. He saw to it that his old buddy and his men would be outfitted with *beau coup* C-Rations and med supplies. Roger had nearly died in the field, and in the hospital, and had astonishing tales to tell.

Roger Knapper had begun his tour by commanding a company of Marine grunts—the finest. His reinforced platoons patrolled the Mortar Belt around Da Nang, clearing any enemy or weapons within the 3500 meter mortar striking range. They saw much action, dealt with continual ambushes and booby traps, and maintained that invisible wall of defense for the garrison troops who in turn supported the efforts of the grunts.

Then surprise orders came down for Knapper to transfer to the 51ˢᵗ ARVN Regiment as a tactical advisor to one of their infantry battalions. He had done too good a job as a commander of US Marines; now the Brass wanted him to impart his skills to the struggling South Vietnamese allies.

Roger had been warned that the 51ˢᵗ had a worthless reputation. Moreover, his fellow commander, ARVN Captain Hoan, had gone through six Marine advisors already. He was to expect trouble at every turn. Roger went to the field to endure the most dismal living and combat conditions known to this war. All resources would be put to the test. But the traits he found in Dai Uy Hoan would rank among the surprises of his tour.

Knapper was advised that the battalion needed to patrol through Xin Dai Market, the infamous lair of many VC. He was also warned that the patrols always got shot at there.

"Well, let's go get shot at then," he replied, with his typical matter-of-fact coolness. He was an effusion of morale. He knew the best defense: *Charge!*

Entering Xin Dai with a cautious yet steady pace, the ARVN patrol soon drew enemy fire. Hoan ran forward, commanding squads to deploy this way and that, leading a bold charge right up the middle of the road. To Knapper's good pleasure, the Arvins in Hoan's command advanced bravely and skillfully, dispelling any doubts he may have reserved about them. Then he saw the courageous Hoan go down under fire.

Knapper was returning fire and barking orders, looking for a way to get to Hoan. Hoan got up, stumbled into a cemetery, and leaned against a large grave mound as he pulled down his pants to examine his own wound.

Knapper pinned in position, exchanging heavy fire with half a squad of VC, but could see an Arvin medic sprinkling World War II vintage sulfa powder onto Hoan's wound, and applying a large compress bandage. Hoan then got up, and ran ahead to command and reinforce the lead squad.

With the skirmish won and the VC vanquished or dispersed, Hoan was still hobbling around with a gaping flesh wound through his thigh, encouraging and praising his men. Knapper saw to his evacuation, but he was right back on the line in three days to visit and check on his men. Then within another four days, Hoan was back to full duty. Like a Marine. Like one who has tasted liberty and was willing to fight for it.

Knapper saw hope for the ARVN. He may as well, becoming engrained in their world of warfare and survival. He existed with very little American contact, subsisting on meager Arvin rations. Once a week a truck came out and dispensed one helmet of rice per soldier. They were also issued a wee allowance to buy basics, such as fish or a small game hen, to split up and share.

Roger noticed his Bat Boy, or bodyguard-servant, had come up with the cutest little puppy with which all the Boy-sans played. Roger dubbed him Rover-san. That night his Bat Boy brought him a bowl of rice with delicious chunks of chicken.

The next morning Knapper did not see the puppy, and inquired after him, "Rover-san di-dau?" Boy-san replied with a smile, "An com!" (Meal of rice!) Rover-san had spiced the rice. Dai Uy Nah-pah learned not to inquire again of certain delicate matters, especially menu contents—or the status of pets. He also came to develop a taste for many jungle entrées as yet *un-et*.

The name of Dai Uy Nah-pah attained legendary status among the Vietnamese for his Shooter skills, bravery, and loyalty. The natives began to remark that he may be invulnerable, escaping so many close calls and even attempts to assassinate him. On one occasion he zoomed down the jungle road in a jeep so fast, that he drove clear across a defective enemy landmine which did not detonate until he was several feet beyond it. Rumor built this up to infer he was a ghost.

He ran errands alone in his jeep, confident the VC would not waste an ambush or risk exposure on a solitary "ARVN private," as he appeared to be. Villagers would often pick at his shirt or pat his arm, to see if he were real; amazed Arvins did the same after he survived a no-way-out skirmish, wondering if, indeed, he were a spirit. After all, there was a legend going around in I Corps about a spirit-soldier some called the *Phantom of Phu Bai*.

One day he passed a civilian bus, then ran over a huge snake stretching across the entire road. The jeep did it little harm as it slithered on toward a rice paddy. He jumped out with his AK-47 and took the snake's head off with a single round. Behind him he heard uproarious cheering from the peasants on the bus, which had stopped to view the spectacle. Roger made a polite bow toward the crowd, then revved his jeep back to camp.

The Battalion CO came to inform him he was now a local hero in the hamlet. He had killed their most deadly form of snake, a species said to be an omen of many evils. The killer is blessed with tremendous luck; all witnesses are endowed with a portion of same. The CO did not want to miss this vital PR break.

In the hamlet, the cheering natives gathered around to admire their new hero. But Roger noticed a "wanted" poster bearing his likeness, and a reward to any who could kill him!

He tore it down and said through his interpreter, "Good people! This is a happy day for freedom and democracy! Just as I defy those who placed this poster, I warn them of Liberty's defeating power which is come upon them. They cannot touch me or my men, nor halt the course of freedom. *Your* freedom!"

Hearts and faces warmed. He then scratched a rectangle on the dirt, and said, "This luck will never fail me in battle, unless you lose faith. If I fall, bury me here on this spot, to curse the VC!" The usually staid society wept with joy. It was a publicity dream.

Roger Knapper fulfilled his promise in many fights. But the unseen foe of contagion took him down. Too seldom could spotter planes drop him cases of rations. Malnutrition brought pneumonia. And he had malaria. And worms. Eric could only shake his head in admiration, and risk protocol to hustle him some well-deserved grub. They talked of targets and victories, glad to see they were hitting in Nam like in Camp Perry. Parting, they shook hands for luck. They solidified the mystique—*they shared the Phantasm.*

CHAPTER SIXTEEN

CHRISTMAS BY 'STARLIGHT'

"CEASE-FIRE" for sacred days is a concept honored by the US military, but a term not found in the lexicon of Communism. Christmas night, 1966, erupted from a state of holiday truce into deadly Pandemonium. Signs of forthcoming battle were already evident when Eric and entourage were convoying out that day to a desolate Marine encampment known as Chinook, between Phu Bai and the DMZ. A primary bridge had already been blown by enemy demolitions. The Marines were stranded in the boonies, hunkered down and anticipating ambush while Seabees bravely arrived to repair the viaduct.

Worse news was passed along the line: a Marine recon patrol had spotted an entire VC regiment moving into the area. The Seabees worked feverishly in the knowledge that Charlie would take foul advantage of the noble Christmas cease-fire to move into attack positions. Just where he would hit was uncertain, but he was sure to hit tonight, and hit hard.

By the time the Marines arrived at Chinook all units were on Red Alert, and amassing on the perimeter for defense. A Major briefed Eric and the other Snipers, who had come to Chinook to train Marines on the M-16 assault rifle, and the Starlight night-vision scope. They went to the

90

perimeter with the other Marines, zeroed their M-16's for close-in fire, and attached their night scopes.

Preparation for battle was otherwise limited to aerial and ground reconnaissance, though no air strikes or artillery fire missions were allowed unless direct attack were actually underway. Some firing was heard about a mile away, rumored up and down the line to be a friendly recon patrol laying down suppressive fire to evade surrounding enemy. Nothing closer was evident by twilight, but the air was thick with breathing death.

There was a full enemy regiment out there, milling about and loaded for bear. But where would the enemy force hit? Would they diversify assaults, or come in direct waves? Or encirclements? Or driving sweeps across all of I Corps? Or would they simply make ominous maneuvers to keep the Americans unsettled on this Day of Peace, then strike as the cease-fire was winding down? When would they come, what would they do? How long would it last? Would they be reinforced? Would a new wave come after them, to mop up the mess? How would tomorrow's headlines read? Who would die—who would live?

These questions hummed through the accelerating imaginations of all the Marines along the Chinook perimeter that Christmas night of ill will. This would be a night to remember. Or forget.

Charlie, true to form, was seizing the generosity of the Allies. Hoping to take advantage of a lax vigilance, of American kindness in not killing them this day, Charlie's disregard for decorum made for the most dreaded of all enemies. And the Marines at Chinook knew it. They knew what to expect: Possibly being overrun, mutilated, tortured. What if support units were too partied-up to respond to a request for backup? Would politically-minded command figures gloss over or deny the seriousness of mounting aggression until—as in Pearl Harbor—their denial failed to stem the reality of disaster?

The Marine in the foxhole and the bunker would filter these concerns out of mind until the only real protocol was bullet to bullet, man to man. Global destiny has often hinged upon the endurance and shooting skills of a single battalion, or squad, or lowly soldier, somewhere far from home and willing to fight with all it takes to get himself back home.

Tonight the Marines at Chinook knew Charlie was coming, and firmed up their resolve to fight to the last man— even stem the tide of the entire war, if the cards so fell. Their appetite for battle was being honed by Charlie's mortal menu. A good Marine reverses the enemy in his own tracks— lets the haunting din of enemy battle drums thrill and drive him as if they were the drums of his own regiment. The blood warms, electric charges pulse the nerves, the senses focus, and nothing but war matters.

Esprit de corps was the cement. Good leadership was the lifeline. Commo was organized, radios tested, positions manned and checked, pep-talk was passed along by leaders crawling out to their men's positions, command staff ran through procedure; contingency plans were laid for ammo, medevac, reinforcement. Still, it was just another scene from the age-old drama of preparing for the one battle which may come to unravel much of the preparation. That is why a Marine is prepared to be his own leader and the lifeline to his own buddy, to carry out the fight until there is no more fight left. *"One man, one war—one duty to the Corps. One Corps, one plan—duty bound to every man."*

There was not one Marine on the Chinook perimeter on Christmas night of 1966, who was not prepared to fight to the death for his buddy. Still, the NCO's continually observed for any weak points in the defensive line where Charlie might break through, "first-and-goal." Machine gunners and men with Claymore detonaters were especially directed to observe for peak moments and places where such a break could occur.

A universal concern to leaders in battle is the bored sentry who gives himself the rest of the night off, and slumps down to sleep in his hole. And now a strange new subspecies of soldier was emerging known as the Pothead, that influential mix of California rebel and Vietcong jungle animal. Thus stern orders were given for absolutely no smoking, even under cover of ponchos, with harsh warnings against any "aromatic" substances—such as *wacky tabacky*—which lure Charlie like flies to a barnyard.

Eric and his fellow Snipers assumed the role of common sentry without complaint. There was little else a crack-shot Sniper could do by night. At least these few had night scopes, which gave a good 30 yards of vision so long as the skies were not overcast. Drawing on light energy radiated from stars and reflected by the moon, the lenses magnified this light to enhance the visibility of nearby ground objects. A reasonable human silhouette could be easily discerned, though it was not always possible to determine whether that moving body were friend or foe. Final word was passed down: Shoot anything that moves.

Such liberal clearance for open fire caused a simultaneous sense of relief, and yet a heightened degree of anticipation. As time itched by, some men drifted in thought or prayer—it was Christmas, somewhere.

Eric jumped into a foxhole with a young buck Sergeant whom he had been training on the Starlight. There would never be a better opportunity for the "practicum" than in the firefight sure to erupt this night. The man was learning well, and was a combat-proven marksman. But scanning with the night scope tended to leave the user a little punchy after twenty minutes. His eyes were about to get the jitters when he thought he saw something move. He wanted to shoot.

"Movement inside the wire, Gunny! Clearance to shoot?" he asked, in deference to Eric's valued opinion.

"What you got, Sarge?" he whispered back in confidence.

"Got a silhouette. Crawling. Right to left. I'd better fire!" He squinted through the scope, then paused to rub his eyes.

"Here, let me see." Eric took the M-16 and peered through the night scope. Slowly he panned, minimizing movement, his own silhouette kept low.

Then he saw it, too. A human body, crawling in the dark. He flipped the selector from *Safe* to *Semi*, and prepared to squeeze off a well-placed round, the first shot of a pending battle. It had to be clean—it had to be true—

for this advance infiltrator would likely be packing explosives to toss at the Marines, unless stopped. He was close. And he could signal. A perimeter breach! And he could blow a larger breach wide open, or he could set off a flare to illuminate positions. Clean and fast, he must be stopped.

A burst of automatic fire would not do. It may strike unseen positions, and would surely spark a mass impulse of friendly fire. Full Auto could also set off the sapper's explosives. But one good precision shot, followed by an immediate command of "cease fire," could avert a cluster-clamor and save friendly lives.

Eric snugged the weapon in and applied his keenest turkey-hunter senses, preparing for a surgical shot to the VC's center mass. Then the advantage of his harmonized senses paid off as never before: There was an irregularity in the silhouette.

Too long, too high, moving laterally instead of toward them, the suspected VC gave pause for analysis. Could he be an American? Was the world's premier Shooter and Scout Sniper about to go down in history for tragedy via friendly fire? Eric England would never commit a false shot. But orders were to shoot. Senses and sensibility delayed him long enough until he heard the silhouette speak! And he spoke in English.

"Hey, Mac. Gotta spare smoke?" the greenhorn whispered to another young rookie, in an adjacent foxhole. Then the careless newbie slithered back to his own borough.

Eric and the Buck expelled faint sighs of relief. But neither man spoke. There was no need for words. Eric England, the Appalachian hunter who grew up living off the woods, learning to shoot with his great-granddaddy's Civil War musket, had tonight served his country well and in the finest tradition of the Corps—by knowing when *not* to shoot. He also prevented a premature outbreak of misguided fire which would have laid down noise-cover for Charlie's advance.

The tactical confusion would only be the beginning; the Marines would also have been blamed for breaking the Christmas cease-fire. Dealing with Generals, politicians, protesters, and the press would be far more scathing than a brush with Charlie. After half an hour of profound contemplation, the Buck Sergeant would whisper his fervent thanks.

When the expected firefight did erupt within the hour, it broke out on the line and the Marines accurately perceived where to place their fire. The hail of enemy 7.62mm rounds was met with warring skill and traditional bravery. Wave after wave of VC squads were repulsed by well-directed, withering fire. But once the VC discerned several Marine positions, 81mm mortars began to rain in on them. Many Chicom frags were tossed; some of them actually detonated.

The Marines hunkered down but continued to blaze the perimeter and beyond with M-16 and M-14 fire, M-79 grenade projectiles, and M-60 and .50-cal fire. The machine guns for the most part were randomly scouring the countryside, but their wall of defensive fire had its effect; Charlie seemed to be slacking off, even in his mortar barrage.

Falling back, the VC lobbed several RPG rounds into the perimeter. Then came the final, desperate assault. Eric could not resist the mental rehearsal of possible hand-to-hand combat. He drew on the experiences of his hero, Sergeant Major John Boitnott, pioneer Sniper of the Korean War. John also fought in twenty-three campaigns in World War II, becoming proficient in repulsing Jap *banzai* attacks. And he thought of his long-time buddy and NCOIC, Master Sergeant G.B. Merrill, two foxholes away from him tonight. G.B. had been stabbed through the shoulder by a Jap's sword, before bayoneting the Jap to death. Tonight could become a night like that.

Eric's rifle skills had never been put to better use, as the final assault came. Yelping like banshees, the enemy came in a mad charge through the veil of night, illuminated at intervals by muzzle flashes, explosions, and white phosphorus flares. He burned round after well-placed round through the running silhouettes, snarling over not having an M-14 .30 cal, or better yet an M-1 with its .30-06 knock-down power in semi-auto.

Some VC went right down. Some kept stumbling forward, a few breaching the wire, intent on tossing their frags and satchel charges—anesthetized with opium and brainwashing—and fired by demons of the dark world of Communism.

He finally had to fire full-auto at a VC who amazingly kept running toward him with an RPG, trying to get into position for a close-in kill to clear a breach for his comrades. Single shots had knocked him down several times already. Still onward he came, apparently intent on blasting Eric's position or one not far behind him, perhaps a gun nest. But the full-burst slapped him down gutless, while his grenade fired straight up into the air. Exactly where it landed was anyone's guess, so many explosions having occasioned the evening. But at least it did not land in Eric's lap.

By the time the Marines were ducking low in their holes to avoid the strings of napalm being dropped by A-4 jets, most of the battle work had already been done. Thanks to the quick thinking of Gunny England, it was possible to keep most of the enemy beyond the perimeter wire, to make them a target for the napalm. Marine casualties were relatively light as well. The enemy body count on the following day was substantial, though the work was difficult owing to the many VC burned and blasted into oblivion.

Visual acuity, so often associated with a Sniper's proficiency in eliminating his foe, had proven indispensable in saving innocent lives by knowing when not to fire. Saving buddies is the greatest victory any warrior can ever claim. Christmas was over. But many more Marines would live to see another.

CHAPTER SEVENTEEN

DOWN IN THE DMZ

SHATTERING explosives and nagging small arms fire pummeled I Corps with frequency. Quiet lulls between actions were a mendacious peace; few A/O's in I Corps could lure anyone into complete serenity. Yet the aesthetic beauty of the countryside often betrayed the mangled logic of the warfare which occupied it. Seldom could the molested landscape of Vietnam be enjoyed for what it was.

Some men are driven to depravity by the incessant barking of the hellhounds of war. Yet some are plunged into deeper currents of spirit. Whether losing one's merits or clinging to them all the more, men emerge from combat rather changed, within and without, and bear much emotional scar tissue.

The staunch Eric England brought his own internal fortress to bear upon the sadistic pseudo-Sirens of Vietnam. It went with him wherever he ventured beyond the concertina-and-sandbag fortress of Phu Bai. He held his own. He projected a natural fortitude upon the framework.

The recon patrol consisted of young, athletic men, who were hard-put to keep up with the 34 year old Gunny England. They were in the tough-n-cool phase of young warriorhood. They were seriously attentive to the unseen, silent dimension of anticipation. They were mentally gearing up for the dangerous operation which lay ahead. Gunny England, half a generation older than most of them, earned and held their respect and admiration. He was always first at briefings, first one on the flight line, last man on the chopper, and the first to step off.

The men would crack the mask of their collective "cool," at one prime grin or croaky witticism from this uncommon legend, who ironically felt at home among the common. Yet he was seriously poised as they—far more attuned to the gravity of the deadly task before them— deeply concerned with these boys' welfare. He regretted their having to risk life, limb, or capture in the duty of escorting and protecting him, and his student or spotter. They sensed his concern; he welded quickly into the recon team framework.

Before the Huey's jet and rotor began to whine, they would consider it good fortune to be endowed with one of Eric's witty remarks, or folksy words of wisdom, conveyed within the modality of his folksy accent. His intonation, rooted in Scotch-Irish ancestry and modified by Appalachian culture, is best described as a blending of the confident brassiness of John Wayne, the genuine dry cheeriness of Jimmy Stewart, the lilting humor of James Garner; and when circumstances required, the authoritative rocketry of Vince Lombardi.

Cousin Harry Turner, his original mentor and now greatest fan, continued to follow his career closely, and enjoyed describing him as much as boasting of him. Harry is known to have said, "Eric emulates The Duke a great deal. It seems that all *tough, good* guys are rather alike. I mean, John Wayne, Gary Cooper, Burt Lancaster, James Garner, Matt Dillon—and *Festus*—to name a few. Some are actors, some are hot-shot Marines. They all are stars, from the same mold. Eric was born to this order."

Today Eric sauntered up to the flight line with his gear, like John Wayne approaching his horse. The recon boys followed him like faithful hounds. They began to chortle inwardly, gagging on their young-warrior need to remain cool and detached. Yet they were delighted. For Gunny England had just spoken, crystallizing the entire Vietnam scene for their encapsulated consumption. Some Marine's pet cur came meandering across the helipad, aimed southward. Eric's vocal motor whined into gear as he quipped, *"You can always tell which way is south, over here."* Pointing toward the mutt with a jerk of his thumb, he clarified, *"Because Ho Chi Minh's best troops are defectin' right to us, with their rear-ends pointin' north, right at 'im!"*

The men absorbed the tonic of humor as the smell of kerosene, and the hum and thwack of engine blades, filled and stirred the afternoon air in prescient preparation for their descent into hell. They were fully confident, with Eric aboard. The rhythm of the chopping blades beat out a steady tempo on the air, as once again they rose—for a time—above the Hades below them. Refreshing was this narrow slot of time for absorbing the beauty of the emerald forests and white dunes interwoven by many streams; yet now and again scarred with stark terrain denuded by chemical defoliants to expose a few of Charlie's nests. All was not well in Paradise; it was infected.

Then came the slightly sickening sensation as they began to re-approach *terra firma*—some flight crews called it *terror squirma*—knowing their momentary escape was over.

Eric had no spotter to accompany him this day. There was a reason. Everyone knew not to ask. The less they knew, the less that could be pried out of them if captured.

The 3rd Marine Division had been moving from Da Nang, to areas north of the Hai Van Pass, creating a chain of USMC outposts along the DMZ. Beginning with Gio Linh and Con Thien on the east, then proceeding westward along Route 9 toward Khe Sanh, the links included Cam Lo, Camp Carroll, The Rockpile, and Ca Lu. US artillery bases could reach across the DMZ, and to the edge of Laos.

The NVA were taking up hidden positions within the DMZ, and the hills of Khe Sanh. The Marines wanted to secure these hills earlier, but Westmoreland had diverted them. By 1966, however, he had ordered Marines into the deadly area under-prepared, as apparent bait and decoys for the hungry NVA hordes. The NVA were so well dug into their subterranean bunkers, even the B-52 raids could not bring them out of hiding. Many good Marines were slaughtered needlessly. They held their ground nonetheless.

In 1966, the NVA had already hit Khe Sanh heavily and had been repulsed every time, long before the more publicized attacks there during the 1968 Tet Offensive. They had also hit hard to the east, in Con Thien, with massive forces crossing the outlawed DMZ at many key points. Intense US air and arty power, and dogged Marine determination, had turned them back.

Yet the NVA hordes did not turn back along the DMZ, so much as they turned downward, digging in like an army of ants, seizing the very grassroots of the region. Large-scale operations were being constantly planned by the NVA. It was essential to spot and eliminate as many of their recons, forward observers, officers, spies, couriers, or sappers—and snipers—as possible. All the heavy firepower on earth was no match for the surgical precision of the USMC Scout Sniper, when the target was high-priority and clearly seen. None of the bomb tonnage dropped on Hanoi had so much as scratched Ho Chi Minh, though he was constantly taking precaution against any solitary Sniper coveting his scalp.

"We're averaging 200,000 rounds per enemy kill over here, compared to 25,000 per kill in World War II," Eric would explain in his Marksmanship classes. "Compare that to 1.2 bullets per kill for the average Sniper. And 1 shot per kill, for some of us." Even with single shots at individual targets, the Marine Scout Snipers were being kept busy along the DMZ— Ho Chi Minh's ragged skirt hem. Today their mission was secretive, but clear: seek out and eliminate whoever the hell was calling in so many accurate artillery rounds onto Marine positions—from *within* the DMZ!

In a series of diversionary moves, the chopper altered its course several times before banking abruptly, then sitting down hard and fast on an isolated ridge in the westernmost DMZ. The foliage was denser than in some eastern regions, but the crown of this hill was burnt bare by artillery and napalm. Eric would not have selected its high exposure and low tree line. He preferred insertion into heavy forest and undergrowth, as seen on down.

No sooner had the team offloaded and begun their move toward the coveted cover of foliage, than small arms fire erupted from each end of the narrow hogback. The promontory was now a hot LZ, as rounds tore through the packs of two men, grazing one painfully across the small of his back. This parapet, which only yesterday had been rated by Intel as one of the least hostile, was a practically inescapable deathtrap.

"Hunker down!" yelled Eric. "Shag it down to the tree line and set up a line of withdrawing defense!"

As the team leader fell into a rapid low-crawl, he joined in with, "Get low! Hit the trees! Tuck your heads and tails!"

Now the patrol was cut off and under fire. The leader barked orders again.

"Down the grade, feet first! Minimal fire until targets sighted!" was his able directive. With this, he kept his silence, slithering backward down the slope, on his belly, trying to fix on any potential targets up above.

Eric went into a natural scoot-n-tumble, just like boyhood days on the Appalachian slopes back home. He rolled and crawled into deep green cover, finding concealment in a small coppice, setting up a vigil for any NVA advancing up the slope.

The well-oiled team gathered up and formed a tight perimeter in a thicket skirting the coppice where Eric lay. They lay prone in an outward-facing circle, boots almost touching, while strategies were hashed out.

They know we're here, we don't know where-all they are, and we can't get out if we stay still," the leader whispered over his shoulder to Eric. "We gotta move. Confirm, Gunny?"

"Aye-aye and amen. I'll stay scotched in here, and lay cover for y'all," Eric offered. "Maybe leave one man with me, with his M-14. Naw, just leave a '14."

"What objective? Where we gonna go first?"

"Move north *and* south, along this ridge here..."

"Sir?"

"...in two units. Lay some fire toward that crest yonder, *if* you're spotted. Recon-by-fire to nest 'em, *or* to draw 'em out. Then move out smartly, away from any fire.

Regroup your units 200 meters east of the LZ, and call for extraction..."

They were interrupted by an unexpected blast of napalm, from an airstrike apparently called in by the chopper pilot. The blast hit before the sound of the A-4 even passed over.

"Who the blazes ordered that!" griped the recon leader. "Now they've got us like a pin on a map!"

"Naw, just lay and watch," Eric said, nodding southward toward more approaching jets. "They'll pepper all around these ridges, just to divert enemy Intel from reckoning where we are."

Sure enough, within moments napes and rockets were hitting in and around the ridges to confuse and hopefully delay any advancing NVA units, who would execute the recon patrol and its Sniper on sight.

"What a lot of Defense Department expenditure! Are we really that important? Or is it just you, Gunny?"
The leader grinned. But it was the grim grin of death. Eric had seen it so many times before. Eric shot him back an encouraging grin, though it was tough to do when the mark of death was so close to taking over the young man's countenance.

Eric calmly continued, "Move now, before any surviving Charlies get a chance to evacuate this way! As you move, you might be driving a few of them back up the ridge and down the other side." Years of deer hunting were paying off handsomely. "I'll let 'em slip on past, if they head on to new feeding ground. But me and my beagle here will tag 'em if they circle back!" He patted the M-14 in reassurance.

"What about you, Gunny? You're trap-bait!"

"Aw, I'm aw-rite. See to your wounded man, regroup your units over yonder, and call it in—in code. The ridge is ours again, for awhile. Move while the smoke cover is blowing this way."

"Yessir." The traditionally territorial recon team leader couldn't resist passing the mantle of authority to this, their own personal legend—their own secret weapon—Eric England.

"I'll look for any observers up on these ridges. See you on the east side. Leave me a radio. Now, *shift up and sling gravel!*"

Eric knew he had to move before any enemy survivors headed toward his hide. He also dreaded an encroaching brush fire generated by the napalm, working its way down the ridge. He had noticed a stream some 200 yards south as they were banking in for their landing. It could provide safety and a route to follow southward, if not an enemy watering hole.

He watched like a mother hen as the men slyly crept out of position, and maneuvered both ways around the ridge. He felt bad that they had not the chance to fulfill the mission as they were best trained to do. But then again they had accomplished this and much more, in identifying the hot spot for what it was, getting several Charlie fried in the process, and reducing the likelihood that Charlie would be making strategic or tactical use of this ridge again any time soon. And no shots fired. Yet.

Seeing his zone clear of hostiles for the moment, Eric began to crawl steadily until he was under the smoke wafting down the slope. Then he rose and ran in a low crouch, until finding a small crevasse or gully covered with ferns. He eased the muzzle of the M-14 through the foliage, avoiding dirt jams while checking for hazards, then he wedge himself into it, to watch. And to wait.

CHAPTER EIGHTEEN

DEEPER CURRENTS

THE gentle music of the trickling stream lulled Eric into a rare moment of tranquility, each intonation soothing dusty sanctuaries of the soul, urging reveries of his beloved Appalachian trout streams. The shallowness of the noisy little brook metaphysically transformed into deeper currents of reflection.

For a thin moment at least part of him drifted back to the waters of North Georgia, Virginia, Carolina—back to the teeming rivulets which carved the mountain gorges the way memories convolute the brain.

His currents ran deeper still, casting back upon a proud cultural heritage. He pondered his father, sufficiently sophisticated to have been named Augustus, yet affable enough to be called Buster. And his saintly mother, Harry's aunt, Mary Nix England—a wellspring of dignity whose honor he could never neglect.

Mary's sensible character and deep spirit provided the balance to Buster's adventuresome energies and ingenious wit. Eric embodies these qualities, always true to his origins. His sister Edie likewise exudes these strong family traits, within a sparkling framework of femininity. Eric calls her Ruth; he has also honored her with various nicknames through the years, a tribute bestowed on very few. He calls Harry "Cuz;" Harry's son Steve, "Pistol." He has dubbed buddies with fitting sobriquets, but few can claim the distinction of bearing a *nom-de-nique* endowed by Eric himself. And Eric has earned a few handles: Hot-Shot, Fruit-Jar, Ear-Ache, Gunny Crockett; Phantom of Phu Bai.

For a fleeting moment he reflected upon his parents' many supportive letters, little envelopes of love and devotion. The values they had passed on to him were a blessing to his fellowman, since as a warrior his chief war was always against foes of fairness, enemies of the right. He owed his people the honor which they had imparted to him. He must conduct himself in this messy war business as honorably as they would expect of him. He never forsook their legacy, at home or abroad.

Would he have opportunity to show mercy to his enemy? It was certainly in him to do so, granted the chance. But chances were slim. So many of them had been killed at great distances, and for just cause. Still, it was merciful that he took them out with a single shot, rather than to allow them to grovel in anguish.

His was not to reason why. As a warrior and NCO, his duty was to focus on the immediate mission, annihilate the foe or his threat, and not grind down his own warring capacity in moody rumination. He was thankful for his fellow Snipers, men of honor selected for this role based on distinguished target scores, sound psychological profile, sense of duty and human decency, and their country's need for the moment. He drew on these deep confluences of purpose and honor.

Then his thought waves began to flow swiftly back to the Nam; to the hell-trap of the DMZ. He first had to save his buddy Marines. Then he had to save himself, out of duty to his devoted loved ones. They would have to come first, before risking any mercy on Charlie, should the choice arise. Yet he would prefer to go home on his back to mourning loved ones, before he would commit any act of dishonor, even upon his foe. To date, he had not encountered any honorable Charlies, nor any occasion for extending mercy.

He leaned forward to take visual inventory of his own personal DMZ. *There he met his new neighbor, Charlie!*

Lt. Charles was just somehow there, stretched out in the bushes, appearing to be unconscious. A Commie "El Tee"—a Lieutenant of the North Vietnamese Army; a *Ti Uy* ("Tee-Wee") in Vietnamese. He had not crept up on Eric. Rather it was the reverse; Eric had unknowingly stalked up on him like a cat on a cobra. Was he playing dead? Did he "need killin'," in the parlance of the Old West? Was there a margin for mercy? The stage setting was, for the moment, entirely under his direction—in a scene due to change. He was both captor and captive.

How long he had lain there was uncertain. His slim green haversack laid against a tree, a courier style of bag suggesting data and documents. His pistol belt hung from a low, stubby branch. His uniform barely showed through the bushes, but his inanimate face and cheaply made insignia were clearly visible.

Eric inched forward for a better look. There was a crudely patched head wound. His uniform was scorched in places. So, he had been with the Marines all along, then singed by the brink of the blast, and likely got a concussion from the shock wave. He had tried to evacuate the ridge with his priceless bag of information, collapsing by the little stream where he had stopped to cleanse his wound and replenish body fluids.

Fate had delivered Ti Uy Charlie into his hands. He owed it to Fate to make his move; his obligation to Honor and the Corps was equally present. From Charlie's mere presence at the water, Eric could deduce that the site was known to other *Bo Doi's* on the hill. Ti Uy Charlie could alert them! Eric needed to seize his captive if he were actually still alive. He could use him as a hostage, if the script ran sour. If surrounded, there would be no way out, no stage door exit; only a fight to the death.

Thinking fast, Eric crawled out onto a flat rock in midstream, using the M-14 barrel to slowly unhook the pistol belt from the tree. Its contents, if not booby trapped, were the essential objective. If going down in a shootout, he could at least destroy the contents and limit the NVA's

106

effectiveness in this sector; or radio in as much of its facts as he could make out. But he had to have the bag first, without a struggle.

Unhitching the bag from the tree, it was weightier than it looked. Binoculars? Booby-trap bomb? It slid slowly down the rifle, by its strap. Easing the flap open, he was relieved to see no wires or triggering devices—only a goldmine of maps and documents, and notes scribbled on the dates of a calendar.

Then came the sound of an approaching Huey from a southerly direction. Charlie lay between Eric and the chopper's intersect vector. The familiar noise, which VC called "Thundering Death," startled El-Tee Charlie awake! Eric's eyes zeroed intensely on his enemy's frozen gaze. Little Chuck had arisen from stunned bliss, into a waking nightmare. Teetering on an acute anxiety attack, Eric thought for sure this quarry may just seize up and die, like a mouse by a mongoose.

Eric slung the captured loot over his shoulder, gesturing for silence, raising finger to lips and muzzle toward enemy. The muffling of the chopper, once close, could handily cover the sound of an execution shot. Charlie could also shout to his comrades any second, before the Huey closed in to drown him out. The balance of Fate was never so equated. In whose favor it would dip would be determined within a heartbeat.

He could try to knock Charlie out. But if they fell to a struggle, he might wrest a weapon from him. Eric would be exonerated for shooting him outright, to protect the patrol and the captured intelligence, if only that danged chopper wold hasten its arrival.

Charlie could bolt and run; Eric would have to charge after him until in shooting sight; blowing his cover and impeding his own escape. Drawing on the deeper currents of his heritage, his greater instinct was to take Charlie alive. After all, who would remember this moment when they were both old men?

Eric slung his .30-06 and stepped on over the stream, lifting Charlie by the collar. He used a green vine to bind his hands behind his back, then took Charlie's pistol belt to bind his arms to his waist—minus the pistol. Then pointing obliquely up the hill, he commanded, *"Di-di! Mau-mau!"*

His captive complied, seeming grateful to still have his life, at least for a few unpredictable moments. After all, he must have folks and friends a few hundred miles to the north—a *minh oi* waiting for him in Hanoi—some reason to live. The enemy until now had never seemed so human as this little officer. He seemed so unlike the peasant guerillas and the more savage among the NVA regulars. Eric could not help but think of his great-grand uncle who as a teenage Confederate soldier had survived a Union prisoner-of-war camp every bit as brutal as Andersonville.

But despite that boy's man-sized troubles, how great was the value of that son surviving to return home, after his 13 year old brother had been killed at Sharpsburg, and another aged 15 had died in Virginia. It is always good for a soldier to come home, if he can come home.

Eric sensed by now there were no remaining NVA close by. The recon team did not even have to fire a shot as the unit now regrouped around the knoll, to the east where the sharp ridge hipped out in a round rise. And Charlie did not cry out at all. By now his own comrades were as foreboding as his captors.

Eric prodded him on up the incline at an angle. The chopper grew thunderous as it sped toward the new extraction point. Eric knew they had to hustle around the ridge, or risk getting left. It was still too hairy to cut across open terrain at the top; he listened for NVA firing on the Huey; there were none. With the noise, they doubled their pace through the brush, staying in the tree line, ever-wary of impending AK-47 bursts or Chicom frags.

How long could the Huey wait for him? He would not imperil the men if cut off. He broke radio silence to announce, *"I'm a-comin'—gotta prisoner. Git gone if ya have to!"*

Charlie glanced back at him, expressing an understanding of his concern. Then Charlie blurted out,

"Come! Can go!"

"Huh?" Eric answered, panting lightly.

"NVA, all gone. Go up! Hurry—can go! Up now! Me, not can go back. You unna-stan' ?"

"You know, I believe I do!" Eric nodded, and they raced uphill and burst from the tree line, and across the burnt crest. Then galloping down the far side they almost fell into the arms of the recon, with Eric hollering, *"P-O-W. Hold yer fire!"*

Pulling Charlie into the Huey, they were aloft in a heartbeat. Ashes swirled up from the rotor-wash. Eric studied the DMZ, rifle at the ready, as the green bird zipped toward South Vietnam. Turning to look at the men, he was surprised at their smirks.

"He's no ten-point buck," he said with a grin, "but my ammo-to-kill ratio is the lowest on season record!"

The men struggled to choke down an erupting laugh. A couple bellowed out loud. The man with the searing back wound laughed until he yelped with pain.

One man kicked at Charlie, snarling, "Yeah, ya little fawn! Without them Chink weapons, you're nothin' but a scavenger!"

Eric shook his head. He gave his POW a sip from his canteen. No blood this day. Charlie got away with his life. But Eric, too, felt he had gained something far greater than mortal life. He felt a surge of heritage coursing his spiritual veins. And he felt sure the folks back home would have liked it that way.

CHAPTER NINETEEN

THUNDER ROAD

ERIC ENGLAND has been said by some to be invincible; impervious to peril. To be sure, he is a rugged paragon, and has survived deathly snares and hardship not only in battle, but on the home front as well. He grew up scaling or scooting down hazardous mountain crags, in heavy storms or cloaked by night—often with a fresh deer kill over his shoulder—utterly defying discomforts and death's sneering hot breath. He could probably grin a bear down. For certain, he has sneered back at many deathly challenges to befall his path. A routine rugged experience for Eric would likely kill the average man.

Nature's wily ways were his youthful domain. Still, technological adventures began to appeal to him as he developed into the teen years. Growing up in the 1930's and 40's, especially in a remote area, never was the universal bond between man and motor more firmly rooted. Speed, style, and performance were secondary only to the actual model of car to which a young man swore allegiance. Track performances of professional race drivers were followed fastidiously. A great many race circuit drivers had acquired their skill through the "apprenticeship" of running bootleg.

The derring-do of some mountain bootleggers was especially fabled.

Eric was already mostly man, years before he was old enough to drive. And it did not take him long behind the wheel, before he could maneuver the mountain passes at death-defying velocity. He would grin like a puppy in a butcher shop, rounding curves at three and four times the limit, and leave the bragging of the event to any passengers who did not faint.

Some bootleg runners had devices installed in their cars to impede the vehicles of pursuing lawmen, which would spray the road with oil, or blanket it with tacks. There were also "blockers" who maneuvered their cars in front of the lawmen as a decoy.

Though Eric never made such illicit use of a vehicle, he nonetheless viewed dare-devil driving as an essential rite of passage into manhood, as did his contemporaries. The preceding generation were content to emulate the cowboy heroes of silent films. Eric's peers were into speed and performance. Ironically, many never survived this "manly" fascination long enough to reach manhood.

Eric took note of one notorious runner who could negotiate 25 mph curves at 100 mph, or evade hot pursuit by jumping ditches and fleeing through fields literally with the speed of a crop duster, then escaping on mountain backroads and hidden roads.

Eric liked his cars hot and fast: he once turned down the purchase of a car simply because it would not go over 140 mph. But if he ever had occasion to haul any white lightenin', it was probably done so nonchalantly that he waved and grinned at any lawmen he met along the road. He probably stopped and pulled a cork with some of them. (He never met a stranger in those hills.) But any sporty driving was, for him, purely recreational. His style was jaunty: fill an old A-Model Ford with jars of "mountain tonic," show up for the Nationals at Camp Perry and parade it around, then hand out jars to the amused Shooters.

Eric was, and remains, a Ford man. In his youth, a person was usually either a Ford or a Chevy man. The distinction was as real as one's political affiliation. To see a family with both a Ford and a Chevy in the yard was usually a sure sign of domestic discord.

He always favored the Thunderbird. He has owned a few, and drives a hot red one today. Of his countless trophies, he most prizes the photo of himself seated in his pal Bill Elliott's NASCAR T-Bird, "Old Number 9."

But no Ford could out-boast the escapades he pulled in his most famous car, a stock 1959 Galaxy. Its exploits are still discussed in admiring good humor along the hallowed Halls of Montezuma. He was continuously ferrying buddies to matches, social events, and duty assignments in the "Ridge Runner." It was center-stage in a one-car train of massive moonshine importation, supplying Camp Lejeune so steadily that his Colonel suspected him of operating a distillery right on the base! Col. Williams spent his free time hiking and boating about the base, intent on finding the still that never was.

An unmodified stock sedan, the Ridge Runner nevertheless performed admirably under Eric's eminent skills and reflexes, in town or country. The tales that car could tell are legion. Jerry Kozuch sure remembers it; he once *shot* it!

Driving home to Georgia from Quantico one day, Eric was bringing Harry a genuine Civil War sabre as a souvenir from Virginia. By now Harry was well into the family-raising venture, settled comfortably on the scenic shores of Lake Chatuge in Hiawassee. Eric pulled over in Virginia near the North Carolina border for a short rest. His method of repose on the road was to sleep suddenly and deeply, but only for ten minutes, a finer point of self-discipline he cultivated over years of travel and military hustle.

As he reclined, a carload of ruffians noticed the apparently unoccupied Galaxy on the roadside and slid to a stop. This alerted Eric, who awakened as the hoods were backing up and parking behind him. In the rear-view mirror which he had tilted down for surveillance, he observed four of the roughs emerge from their car. They paused in their tracks for a moment when they saw him on the front seat. Then, two of the four pulled out switchblade knives. Another produced a blackjack.

They walked on toward the blue Galaxy, popping their blades. With icy movement, Eric slid the sabre up to him. Then with an ear-piercing Rebel Yell, he bounded out of the Galaxy and ran fiercely toward the robbers, waving the long sword over his head in a two-legged cavalry charge.

The goons froze in their tracks, their faces fixed in shock and horror, as if a load of dead skunks had been dumped on them. They turned and darted back to their car in a fearsome frenzy. One dropped his switchblade in the mad dash. Turning to retrieve it, then seeing Eric closing quarters on him, he stumbled all over himself and let out a shriek. The car was peeling away and slinging gravel before he could even climb in, diving through a window and hanging out at the waist, kicking and screaming as they tore down the highway in full retreat.

Eric picked up the switchblade and examined its faux-pearl handles, holding it alongside the big sword and grinning. He grinned as he raced for the Carolina line. He was still grinning when he presented the sword to Harry in Georgia.

Eric has cars in his blood; especially race cars. He follows the sport like a hound on a hot trail. He has always been well acquainted with race drivers, both common and celebrated, and could always hold his own behind the wheel—whether dead-heat racing on the tracks just for fun, or terrorizing the roadways in his less judicious youth. But he has not always been entirely fortunate with the automotive aspects of his life.

One night in 1959, while on leave in the North Georgia Mountains, he was crossing the infamous winding pass across Blood Mountain. Centuries earlier, the Creek and Cherokee nations fought such a gory, ensanguined battle there, that the streams ran red with their blood. It was the wrong night to disturb the sleeping warriors of Blood Mountain, for Eric suddenly found his Galaxy losing its grip on the damp, narrow road, the sentinel-spirits betraying his otherwise superb driving skill. In a heartbeat, he was tumbling, sliding, and flipping horrifically down a steep slope and into a dark, deep gully. Devastating damage was incurred within sheer seconds. He received a bloody blow to his crown which stunned him for a time.

The magnitude of the spectacular crash was equaled only by his miraculous survival of it. Slipping in and out of consciousness, he began to painfully worm his way out of the mangled wreckage. His clothes were torn and bloody. A shoe was somehow yanked from his foot. Vines ensnared him. Then came the hissing: was it a punctured radiator? A snake pit?

He fumbled around to check his wallet, and felt it was gone, torn away with the pocket. He lost a good deal of money. And he lost his fabled Ford.

Slowly he crawled up the slope, aching in every segment of his being. Only by a combination of shock-induced adrenaline, hope, willpower, and assorted intervening miracles did he manage to inch his way back up to the road. He needed help, though none appeared forthcoming. Setting his bearings, he began the arduous task of trekking down the mountain.

The area was still true wilderness in those days. Mountain lions and panthers still inhabited the woods. There were no lights but for the stars. The road, an ancient Cherokee trail, had existed for all but the most recent years of its life as a crude and unpaved route. In his Granddaddy's day it was little more than gullies and ruts. In recent times it had been roughly paved, but was still no place for a battered crash victim to be stumbling in the dark, fresh blood leaving a scent for killer cats, dodging pitfalls and cliffs.

Finally headlights appeared. He flagged a ride. The tattered Eric asked to be taken to help—not to a doctor (there were none for miles)—not to his mother's (he must spare her the shock)—but to Harry's lakeside retreat around the next mountain, in Hiawassee.

Harry's brood stood watching in awe as Harry dressed Eric's head wound, witnessing how tough Marines tend to these matters. Eric had already taken his anesthesia. There was essentially little more that could be done but to douse the wound, irrigate the open gash, then apply a

114

temporary bandage. Having no peroxide on hand, there was no choice but to flush the wound with alcohol.

Eric looked downward and clinched his eyelids, grimacing like a wet bull caught in an electric fence. They were far from a doctor, though Harry strongly admonished him to see one. He changed clothes and kept his wound covered with a cap. It was all Harry could do to talk him out of climbing back down the slopes of Blood Mountain in pursuit of his wallet and shoe. He struggled to walk without a limp, and to conceal the serious gash from his mother. Congress could strike him a thousand medals, and they would yet be a lackluster compensation for the heroic endurance he mustered.

Reporting to Sick Bay on his return to Quantico, the doctor and corpsmen were astonished at how long he had held out against the avalanche of anguish. Soon he was visiting home again, grinning as he showed Harry's children the gob of stitches beneath his green campaign hat. To them the wound was emblematic of courage. They had already seen his bashed-in car. It matched his scalp. They now saw him as indestructible.

They had been to Blairsville to view the remains of the Ridge Runner. It was squashed nearly flat. The roof was caved in with a conical point. Motorists would stop just to marvel at the wreckage, then marvel anew on learning that the driver had somehow survived; even salvaged himself by climbing mountains in the midnight. He simply had too far to go, for Fate to deal the death card that night.

Yet his car calamities were not over. In the early 1960's he was negotiating the notoriously winding road across Turkey Gap, from Hiawassee to Clayton. A tire blew, sending him into one of the Gap's many deep gullies. He was thrown from the vehicle, and by the time they both completed their tumbling course, the car rolled over onto him. He was pinned under it all night.

In the morning a passing motorist noticed the several tree tops Eric's sailing car had clipped off, and stopped for a look. The gully was too steep to descend, but peering through the trees he saw what appeared to be a corpse protruding from beneath the wreckage. The old man almost fell down the precarious incline himself, on seeing the "corpse" awaken and calmly ask him to call for assistance.

Removing the car was an engineering marvel, but as rescuers tried to pull him out and transport him, he wobbled to his feet independently, and climbed up the near-vertical grade with them. They could hardly believe Eric had not been mangled, burned, or bled as pale as a pink pig.

"Why, none of that amounts to pain, compared to trying to get some shut-eye under that steel sleeping bag!" he joked.

In his exposure to many things and ideas after years of military service and world travel, he grew slightly less prejudiced against other makes of cars, especially if they held some utility or value. Though forever a Ford man, he took a radical step and acquired a Volkswagen Beetle for making his long runs between Lejeune and Georgia, through the mountains, or up to Camp Perry. It was in a time when some still referred to the VW as a "Kraut Bug." But he defended the good service and economy it gave him. He was good advertising for VW, and was seen in his Beetle everywhere, going hunting or fishing or to the ranges, putting it through off-road tests like a jeep.

The Ford boys back home ribbed him some, but everyone stands back and respects Eric England once he has spoken in favor of something. And they all knew his exploits behind the wheel of hotrod Fords surpassed any of theirs. "Besides," he would explain, "the more gas money I save, the more tonic I can carry back to Lejeune!" And his passive little VW was never suspected of running 'shine, the way the hillbilly-hotrods were.

One night he was returning to base rather late. Tired from the long trip, he took an exit he failed to notice was closed off. Crashing through the barricade, he careened wildly before coming to a four-point landing. Before he could extract himself from the floorboards, his blue-tick hound, Old Reb, awoke on the back seat, startled, and attacked him! Unable to calm Reb down, he had to bite his ear before he would recognize his master, and comply with the *at-ease* command.

The same Vee-Dub was well known by Carlos Hathcock, who shared a wreck with Eric on the back roads of Camp Lejeune. They had been testing captured Chinese and Soviet weapons under various adverse conditions, rifles they would both be facing when they became Scout Snipers in the new war in Vietnam. Rounding a turn, they were surprised to see a bar-gate closed and locked. They ran under it, tearing the roof nearly loose from the car. When asked if he remembers the incident, Carlos grins and bellows, "Why, ya never forget nearly having yer head cut off. And I liked-ta got mine!"

Keeping current with NASCAR results—and plotting ways to get into racing himself—kept Eric's spirits alive as he lay in a Naval hospital years later, facing possible medical discharge as his Vietnam wound healed. Some men shoot and hunt; Eric excelled as a shooting *competitor*. Some boys race cars through the mountains; Eric's nature would insist on official, measurable racing competition. Fierce yet friendly competition: to Eric this is the zestful essence of life; the fuel for living.

His interest in stock car racing was never keener than it is today. And as Fate keeps turning his pages—with Ford turning his gears—it is natural he would cross paths with the likes of NASCAR great Bill Elliott, whom he admires despite his being Eric's junior. "Awesome Bill From Dawsonville" had the honor of taking private shooting lessons from Eric. Eric is equally honored to have been asked by Bill to transport his NASCAR T-Bird to racing events as far away as Seattle. "Wild Bill Elliott," the King of Thunder Road, sees and respects fellow sportsmanship in Eric, King of Range and Ridge. And to Eric, who once aspired to dominate Thunder Road, that is good enough.

CHAPTER TWENTY

RETURN TO KHE SANH

FULL-SCALE WAR rocked Vietnam. It was no diminutive conflict—no mere "police action." In the heavily embattled I Corps below the DMZ, the fury of 1966 rolled into 1967 with no sign of letting up. Indeed, many great technological advances related to warfare were just being developed as a result of the growing magnitude and complexities of this war.

New assault helicopters, weapons, and tactics—even most aspects of uniforms and field gear—were being adapted to the protracted struggle. Adapting for Vietnam had become a way of life for an entire generation of the US military.

The M-16, developing since the 1950's, was just coming to center-stage. The Army had it since 1965, getting the bugs out of it and its revolutionary ammo. Shooting with the M-14 had been fine for the USMC. Now, the Marines were ordered to have all personnel in-country using the M-16 by *01FEB67*.

Gunny England and Master Sergeant G.B. Merrill, among other top Shooters, were diverted for a time from the duties of Socialist-sniping and Proletarian-pawn-plinking, to orienting the line units to the new lethal toy.

For Marines just coming in-country who had already trained on the novel weapon, marksmanship improvement was being taught. Honing these skills was increasingly crucial to the war effort, and in preserving the lives of fellow Marines in their bloody duty.

In a typical skirmish with Charlie, (if typical ever happened,) Marine patrols ranging from squad to platoon strength might be surprised by a sudden hail of rifle fire. Pinned down and firing wildly in all directions at the ambushers, the battle with an unseen enemy could grow savage and bloody, necessitating air and arty support, medevac, reinforcements, or even extraction. If immobilized, they were fixed for enemy mortar fire. The pathos was repeated all too often.

In countless instances, the enemy would be on the run before reinforcements or aerial surveillance could arrive. Charlie did not have to stay and lay claim to his turf. It was always his, and he could return at will. The US troops could not remain in place for every square yard of turf gained, and would usually withdraw and send follow-up patrols or bombardments to keep Charlie stirred up or scared off. The Americans brought formidable resources of power and technology to bear, and always won if Charlie would stand and fight. Still, all too many Americans were dead, with all too many VC getting away. Charlie always tried to drag off his dead as well, to demoralize the Americans despite the much higher body count of VC dead.

Accurate and effective rifle fire was deemed to be a key factor in nailing Charlie before he got away. To lower the bullets-to-kill ratio would likewise increase the friendly-to-enemy kill ratio.

Merrill, the NCOIC of the 1st Marine Division Sniper School, was a three-war man: World War II, Korea, and now Vietnam. He was cool, confident, and yet forever alert. His warring skills were legendary. Eric enjoyed his camaraderie, and trusted him completely in matters of protocol, on or off the field. They made a great team. They had participated on so many USMC match teams together, and would again, that to them Vietnam was almost just a freak match tour diverting their real careers back Stateside.

Against their preferences, they quietly mastered the M-16, and began to analyze the obstacles Marines were having with it in combat. There had been mechanical problems, ranging from improper powder to defective shell extractors.

Now, the newer Marines were in a lull concerning not only body counts and kill ratios, but a gap needed to be sewn up quickly before the enemy exploited the additional lag in changing the seasoned fighters over to new weapons and tactics. Eric and G.B. detected what shooting and tactical skills needed improvement, and took their solution to the scene of battle.

A typical week would run thus: chopper out, or convoy out on a "Rough Rider," from Phu Bai to Chinook; proceed thence to Dong Ha and The Plateau; on to The Rockpile; to Cam Lo; back to Dong Ha; then take a Navy patrol boat down the river and then up to Gia Linh; then home to Phu Bai—all in five days.

They often took surprise enemy rounds on the boat rides, returning automatic fire—or a well-placed .30-06 or .308 round when an enemy silhouette was clearly sighted—supplemental to the Navy's machine gun fire and sometimes "zippo's" (onboard flame throwers.)

While instructing in camps, they often had to dive for cover due to incoming mortars or rockets. Charlie was also observing the training and preparations of the Marines as occasion granted, eager to test the Americans any time a new plan was being implemented; always eager to kill Sharpshooters and Scout-Snipers especially. Eric and G.B. stressed to their trainees the need to limit NVA observers and arty men with Sniper rounds, and to get more good hits on enemy regulars out on the perimeters and in patrol actions, by knowing and applying their new weapon.

In some instances they found their chopper or ground transport delayed due to weather or combat action, resulting in their serving on perimeter defense, or even impromptu patrols and Sniper missions, while guests of a besieged camp.

Khe Sanh, though not in the same Division, was relying on them a great deal as they became "on-call"

Shooters for the infamous Hill 881 sector. Many of their confirmed kills were logged during times of routine weaponry instruction visits to Khe Sanh. Marines there were facing moderate combat casualties again.

The Pentagon tended to blame the rising casualty rate solely on the masses of enemy regulars pouring in from North Vietnam through Laos. This way they could gain political and civilian sympathy, and hopefully obtain higher funding and troop increases. But as a potential General in NCO stripes, eyeball to eyeball with the real enemy, Eric's first observation was the truer one: that many newbies' marksmanship skills had eroded seriously since Stateside training. He couldn't change Washington and he couldn't pin on a General's stars, but he could change the war— by changing the individual fighting Marine into a more effective marksman.

True, the NVA were pouring into the region in alarming numbers. But Marine casualty reports showed an increase in one-shot kills from NVA sniping efforts, in addition to the routine diet of mortar shells. The Americans had the means to stem and reverse the influx. Ever mindful of their duty, Eric and G.B. were determined to do their share. They could operate effectively without political restriction, right in their own backyard. Thus while training and supervising the line Marines to defend the perimeter, they planned to carry out as much "extra-curricular" counter-sniper recon as possible. And the plan could not be implemented a day too soon.

Then a new burden was added to their hectic schedule, with orders to begin training all non-line and support personnel on the M-16 as well. Dental companies, motor pools, supply personnel—all had to learn the M-16, and fast. There was surely sense in it: noncombatants in Vietnam routinely performed hazardous perimeter guard, convoy escort guard, and other deadly duties; indeed, if overrun, a base could and did summon all available men to take up arms.

But already short of manpower, the USMC was not sending enough qualified M-16 instructors to fulfill this duty; they were back home teaching the recruits inadequate or easily forgotten rifle skills; the best instructors were already in Vietnam to perform as Scout-Snipers and Sniper Instructors! So in a typical military brain-bind, the Corps' elite Shooters were far from Parris Island and Camp Pendleton, teaching routine shooting to non-shooters in a non-routine-shooting war.

Expedience was therefore the unwritten order of the day. Eric and G.B. devised a plan for a three-day class on the side, to ready a passable mock-up of a recon-counter-sniper team. They coveted more field time, being bogged down with the mundane M-16 classes.

Eric would begin a typical M-16 class with Leatherneck sternness, captivating attention. The more experienced men knew who Eric was, and were all ears. Before this dazzling cavalier could utter more than two minutes of salty sage advice, all were captive fans. He exuded an entertaining Marine confidence they all admired.

"I am Gunnery Sergeant England," his commanding Drill Instructor voice would crank out. "I have been involved in Marine Corps Marksmanship for over 14 years, on ranges and USMC teams. I know what I shoot for, and I shoot it." He did not have to mention that he was a Leech Cup Champion, a celebrity Shooter, or one of the top-gunning Commie Killers in-country. His confident style and commanding presence spoke for themselves.

"Now enough about me. What about you? Let's talk about why you're expending so many rounds, and not drawing blood. Charlie knows your deficits on the M-16 already, and he is swarming to come eat you up. A show of hands—how many had even trained on the M-16, back in The World? Okay, now—how many have not even touched one since training?"

With a penetrating eye screening for problem-profiles among the boy warriors, he would resume, "My first love was an M-1 Garand. Back in 1954, Chesty Puller pinned a medal on my uniform for winning a waltz contest with old Emmie. Well, that gal is up and gone. I got over her, though. Met the M-14, out ridin' the range. She treated me well. We got along fine, 'til she run off with the Quartermaster. Now there's a new gal in town: the M-16." He would pause to shake his head and spew tobacco juice to one side, fighting back a grin.

"The M-16 is, and I repeat, *is*, a fine weapon, suited for many types of warfare conditions. You may as well have confidence in her; you're stuck with her. And you will not go home on your feet if you do not develop a great working relationship with this weapon. You will come to feel married to the M-16. The future of freedom depends on how well you have courted her."

They knew this England guy had "been there." Their trust grew with the realization that this target-master of Olympic stature was down in the dirt with them, because he cared enough to help.

"Nobody's here to lead you around like in Boot Camp. You gotta do this all by yourself! Loose sights? Mud in your muzzle? Who's gonna check it for you? Your baby sitter? Did you bring a caddy from the armory?"
A pause and a grin.

"Mud in your muzzle means blood in your guzzle! And you'd dang sure better not let me catch you risking Marine lives just because you treated your weapon like year-old Easter eggs!"

"And who's gonna call your shots for you? Let's face it, we're getting paid all this money to do one thing over here—in addition to enjoying the vacation. We are here to kill the enemy, and the faster we do it, the faster we we'll git on outta here and git back home!"

"First, let's talk about daylight shooting. Just those times when you're looking over that perimeter, or patrolling these stinking hills. You wanna make 'em stink with Charlie's blood, not ours! Remember, when you walk this turf, you are treading on blood spilled by your fellow Marines!"
The trainees grew more somber, but remained as fully attentive.

"Now, by day you're getting many chances at good open shots, at 50-100-200-and 300 yards. But you are expending far *too many* rounds! And *not* getting *blood!* The reason? You are shooting just as *fast* as your finger will jerk.

You don't aim for a hit. You go diving and slinging lead, and giving away your position. You're pinned down. And you're gonna *die* down, if you do not make that first round stick like slop on a shoe!"

Distant gunfire in the hills caused them all to wince briefly. Eric resumed his stride.

"Aw-rite, now think. You men are not thinking of what you're gonna do, *before* you have to fire. You are just pointing the weapon in the general direction of the enemy, and going *ape-shape!* The best shots in the world can't get blood thataway, and *you* trigger-tamers sure can't, either! This is basically what you're doing wrong. Now, here's how to correct it, *and* get blood on the *first shot!*"

"Know the zero of your weapon. We will zero every man's sights later. Now, concentrate on the *first* shot you are going to make, and on getting blood. Get a steady position, and use the sling to brace-in with if there is time. Now, you know the rest: proper sight alignment, and trigger-squeeze. And forget about your drawers! A tight grip and a solid, eyeballed shot. Do that for at least the first round, and then if you *have* to go ape-shape on full auto, and shoot all over creation, you have at least tried one well-placed round. And that first round *can* get blood, *and* demoralize Charlie, up-front!"

A low-flying Chinook interrupted the lecture. He went on. "Remember Charlie. He lives here. It's *his* hunt club! But we can outsmart him and outshoot him by trusting our weapons—training our minds to react with proven tactics. If Charlie's shooting all over you, chances of him hitting you are about as good as you hitting him. No takers in Vegas; even the odds. Hold your target—follow him—if he is moving fast, lead him. Anybody here ever hunt deer..."

CHAPTER TWENTY ONE

HOVERING OVER HELL

BY TWILIGHT'S last glow, Eric and G.B. would typically be slinking off from Khe Sanh with a recon team for a bit of night hunting, setting up listening posts, or fixing a sniper hide before sunrise. Or they would be out for one to five days training the counter-sniper men, often reporting one to six confirmed enemy kills as a matter of course; sometimes more. Then they would coolly return to teach their classes without a flinch. This would fire the zeal of the young Marines to go to the field and effectuate singular victories, one at a time, in this statistics-driven war.

But the field analysis continued to point an earnest finger at the need to stem the NVA's version of snipers, via counter-sniper tactics. G.B. and Eric kept exhaustive notes on their observations. One point became clear: the hills of Khe Sanh had too many crevices, cavities, and other natural modes of concealment facilitating the NVA's ability to pop up and fire unpredictably and repeatedly.

"Shall we give it the old *Con Thien Turkey Shoot?*" asked G.B. with a grin one day.

Eric returned the grin and replied, "How about the Boitnott Boogie?" They both laughed. Ace Korean War Sniper John Boitnott, essentially the founder of the first Sniper School, would direct a dedicated volunteer such as Sgt.

125

Henry Friday to run rapidly along a trench line, drawing North Korean fire. John would then spot them, and nail their hatches down.

"No time for trench digging! And the runners would file a grievance these days, I'm afraid!" More laughter.

"Well, we gotta draw their fire before we spot 'em, it appears from the set-up."

"Yeah. And I don't think John can get a permission slip from the Pentagon, just to come help us!"

Eric shook his head. "Imagine a warrior like him, stuck with a Pentagon interservice liaison job—dodging politicians like they was fire balls—an acting Sergeant Major with the power of a General in some ways. But he'd rather be over here sniffing out Charlie and pinching off his gnatty little noggin', I bet, and we could sure use him too!"

G.B grinned and nodded. "Well, aerial photos and electronic surveillance have fallen short of spotting their lone sniping elements. We simply gotta draw 'em out. How are we going to adapt John's technique for drawing fire?"

"How about low-flying, slow-going recon choppers? And have several of our own Snipers, already situated on as many hills, in as many bushy draws, as we can secure. Chopper crew armors up as much as possible. Charlie shoots up at the green bird, compromises positions, gets spotted by the chopper crew. Our men take shots in rotation as Charlie's heads pop up. Recon works their way up to the sighted enemy. Either way, it's *spot 'em, blot 'em, and shot 'em!* "

"Gotta be wild kids to do that. Real hot-rodder pilot jockeys. Young, dumb, and chewing gum!" More laughs.

"Of course, we can't trade-off any Marines' safety. Let's talk to HQ. Maybe some variation can be implemented."

G.B. reflected a moment. "Could you snipe from a chopper?"

"And hold a wobbly target? Hardly match condition! But might could do some creative plinkin'!"

"Yeah, and becoming a real bull-butt target at the same time! But just once, let's go up on a flight, and try some recon-by-fire. Just see what we can flush out. At least, observe some possible NVA positions."

Eric grinned again. "Yeah, if we're gonna ask others to draw fire, let's be the first to do it! Only fair."

G.B. returned the grin, nodding another unspoken affirmation. He valued Eric's courage. "Yes-sir, a first-rate teacher learns first-hand."

Eric admired G.B.'s integrity. "Gotta know it, before ya show it. We'll prepare 'em a good lesson on it, too."

The next day they were in a Huey, visually scanning for NVA hides; starting from a cruise elevation of 1500 feet, then after a slow fly-by, descended to 1000 feet. They had not drawn fire until they had just finished canvassing an area, and were leaving it. They felt a round strike underneath, between the tail-boom and the door gunner. On banking back for another view, the trigger-happy culprit would not be visible. The aircraft commander would not descend lower without increasing speed, and limited them to one last fly-by.

"Y'all know this here ain't the way it's done, donchee?" the crew chief hollered over the rotor-racket, his hand over his helmet intercom mic.

"Ain't *nothin'* done like it's done, 'til it's done *done!*" Eric remarked back with a sly grin.

"Try flushing them out," G.B. yelled over to Eric. Then he put a flight helmet on and said to the A/C over the intercom, "Sir, can you come about broadside, and hover a minute. We will fire for effect."

Eric selected a target 1000 feet down, at any angle of 135°, a flat hilltop east of Hill 881. What appeared to be low bushes along even terrain, difficult to hide in, had a sort of little ravine or ditch coming out of the edge of the clump, deep enough to conceal a shooter of Charlie's stature in prone position.

Eric fired a single round from his .30-06 into these bushes. Suddenly there was reflexive wiggling in the bushes, and then a round was fired at the chopper's right skid just below Eric and the gunner.

"Want me to take 'im out, sir?" the gunner asked.

"No. No, wait," G.B. replied, then walked four slow-paced M-16 rounds up a bushy draw leading toward the clump. Again there was a thrashing in the shrubs, and another round was fired toward the chopper, striking the tail boom as it turned about to leave.

"Swing around, atop the hill, come in on that little draw, from the *other* side," G.B. directed.

"We'll take on some more altitude first, before we expose our belly again!" the A/C said back.

The pilot maneuvered the craft precisely as G.B. would have wanted, and sure enough, two NVA covered with natural cammo scurried up the draw toward the top of the hill.

Apparently thinking the chopper was leaving for good, they aspired to give it a few parting shots. It proved to be the last mistake these Bo Doi's would ever make. One shouldered what appeared to be a Russian scoped rifle. The other uncovered a mounted .51 calibre.

"Look at their faces," Eric chimed as they banked around. *Pop,* and then *pop,* and two NVA lay dead, major leaks in their plumbing. The one with the sniper rifle was hit through the chest. The other hit was the wiggler, who had stood up from his clump, blood on his entire left side. He was taking aim with an unscoped bolt gun when he was also blown down, with a devastating hit to his center-mass.

"Take out the .51," the crew chief called to the gunner.

"Get that big gun down there," the pilot supplemented.

The right M-60 machine gun spewed a line of fire toward the superior .51 Cal, but hit nothing more strategic that sandy loam, as the helicopter jerked hard away in response to a burst of automatic rifle fire striking around the chin bubble. Red tracer rounds from the M-60 shot skyward, arching in a fiery bright red rainbow.

Any remaining NVA snipers apparently chose to lay low, as the sky started to fill with green tracers from NVA standard-issue small arms fire. The vertical green and oblique red angular fireworks made for a brief moment of entertainment.

As the Huey spun about to evade fire, the crew chief opened up on the gun emplacement, walking several rounds forward through the leaping puffs of soil, striking home as he hit the NVA nest. The NVA gunner's career was abruptly ended as he was, for all practical purposes, ripped in two.

Lids started popping open on "spider holes," muzzles extended from the concealment of bushes, and suddenly stinging rounds of 7.62mm hornets were buzzing at the big green dragon fly, from at least eight different positions in the hills and draws.

As the craft sped away, G.B. remarked, "A job for air and arty—*if* they could fix on 'em. But the goons shift around by night. And too tunneled in or fortified underground, to really scorch their mangy hides. Why, they'd need a thousand tons of delayed-fuse bombs, polished off with a heavy frosting of napalm!" He and Eric just sat shaking their heads.

The A/C was calling in the coordinates for whoever cared. It was just another fire mission or napalm run for the unseen purveyors of pyrotechnic power.

Soon they were approaching Khe Sanh. Back to base; home-free, until the next round of "terror-tag."

G.B. continued to Eric, "Anyway, that's they way to hold 'em, Cochise! Wish our classes could have seen that! They won't believe this at Camp Perry!"

Eric shook his head again in amazement. "Ree-con's got a job to do. It's a ground job. Why, it'll take *regiments* to take these hills and spider-hole snipers, otherwise." He pulled plugs of beef jerky from his pocket and offered the men all one.

"Or a coon hunter, with a good pack of dogs," G.B. said with a laugh.

Eric chewed and pondered the terrain passing under them. "I got an idea. I got an idea."

CHAPTER TWENTY TWO

HIT 'EM WHERE IT HURTS

INFANTRY battalions of the USMC each had their own Sniper platoon, consisting of thirty-nine Top Shots and their cadre. They worked with reconnaissance teams, went out on infantry patrols, scouted, and were sometimes pressed into helping defend the perimeters when enemy advances were heavy or eminent. Eric England and G.B. Merrill grumbled in their temporary tent at Khe Sanh, about how to reduce the well-dug-in NVA snipers. The USMC Sniper Instructors in Vietnam had turned out many fine students, and the mandate had been established to use them as Snipers, not as routine guards or security—as Snipers only.

"Those NVA pop-up snipers are too well concealed and dug in to fix 'em for air and arty," G.B. groaned. "Probably move around at night, and get steady reinforcements. It's a recon and sniping job, to get any edge of control on 'em."

"Draw 'em out," Eric dryly remarked, staring at the green canvas roof from his cot." We're only in Khe Sanh as bait anyhow. We need to create a diversion that'll draw more of their shooters out of their holes and into a trap."

G.B. nodded with a broad, wry grin. "I'm with ya so far, Moonshiner!"

"Moonlighter! We'll call it *Operation Moonlighter!* We'll leak the word out and make Charlie think we're on night maneuvers. Let's get a notepad..."

They worked for hours on a potential counter-insurgency attack plan, to pass up to Command. If the brass didn't readily see its value, the Gun-n-Garden Club would likely deploy their own clandestine version anyway. The idea was to send patrols away toward the northwest by night, pretending to be shifting infantry units for a campaign, all the while dropping off Sniper teams and recondos at strategic sites for ambush and observation.

By night, a few Marines would create artificial or "decoy" hides, shelters, foxholes, and other obvious "positions of fire," to lure Charlie and quench his vile thirst for precious American blood. All the night movement would cause Charlie to assume the Marines were conducting night maneuvers and attack modalities, and would be less wary in daylight hours—when the designated Marine attackers would be rested.

Once a significant number of NVA were in the open vales, including several inevitable NVA snipers, the trap could be clinched, wringing out the enemy's rising morale.

Marine Snipers would be positioned at the choicest sites and maximal vantage points, usually atop or on the side of ridges. They would serve in the counter-sniping role, while the dug-in recons ambushed any moving NVA. Evasion plans would also be worked out to a tee, maximizing use of natural terrain and cammo; where appropriate, withdrawing patrols would loop back and outflank or rear-attack NVA stalkers.

Charlie would likely expect a campaign of from two to four days, and would extend their supply, evacuation, reinforcement, and communication lines for this spur activity. Then, US sniping and flanking patrols could result in dozens of NVA kills, disrupt their Intel and morale, and divert troops. If The NVA responded by moving larger elements into what they perceived to be a major developing campaign, they would likely expose themselves to greater aerial and artillery bombardment.

131

Walking toward the club, they were sad observers of four Marine dead, all shot through the head or upper chest with single rounds. NVA sniper rounds. Bags were unzipped by corpsmen as a chaplain checked their dogtags for religious preferences. No sooner than the body bags had been readied for transport to Graves Registration, than the ever-familiar (yet never-routine) ba-*woompf* of enemy mortars began to pummel the interior of the perimeter.

As they dove for the cover of sandbags, G.B. remarked, "There's no time for our plan. We've got to act *now.*"

Eric replied with a wincing and somber nod, as they lay listening to the ear-splitting intrusions of the 81mm blasts. After the barrage, they double-timed to help the wounded. Reflexes and sandbags saved most of the men from wounds or death. One Marine was killed, behind the wheel of his jeep. At least seven received searing shrapnel wounds necessitating their evacuation.

Afterward, they hassled the young E-5 manager to come back out and reopen the NCO Club. They sat and returned to their notepads.

"Just go set up a lot of phony positions, by night. Do a lot of phony chopper insertions, by day. Fall back, and wait for 'em to go out there for a ghost-fight," Eric suggested with a frustrated groan.

"Yeah, maybe so. Maybe so. And cut off their lines. Might wipe out a company, plus a few of their jack-rabbit snipers!" G.B. was focused; his vision was honed by his sense of duty.

"Hit 'em where it hurts!"

"And most of alll…"

"Them *jack-rabbits!* Just skin the squinty-eyed devils. Settle the score and clear the field. But where's the ball field? What on earth is going on up at HQ and Operations?"

G.B. jabbed his finger at the map. "Here. This little flat valley between these knolls, just below Hill 881-South. I need to go have a talk with the brass. They all know the scoop, but don't pass down the strategy fast enough. Charlie seems to get the plans before we do! The big plans; that's why we need to keep our plan small, secretive. Worm our way through the big picture."

Eric peered at the map studiously, as he unscrewed the lid on the pint of Grade-A Georgia Moon. He got his tonic shipped to him exclusively by his gal, Sue Berrong. Though she was not an imbiber, her father Shorty was a supplier-hobbyist. A saintly man in every respect, his only departure from doctrinal persuasion was as part-time purveyor of high-grade corn squeezin's, to the select partakers among the professional classes and gentility of their Appalachian Shangri-La.

"Lot of NVA movement to the south of those hills," Eric noted.

"Better belay that snake oil," G.B. laughed.

"Yeah, I'll give up these *pints* when they ship me home. Then, I'll get it in *half-gallons* only!" Eric would chortle back.

"No, this plan won't work. Too many *ifs*, not enough *jiffs*."

"Hmm." Eric put his jar away and studied the trails.

"The Marines like everyone else are working hard at attacking infiltration routes, that stem off *The Trail*..."

"Uncle Ho-ho's little Pathway to Paradise..."

"...and I bet if HQ uses us any more here, it will be to interrupt infiltration."

"Bound to happen. Meanwhile, let's implement a mini-version of *Operation Moonlighter*—just enough to draw off a few of their *jack-rabbits*—get 'em sniffing on our blood trail, then..."

"You've zeroed it!"

"This is a personal showdown, us and them. Sniper to sn..."

"Sniper to jack-rabbit! In the finest tradition of the Corps."

They set about designing a more abbreviated counter-sniper plan. They formed a team composed of a corpsman, radio operator, and six Snipers including themselves. In the urgency of the situation, HQ eagerly loaned the needed men, but at their request did not clear their operation through channels for at least two days, to maintain secrecy. This would mean they were fair game, to friend and foe alike, if exposed.

The team was briefed on situations, tactics, and the need to get blood. They were selected primarily for having considerable experience in the field already; they were at one with the bush. And even the non-Snipers on the team had high rifle scores.

The NVA were becoming so at home, they were increasing their numbers of spider holes, or pop-top foxholes with camouflaged lids. Charlie would pop up, shoot up a Marine or half a squad, and vanish. The NVA version of snipers often dug into little cavities in the slopes, whose openings were concealed by brush. They were near invisible yet enjoyed a wide field of fire. The one advantage to the Marines was that the cavernous hides may amplify the NVA's rifle crack. And although the NVA usually were limited to an inferior sniping rifle and scope, they were getting good at long-range shots, distant enough that their noise dissipated before it was discerned.

Within hours before they went out, Eric mentioned to G.B., "We still need a variation of the Boitnott Boogie—maybe using *four-legged personnel!*"

A bright smile of approval beamed across G.B.'s face. "That's it! Need a good hunting dog! A K-9 Combat Tracker. But I hear the dog-handlers are tightening up on the deployment of their dogs right now. Taking too many *canine casualties.*"

"Well, we'll have to barter. A little *appropriation lubrication* should do the trick!"

"And if you talk *coon-hunt* with 'em, they'll see right off that you'd never risk a dog who is worth his chow."

Eric got on the horn and talked tracking and hunting with the NCOIC of the kennels back at Camp Kaiser. He tried to warm him up to the idea of letting him borrow a dog. No dice.

"Long distance won't do it," Eric announced briskly to G.B. Gotta chopper over there, and get us one of them dogs. They got the best ones in-country; they track, point, even tree without barking!" They went over and talked a deal for a flight over to the K-9 kennels at Da Nang and

Camp Kaiser, but they would have to arrange their own ground transport once landed. "Aw, I got buddies who'll get us a jeep," Eric reassured, and went on the flight alone. By afternoon was talking with the Top Dog of dogs, in person. Eric listened attentively to the man's accent. Kentucky, he was sure of it. He pulled out a Mason jar of mountain dew, and re-opened negotiations. Eric wove the conversation through hunting in Kentucky, the care and breeding of quality dogs, and a line or two on the last coon-hunting contest in Paducah. Within a half hour, Khe Sanh's newly formed counter-sniper team had procured not only a finely trained Black Labrador, but a concomitant handler as well.

The team of exterminators moved out just as the dog handler resumed consciousness, the Lab licking his face and whining for him. Top Dog was surprised to find himself and his prize pup slinking around in the bush with a band of jack-rabbit hunters, marveling at all the holes and burnt earth from artillery and bombing, and wondering just where he was.

As they approached their A/O, a round whizzed past Eric and struck the corpman's aid bag. A small bottle of D5W I-V fluids was hit, and the sudden sensation of liquid on his leg alarmed him as they all went diving for cover. The Lab was itching to tear loose, but maintained discipline. The handler sent him forward, and in several seconds he was "pointing" this Bo Doi bushwhacker's hiding hole.

"Didn't know retrievers could point," one of the team remarked under his breath. "Cross-trained MOS, or what?"

The team eased their weapons into position. Eric whispered to his spotter-trainee, "Can't get eager for a shot just yet; we'd compromise our position, and might be captured and executed within minutes." More observation was in order.

But by now the Lab was softly growling—sort of a muttly mumble—at some hidden terror in the bushes. Eric slithered forward and motioned for the handler to follow him. Pointing and gesturing, he conveyed his tactical intent. Top Dog complied, and signaled the Lab to jump into the spider hole as Eric pried up the leafy lid with a long stick. The dog went into that hole as if assaulting an overturned meat truck. The NVA sniper yelped and panicked, tossing the Russian scoped rifle into the air as he scurried up a hill. The dog was right behind him. Eric suppressed the impulse to fire, watching with one eye for other NVA who may reveal their positions, as they lost composure in the face the novelty now before them. Or, another NVA may shoot this comrade to prevent his capture. Anything could happen in this two-way shooting gallery. With his other eye, Eric followed the scared little jack-rabbit just to see where he may retreat.

Then the dog took the Bo Doi down and pinned him, teeth on neck, as the little terrorist screamed. Top Dog used his silent whistle to order the Lab to drag the prey downhill, out of view. But thrashing violently and getting his hand on a knife, the tough little soldier tried futilely to stab the dog. With a reluctant nod from Eric, one of his young Snipers plugged him, saving the dog and ending the public spectacle.

"Wish we coulda had 'im for a prisoner," Eric lamented.

"Yeah, but we hadta snuff 'im," G.B. consoled. "Anyway, we gotta move. Let's advance at intervals, laterally extended, and let Black Jack Pershing flush these knolls for us!"

The dog had a field day, prancing and slinking and at times crawling about the bluffs and foothills. Twice he pointed at the innocuous shrubbery; twice the men placed rounds into the deceptive foliage, netting profitable results.

G.B. and Eric scanned the hillsides cautiously. They were still more experienced and savvy than the others. G.B., a Korean War vet with brutal battle and survival experience, was in his forties already— but could "carry his own" in the bush. Eric could remain in the bush for months on his own, if need be, and feel right at home. Their perceptual skills, honed by keen foreknowledge of the enemy and his outdoor lair, were the ultimate lifesaving tools. Both of them had spotted NVA shooters moving about for a shot at the galloping Lab.

The order was to let him gallivant awhile, rather than run directly back to the team and reveal their cover. They kept the dog covered, hoping to fire on NVA before any could shoot the dog, but the handler was fuming at the gamble. But Eric and G.B. had loaded the dice: they each showed the students how to send a single round into the enemy dens. Awkward thrashing was heard within the bushy targets.

The Lab lay panting beneath the bushes surrounding one of the hills. The team dared not move. The had bagged four NVA jack-rabbits within an hour, had lost no blood, were not under fire—yet felt as trapped as a possum in a tow sack.

"Let's radio back," G.B. whispered to Eric, "and declare this ravine secure enough for a larger patrol. We'll remain in place, send the boys back, and watch for enemy stalking 'em. From here, we've set up a real shooting gallery."

Eric directed the team, "Y'all work on back. Me and the Canine Commando here will hold rear guard. We'll get the dog back down to us, and outta here once we hear the patrol a-comin'. Request they chopper in. We need noise cover."

Top Dog was muzzling as much frustration as a bull on laundry day. Eric grinned and pulled a fresh pint from within a clump of ferns, hidden on a previous solo recon. They talked of dogs and 'coons and Old Kentucky.

CHAPTER TWENTY THREE

MOUNTAIN PORCHES

ACROSS the top of Georgia the rolling hills of the Blue Ridge come to a peaceful rest, running down the long Appalachian Chain. The remote area was not settled by whites until a century after the coastal Georgia colony. The area was opened up to white settlers in 1838 following the tragic forced removal of the Cherokee natives. The remote area was not settled by whites until a century after the coastal Georgia colony. The region was opened up to white settlers in 1838 following the tragic forced removal of the Cherokee natives. Eric England's forebears were the true pioneers, already residing in this pastoral pocket well in advance of the others, arriving in 1832 from the Carolinas and Tennessee, settling in harmoniously with the Cherokee. Many of these trailblazers' descendants, including Eric, are proud bearers or a goodly portion of the noble Cherokee blood.

Eric pondered on the few remaining cabins there, built in the 1830's and 1840's, and how important it was to

138

have both a front and back porch. The front porch was for polite visits, receiving company, Sunday attire. The back porch was for stringing beans, spitting, and casual visits with more personal acquaintances. The custom lives on today. When Eric comes calling on mountain folk, he knows which homes expect a back porch approach, and which require the more formal front porch social call.

In 1980, cousin Harry acquired the estate of his Turner ancestry in Arkequah, by Choe Stoe. The porches, broad and roofed, were ideally suited to receiving all categories of callers. The back porch overlooks a vast meadow running toward the base of the highest of the mountains in Georgia, which they could use for target practice. They still get together there, and recall the old times. They relate how their Grandpa Nix had kept a pre-Civil War buggy in his shed, and how they used to ride in it as boys. And how Harry's Grandpa Turner worked the hand-terraced fields of this farm, "Turnwold," for nearly a century constantly overturning Cherokee artifacts. Hernando DeSoto was even said to have crossed the land, in search of Cherokee gold along Arkequah Creek. Their Grandmothers were experts with genealogy, etiquette, spiritual leadership; and the use of herbal remedies, a skill both men still dabble at.

Eric typically shows up at the big back porch bearing a gift, such as rare mountain herbs or some antique artifact. They grin a lot. A little prying will get them to relate the humor and adventure of their early years. One winter they decided to go camping near Bald Creek. Harry's field jacket pockets were filled with frozen steaks. They arrived in the pitch of night, and Eric proclaimed, "No need in both of us getting wet. Hop on, piggy-back, and I'll tote ye over, Cuz!"

Harry hopped on, and they both fell into the freezing water. Thankfully, Eric's fellow USMC Shooter, Sergeant Dick Scully, had a roaring fire going. He cooked the steaks for their breakfast, which was about when they finally dried off and thawed out.

They carried the rough-n-tumble outdoor adventures of their youth well over into manhood. Sometimes cousin Harold Harkins would join them. Harry and Harold could not rest until they had perpetrated a keen prank on Eric. One night as they camped on Bald Mountain, they found a flat potato and shoved it into Eric's rear pocket as he slumbered. He scratched at the ground all night, trying to remove the rock on which he supposedly lay. Exhausted by daybreak, he arose to slip down the trout stream for an early catch. He counted on the can of tonic in his jacket pocket, to patch up the abrasions of this rough morning. But Harry and Harold had replaced it with a pack of fig newtons. They chortled at the thought of him wading a mile or so downstream, and reaching for that AWOL can.

Harry always liked to kid Eric, and is perhaps the only person who could get away with it. Eric just grins, or snorts and shakes his head. Once, in the late 1950's, they were plinking in the Chattahoochie National Forest, and Harry kept hitting the tin-can target with a .45 from 70 yards. Harry hit it three out of three. Eric missed it, blaming some technicality or another. It was odd indeed, Eric being a noted champ with the .45. But Harry kept the can in his kitchen window, and whenever Eric would visit, Harry would just point at the can and grin at his hot-shot cousin. Then one night when the family got home from an outing, they were surprised to see the can was gone! Eric had slipped into the house and swiped that can, probably grinning like a possum at a persimmon picnic.

Eric has never been known to do much informal plinking with unfamiliar weapons since then, sticking to match-conditioned guns and standardized ranges where he rules supreme.

The only trait equal to his competitive nature is his non-stop humor—dry, wry, and natural—which makes it so lasting in one's memory. When city-slicker gold panners crowded his favorite trout stream, he casually sauntered over and showed off a gold nugget he carried on his keychain. Suggesting to them that he had found it some 3 or 4 miles downstream, the invaders of his solitude hastened their departure thither.

Too restless to sit long on even the most hospitable porch, Eric will begin to pace and grin as the visit wears on. Harry will coolly continue the revelation of their past antics with a remark such as, "There was this time when we were crossing a foot log, and I was toting a gallon of 'bitters.' We were betting on who could throw the other one off. I flung Eric in the creek, and he came out mad as a hornet. He remounted the log and tried to sling me off. I lost balance and fell, but landed on my back to cushion the jug. Eric was so thankful I had saved it, that he apologized profusely for being a bad sport. We were wet and cold, and knew we needed a medicinal tonic!" Porch talk is reflective.

Eric would see thatched villages in Vietnam, and wonder how they would ever reach civilization without porches. As he spied on them with his scope, he wished he was back on a mountain porch, plinking at cans. He wished Harry could see how hot his shooting there was. But he was glad he did not have to save the targets.

CHAPTER TWENTY FOUR

TURN 'EM LOOSE

GRATITUDE shone on the faces of the Counter-Sniper team formed at Khe Sanh, as they bade farewell and *Semper-Fidelis* to the visiting instructors. Eric and G.B. felt a sense of gratification as they crossed the river and boarded a Rough Rider back to Phu Bai on Route 9. They hoped their effort at Khe Sanh would hold the attention of Battalion HQ, and would be further developed. But partly for secrecy, partly politics, not all the Sniper-kills went on the morning reports and after-action reports as anything more than "combat KIA's." So the commanders got credit for enemy kills, and everyone up the line was happy, but would the Sniper program continue to receive the support it so needed?

Back at Phu Bai, they continued to have their work cut out for them. Missions to Cam Lo, Dong Ha, Gio Linh, and the DMZ in general were now commonplace, in addition to their Sniper School and their M-16 classes.

Operation Chinook had been in effect some two months by the first week of February, 1967. They were frequently called upon to cull out and eliminate key enemy figures, or to simply confound their operatives with bewildering clandestine fire. Operation Chinook was a dozen miles of Nam-ish turf north of Hue. Over two hundred VC had already been killed in the past six weeks by Marine forces there. Snipers trained at Phu Bai played a key role, creating havoc and confusion and reducing capable leadership among the VC; or driving VC units toward infantry traps.

Student Snipers, going to the field with their instructors, were put to good use. Their casualty rate was low, while their enemy body counts were steady. The 1st and 3rd Divisions had promulgated a remarkably effective and cohesive sniper program.

The skills of the new Sniper School graduates were having a far-reaching impact; they were furthering the Phantasm. During Operation Deckhouse IV, nineteen USMC grunts with one Sniper held off well over a hundred NVA, killing dozens and losing not one Marine. A captured Bo Doi told US Intel his unit thought they were up against a much larger force, based on their high number of casualties early on. Nearby, a recon patrol with two Snipers killed two squads of NVA with ease.

In Operation Prairie, smack on the DMZ, heroes and fabled feats were being documented wholesale. In one pitched skirmish, a Marine platoon and their Sniper team faced down a battalion of NVA, outnumbered ten to one, point-blank. The NVA went down so fast, it was almost like the Battle of New Orleans all over again. Marine casualties were reducing. Eric England and his Top Shot brotherhood felt a pride well-earned.

Over three days, a five-man recon team with a Sniper and his spotter came up on several platoons of NVA digging in. Calling in an air strike, they utterly decimated the superior force. But during escape and evasion moves, some VC sighted them. In a hot half-hour battle, the seven held off sixty VC, then another fifty, coming from all directions. At one point they were being charged by thirty desperate VC, and at close range both sides became involved in a volley of hand grenades. The Sniper was picking off an average of four VC with every five rounds fired from his much slower bolt gun. He totaled dozens of kills and undoubtedly saved the team. His spotter, with an M-16 automatic rifle, was hard-pressed to nail half as many kills.

The seven young men repulsed charge after charge. Almost out of ammo, they fell into a tight perimeter for a last-ditch defense, each calling his shots singly as the Sniper was having to do. Two Marines were wounded, but never gave up the fight. At last, a Huey was able to reach them for extraction, flanked by two Huey Gunships (the Cobra was still being developed.) A handful of brave, dedicated men, by holding off a vastly superior and hostile force, demonstrated forever the value of well-placed rounds not only in clandestine missions, but in a do-or-die fight.

Even more Snipers were needed, both as scouts and forward observers; and to oust vital enemy figures such as officers, heavy weapons men, radio operators, saboteurs, and couriers. Eric was taking Sniper students to the field on an increasingly regular basis, getting less solo time or missions with seasoned pros, but the trainees were benefiting from all he had done, from Phu Bai all the way back to Arkequah. He worked all his faculties to the extreme, drawing on every fiber of experience and intuition, to ready these boys to fight—and to get themselves back home alive. Seldom has there been a combat training scenario wherein the instructor is still around at fighting time; he took the boy's safety as a personal challenge, which in turn augmented their skills and stealth—wreaking greater havoc on Charlie down the line.

Meanwhile, thanks to the good efforts of Eric and his fellow Match Shooters, the sniping program was having such a reliable effect on the enemy, that it became a regular function of the US military system throughout the remainder of the Vietnam War. Then afterward, due largely to the efforts and reputation of such acclaimed heroes as Carlos Hathcock, the USMC established at Quantico its first permanent and truly formal Sniper School. The US Army followed suit and established permanent Sniper training schools, fully integrated into the military structure.

What the 1st Marine Division Sniper School at Phu Bai had done was turn out steady streams of excellent young Snipers, like packs of hungry hounds. Nothing frightened

Charlie nor restricted his movement so much as these purveyors of distant death; he feared them more than B-52's and artillery strikes, because they could and did strike anywhere without warning, an invisible and unknown attacker who made individual VC quite visible and directed their death so personally.

Into each of his students, Eric England instilled a goodly portion of his own solid and winning nature. He was sending in among the enemy these live extensions of the Phantom himself. And he kept going to the field with them, in an unquenchable thirst to help them win the day. Over the coming days and weeks he would come to cement the legend of the Phantom of Phu Bai forever—conceived in destiny—executed in loyalty—and sealed in blood.

CHAPTER TWENTY FIVE

STAGING POINT FOR HELL

INSERTED by chopper with six infantrymen to back them up, Eric and a teenaged trainee, already in-country four months and with eight confirmed—and nearly two dozen unconfirmed—kills to his credit, worked their way up a narrow wooded ridge until reaching a small hilltop. The escort remained concealed in the bush below.

Eric sensed that the little pinnacle, with its panoramic view of the flats near Gia Mon, could well be occupied by an enemy observer from time to time. The site overlooked a well-trodden trail leading out of the DMZ, into I Corps, in violation of international law. He also knew this was far too serious and dangerous a mission to take an ordinary trainee on, but this young Corporal was a hard-holder with naught but *esprit de corps* flowing through his veins. He was combat-proven, rough-n-ready. He had come to Phu Bai in much the same manner as young David came to King Saul, and bolstered the King's armies with his gift for fighting and commitment to the cause. He was being groomed as a prospective Scout-Sniper instructor.

Eric crawled slowly, with stealthy precision, prepared to seize this vital viewpoint. They crawled obliquely uphill for over three hours, covering less than 300 feet. Now, within 10 feet, seated atop the peak was the surprise he dreaded: a Marxist minion.

As Eric began to draw his K-Bar knife, he saw Charlie start to key the mic of his captured US PRC-25 radio. Charlie was peering intently down on the northward terrain below, as though about to report important news. Indeed, there was US troop movement in the area. And yes, Charlie had definitely seen something newsworthy. The little terrorist was also holding a Mosin-Nagant, a Russian scoped sniper rifle in 7.62mm bore, more than a few of which the Marines were turning up in the enemy's hands. Charlie held it as though he had use for it.

Noting no other VC, Eric sprang upon his vile foe and yanked the mic, covered his mouth, slammed a morphine syrette in his thigh, taped his mouth and eyes, and bound him with plastic cuffs before the spotter even detected him. The trainee crawled over to admire the work, then helped bind his ankles.

Eric calmly placed the muzzle of the Russian rifle in the low forks of a tree, and bent it out of line. He then bent the narrow scope with his hands until the lenses popped loose. "They'll wonder who busted up his little toys," he murmured.

"This-here's a sore spot to be sittin' on, Gunny," the aspiring Sniper whispered forcefully. "We're gonna be in *Deep-Serious.*"

"Aw! It's all the better!" Eric smiled confidently, the encouraging words of bravery sifting through his hushed teeth. "Who's gonna look for us up *here?* As long as none of them *Bo Doi's* make a prescheduled call-up on that durn radio, they'll think our shots are coming from old Possum Charlie here!"

The trainee's capable eyes spotted the Marine reconnaissance patrol sweeping some low scrub brush from the east. They were exposed to potential enemy fire from a forested area 400 yards to the west. The recondos were 500 yards from Eric's ridge outpost. They were supposed to set up an ambush along the ancient trail running northwest to southeast, right off the DMZ, coming from the area of Cam Pho inside North Vietnam. Cam Pho had been destroyed in the war earlier on, but its neighboring trails continued to buzz with the feet of many southbound NVA infiltrators.

The entire area was easily accessible on foot, from Gia Mon on south, through flats and valleys well beyond Ha Thanh; and southwest past Phuoc Thi and Lai An, both erased by warfare. Thus were they situated at the fulcrum of massive enemy infiltration.

No combat commander dwelling within the bounds of sanity would chance a patrol in the area. Being outnumbered and captured was almost certain. But there were many key NVA players moving through the zone in preparation for fresh campaigns against the US in I Corps; an interruption—if only momentary—could delay enemy plans and communication just long enough to provide the US and allied forces with crucial time and intelligence culling, and captured NVA to interrogate.

Swift, clandestine action was needed, and few but the Marine recon team down below could—or would—pull it off.

The spotter noticed a handful of NVA running out of the west side of the scrub, as the Marines advanced, probing for them. He urged Eric to open fire. Eric waited, waited—then blasted a round through a rear-guard NVA sniper seated in a tree 50 yards west of the Marine patrol. The other half-dozen NVA continued to run from the sweep. Eric popped two more NVA from 500 yards, as they slowed from a dead gallop to a winded trot, leading them like North Georgia whitetails. Down they went, one of them tripping a third who then arose, then was slapped back down for good by Eric's next round. A fourth NVA made it to the tree line, from whence a .51-cal. was being brought forward by two others.

The recon patrol had fallen for cover, then arose in a low-crouching charge toward the trees, some of them attempting to flank out left and right. They knew the only way out of an ambush was to charge directly into it. Any defense or evasive tactics meant being pinned down or gunned down. They knew Sniper cover was supposed to be active in the sector, but they knew not where. Still, they advanced with boldness and with the intent to prevail. It was not a good place to be injured or cut off. It was absolute *Injun Country.*

Then one of the charging Marines stepped on a landmine, holding up the intrepid advance. As they lay momentarily trapped, Eric could see their muted speech through his scope. Then he looked to the west again and saw the .51 being set up and readied to fire. Another round from Eric's .30-06 silenced the gunner before a deadly burst could be fired at the patrol.

Two more NVA, staring in disbelief at the sudden silent collapse of their comrade gunner, soon joined him in peaceful slumber—compliments of 173-grain sleeping pills.

Three gunners had been put down by as many well-placed rounds, from 500 yards, all in under eleven seconds. The exuberant trainee reached over and patted Eric on the back, then silently apologized for this serious breach of protocol.

"Man, wish we could stay up here forever! Good huntin' from up here," Eric chimed, through a slight grin. He had just bagged
several spikers—not trophy bucks, except in the sense of their strategic importance—and was poaching on a restricted reserve where, ironically, exceeding the bag limit was encouraged. Then a source of true joy came in his seeing one of the Marines tending to the buddy who had stepped on the mine, and that he had miraculously beat the odds by actually surviving. But now his evacuation, versus execution, was highly contingent upon Eric and his spotter remaining in place a few more perilous minutes, to help secure the field just a bit longer.

"Keep an eye south-n-eastward, to see if we were followed," the salty Shooter continued. "Look for escape clearance through the woods to the west, too. And check th' prisoner."

Scanning the enemy trail below him, Eric announced softly, "We may *have* to stay up here for awhile. Lookee yonder! Buck season's extended."

Turning his head, the spotter saw it too: a squad of NVA coming down the trail, fresh out of the DMZ, in a fast walk.

"Your turn, Corporal!" Eric whispered, easing the .30-06 over to him. "800 yards. Take out the back man first—

block their retreat. Then work the first one or two. Wait'll they're outta the scrub, and got no natural cover." The corporal began to align the crosshairs of the scope. Eric added, "Then work the rabbits—the flank runners. Stand by for possible fire on the M-16 here."

Alignment, windage, range—squeeze—and then *bang!* And *phoof* went a round through the rear man's forehead. Though deafening to the Snipers, the man was dead before the sound got there, and the distance diffused and muffled the muzzle report to the Snipers' advantage.

Eric watched through the binoculars. "Under 1000 yards—aim at the groin, to hit the chest," he admonished.

Then again the process brought down the lead man, his chest bursting out and splattering onto the man behind him. Then a surprise tandem-kill: the second NVA went down with him, as the exiting round struck him as well. Two-for-one discount day; Uncle Sam got his money's worth.

Rapidly yet smoothly ejecting and rechambering the bolt gun, the young man popped two of the middle men in the single-file, and had wounded another. Eric grabbed the rifle and quickly reloaded another five rounds, as half a dozen frenzied enemy bolted in a dozen directions. One stepped on one of his own mines and went sky-high.

"Bonus coupon day," thought Eric. The blast of the mine took out one NVA, but also caused sufficient stun-time for two of his fleeing Bo Doi buddies, for Eric to eliminate them in their moment of hesitation.

"Get up to the prone position, get the M-16, and shoot at them runners going west!" Eric coolly commanded. "See if you can drive 'em back toward the sweep!"

The Corporal fired repeatedly on semi-auto. Two of the NVA turned back east, on seeing two of their comrades fall dead. They were good, clean 400 yard kills, not bad work for an M-16.

"We're past check-out time," Eric announced, turning to crawl back down the ridge. He stopped to search the prisoner for maps or Intel data, finding several documents, and wanted posters bearing the likeness of two of Eric's former students. He kept them, then wrecked the US radio with his K-Bar; it was too cumbersome to hump back with them.

His protégé lingered just a moment to watch the rest of the unfolding plot, as the remaining NVA fell to the Marine patrol's withering fire.

"C'mon boy," Eric whispered sternly to him.

"Wait, Gunny! I see one crawlin' toward the Marines!" he whispered back, fervently.

Eric remounted the pinnacle and looked. He yanked the boy's rifle upward and said, "That-there's a fellow *Marine*, crawlin' back from a forward position!" His eagle eye was priceless to the Corps, one call at a time. "Now, let's *lizard-out!*"

He did not have to drill the lesson into the young warrior; the point was well learned in such an intensive, dynamic classroom.

Eric and faithful apprentice scurried cautiously down the west slope to team up with their awaiting escort, Eric dragging the prisoner by a cord looped through his easily detachable pistol belt. Then Eric spotted a lone VC crawling up toward their vacated perch. Could he see them? He did: he stopped when they stopped. Eric eliminated him with one round from his .45, paused to observe for others, and looked back for his spotter.

The Corporal, sighting him too, had squeezed off a single round at him with his M-16. He and Eric lay still a moment, so intense it felt like a century, gazing at one another in dead earnest while visually communicating their next move.

Eric motioned with his eyes for him to turn south and work down the way they had come up, sensing that Charlie had deduced they would not come back down that way. It was as though they had killed a deadly snake, and days later its mate slithered into their camp, following the dead snake's scent on them. The terror of being in VC country never shut off; one never knew when Charlie saw him or when he would show up. But he always showed up, even if never seen!

Eric paused to look back again, to communicate a positive word with his eyes, knowing one or both of them might die yet, without the boy ever having redeemed himself for his grave spotting error back on the hilltop. Eric's eyes and brief nod conveyed to the Corporal that he had indeed reclaimed himself somewhat, by his early detection of the encroaching VC—and remaining cool enough to dispatch a single round—not the tell-tale burst of full-auto, which is such a temptation in the sudden face of sure death.

With the undoable job done—against impossible odds, and no witnesses left behind but for the silent testimony of the dead—renewed tales of the Phantom were sure to impair the hearts and slow the fighting spirits of the endless streams of North Vietnamese locusts. The tide would be stemmed long enough—maybe just enough—to extend the lives of American freedom fighters. And if the patrol captured no NVA, he had one to offer.

For now, Eric knew of two Marines' lives which needed serious thinking about: the ones on the captured wanted posters.

Once off the slope and into the woods, he sighted in the bushes what he was sure to be one of his recon men. He silently issued the challenge sign, "*NASCAR.*"

The recon team leader countersigned with, "*Daytona!*" They were once again in the comfort of friendly company.

"Call this hilltop in for a zippo defoliant," Eric ordered. "Got to eliminate that observation point up yonder!" The little pinnacle was a VC shooter's dream, for any who could hold it.

A half-mile of hustling to their extraction point, and the men were soon reunited with Brother Huey. A night of rest at Dong Ha, a shower, and resupply of rations and ammo, and the death-defying Phantom of Phu Bai would be shuttled as quickly again into the heart of hell.

CHAPTER TWENTY SIX

OLD REB ... A GOOD MARINE

WHAT makes for a good Marine? Old Reb was a good Marine. Undoubtedly the first and only blue-tick hound to serve in the Marksmanship Training Unit at Quantico, he was also the only one taking up residence in the barracks down at the range. Reb was Eric England's pride and joy. Reb felt as much at home in the barracks as any Marine there; and owing to the state of near-autonomy of these Distinguished Shooters' billets, Reb enjoyed a full run of the place. Reb and Eric were practically alter-egos of one another, and no Marine with an inkling of common sense would dare question the squatter's rights held in these barracks by Eric's prized purebred hound.

Jerry Kozuch, famed Shooter and Sniper, lived in the same barracks then. "Kazootch" and Eric hunted together frequently and intensively, along with other great Shooters the likes of Bartlett, Dunham, and Hathcock. Soon Kazootch was housing his own redbone hound in the same barracks, too. Guns and dogs were quite the pivotal point in their lives at that juncture. The dogs served as a morale booster for the Rifle Team, and solidified the camaraderie. So long as the team was winning and great marksmen being produced, an indifferent eye was turned away by those who could order the hounds evicted. No one can calculate the positive

153

effect those morale-mutts had on the Marine Corps' shooting overall, but they certainly had a great deal of influence with their respective masters.

Eric worried and fretted over Reb likeunto a newborn babe. They were in each other's company most of the time. Reb could soon hunt any type of game, walking or flying, small or large, and seemed to instinctively grasp the type of game they would be pursuing even before they got to the woods. They were that close. Reb could read Eric's mood and intent.

Old Reb could track, chase, and tree—even point and retrieve—to the marvel and delight of all observers. He had an intuitive grasp, almost a foreknowledge, of Eric's thoughts and wishes. It was the spirit of the woods. It was their playground and workshop and battlefield, and they were well teamed together.

But Reb knew his place. Eric was not only his pal, but also ranked over him as his own personal NCOIC—his own Commandant—and he had to sleep on the floor beneath the bunk, not on the bunk. When Eric would come in and see Reb on his rack, he needed only to snap his fingers and he scampered. If hesitant, he got bitten on the ear—by Eric!

Occasionally a new Marine would move into the MTU barracks; a new marksmanship trainee, or new young Buck Sergeant or Corporal unit cadre. Unwittingly a newcomer might question the protocol of dogs inhabiting the same billets as Marines. Usually these fresh fish would hook on a fast lesson.

One rather obstinate new arrival mouthed a complaint to Eric directly. The barracks fell silent as a tomb, in anticipation of this underling incurring the wrath of the hard-core Old Salt himself—Eric R.-as-in-Rebel England.

Eric started to release steam through his ear-valves, then mercifully reined himself in to a mere growl, "This-here is Old Reb. And he is a good Marine! Now, just you watch this!"

Eric snapped his fingers and pointed at the foot locker, and Reb immediately climbed onto it, all paws squared, and back and head poised like a show dog. Eric repeated the signal, this time indicating the wall locker. Reb leapt up onto the bunk, then sprang and clambered atop the wall locker. Another signal toward the new man's bunk, and Reb made a flying leap down onto it, poised as if at attention. Yet another crisp signal, and Reb was home free, under Eric's bunk again.

"Can *you* do that?" Eric quizzed the astonished young NCO. "Then you'd better *salute* Old *Reb*, 'cause Old *Reb* is a *good Marine!*"

Suppressed snickering began to erupt throughout the barracks as the new fish stormed over to make a complaint to the First Sergeant.

"Sir!" he ranted. "I do not feel I can live in the same quarters as—as—that *hound dog* of Gunny England's!"
The First Sergeant, entirely unaffected, merely replied to the lad, "Why *that's* Old *Reb!* Old *Reb* is a *good Marine!*"

Exasperated, he returned to the barracks, but was not there for long. He was not a favorable prospect for the Rifle Team by any measure of character, nor stable enough to serve as a Scout-Sniper. Team spirit was not in him—not nearly so much as was in Old Reb. He washed out of MTU before long. This might have been predicted when he failed Reb's screening test.

Eric took Reb almost everywhere. There were too few whom he could entrust to baby-sit Reb. One exception was the Hathcocks. Carlos Hathcock, the world renowned Scout-Sniper and Wimbledon Cup match champion, was a close buddy and an integer in the tight circle of the world's foremost Distinguished Shooters. His dear wife Jo, ever supportive of his career, shared Carlos' bond with Eric and his sidekick, Reb. She agreed to board Reb a few days while Eric was away on duty.

Carlos hit it off with Reb from the start, having been on hunting trips and untold social gatherings where Reb was center-stage. Jo even developed a fondness for Eric's sad-eyed shadow—an affection which was about to be put to the test!

Jo had purchased a new upholstered living room chair. Reb lay on the floor so mopey-eyed and serene, she felt it safe to leave him for a few minutes while she ran some errands. In the short time she was gone, Reb had chewed, clawed, and torn that new chair to shreds. She was stunned at the sight of stuffing strewn all over the house—and melancholy Reb still lying in the same dormant position on the floor.

"What's the matter, you can behave in a barracks, but not in a house!" Jo interrogated him.

Reb perceived her disappointment, whimpering and lowering his head. He whined so like a baby that she soon forgave the pitiable culprit, even aided and abetted in concealing his crime. She simply thought too highly of Eric to disappoint him; and she was still fond of Reb, the four-legged Marine. Eric was never informed; Reb got no ears bitten, he repented, and mended his ways—at least at the Hathcocks'.

Even when Eric was home, calling on his future bride Sue Berrong, Reb would often accompany them in the car. Sue didn't mind the occasions when Reb rode along as "third wheel;" on Eric's long trips home, Reb had acquired good car manners, and was seldom a nuisance. Besides, to leave him at the house while they went out was quickly undermined by his mournful expressions. Soon Eric would relent—"*Oh, aw-rite, c'mon*"—and he would go bounding happily into the back seat.

He tried to stay out of the way, but could become jealous if left out of conversations. The perfect chaperone, his head would nudge between theirs, should theirs become too close.

After one particular date, Eric had taken Sue home. They sat in his car saying their goodbyes. As Eric turned to kiss Sue goodnight, Reb thrust his face between them. Eric planted a sincere, heartfelt smooch upon—Reb's cold nose! Eric howled with startled anger. Sue wailed with laughter. Reb fell back in his seat with a whine. Some kiss.

Another time the three of them stopped so Eric could go into a store. Eric had sternly admonished Reb to remain in the back seat, and not be a nuisance to Sue. As Eric returned to the car, he was surprised to see Reb had taken his front seat without authorization. He began to give him a verbal dressing-down, but Reb would not budge.

"You git in that back seat!" Eric ordered. But Old Reb only cowered, head down, sobbing. Jealousy had gotten root in him.

An elderly couple walking by could only see Sue in the car. They had no idea Reb lay on the seat beside her, and for all appearances Eric was yelling at Sue!

He snapped briskly, "I *told* you to stay *outta* th' front *seat*, dummy!"

The old folks turned, looking toward the car as Eric's old Drill Instructor voice took command.

"I *said*, git yore *mangy hide* offa my *seat*, and lay down in the *back*, like I *told* ye!"
Eric had the spectators' full attention at this point.

"Look here! If you don't git yore sorry tail in that back seat, I'll grab ye by the ears an' *throw* ye back there! You dumb dog!"

The old couple hastened their pace, fearing for themselves as well as Sue. Sue figured out what had happened when she saw them vacating in a startled trot. Eric overheard the kindly woman remark to her husband, "Why—he shunt-na called her *that!* Why—she's actually nice lookin', and seemed so *sweet!*"

Another time, a black bear had killed a hog belonging to Sue's father. Eric and Reb were home on leave, and Eric determined they would get that bear. Since it was winter the hog had not spoiled much. Eric dragged it with his car to a spot between the pen and the mountain, where he and Reb calculated the bear had gone. All night they sat in the car, braving the cold, watching for the bear to come claim his spoils.

Three nights passed, but no bear. Eric shifted the hog's position, concealed his car, even scattered hog scent to cover human scent. Still, no-show. Eric could not stay awake another night. And the hog was really beginning to reek. He got Sue to sit up with him and take turns watching. He put Reb outside, hoping he might catch the bear's scent over that of the hog.

Late into the night they both fell asleep. Reb became anxious to get in, and with his paws and face against Eric's window, he barked for his attention. The two slumbering sentries awoke, and in their startled state perceived Reb to be the bear, in hostile aggression.

"*Wah-h-h-h!*" they both yelped, tumbling all over each other as Eric tried to get out through Sue's door, rifle in tow, and she not planning to get out at all for the moment! Then Reb ran around and bounded in upon Sue's lap with full force, sparking another yelp from her. Eric wailed out in a Rebel Yell, to frighten the beast as he jumped in the doorway to save her. Reb got so scared, he began yelping, and nearly tore their clothes in his attempt to escape whatever was scaring his human friends.

"Be lucky if the bear comes at all, with this racket!" Eric complained. Then they just sat in the moonlight, sharing an embarrassed smirk.

But on the fifth night, the bear did come. Eric saw its dark silhouette against the bare winter trees of the mountain. It could not resist the odor; as Eric would later explain, "*A bear is drawn to a rotten carcas, like a lost camper is to sizzling bacon!*"

Eric shot it squarely through the chest with a .30-06, range about 100 yards. The beast was larger than any he had ever seen. The bullet at this range should have shattered heart, lungs, spine, and all. It fell to its haunches momentarily, but to Eric's dismay, rose back to all fours. He cussed his luck as it growled, and scampered back up the mountain! He heard it grunting and thrashing its way up a quarter mile of the steepest, thickest slope—then it collapsed, and crashed violently all the way back down. Even in death, it was a formidable creature, for it had mowed a long path of saplings and brush with its rolling mass.

It was huge, alright. Eric had it hoisted with a tractor and taken to be secretly weighed. It was the largest bear ever killed in the state, pushing 600 pounds. But he could not report it to the Game and Fish Commission! (*"Just a nuisance kill,"* Eric would call it. *"Not the kind you go talking about."*)

Eric's cousin Randall Turner (Harry's brother) could tell many a tale about nuisance bears annoying his bee hives. A renowned producer of Appalachian sourwood honey, he had upwards of 1250 hives at a time when the state Wildlife boys were restocking the vanished black bear in great numbers. Yet his nephew Bill Collins, Eric's second cousin, was a Wildlife Management official. It was all so complex. Reporting the bears was about all Randall could do, as they attacked his hives. Eric had the option of getting out of state, and the obligation of helping Sue's father. And he had a craving for bear meat.

Some 15 years later, a driver ran into a black bear at the mountain junction of Turner's Corner, setting the *official* record kill in Georgia of 580 pounds. But Eric still held "the record," even a confirmed rifle-kill; yet all he could do was grin and "bear" it.

So Eric had set yet another rifle record. But due to technicalities inherent to the incident he could never claim his crown. Not if he and Reb wanted to come home again. But he had his bear. And it was good! Shorty Berrong had his farm back. And the trio—Eric, Sue, and Reb—bonded by their mutual accomplishment—began to feel like a team. Soon Eric was able to leave Old Reb at Sue's home for extended periods.

One day as he was departing the Berrongs' to return to base, he drove all about the farm trying to find Reb, to bid him farewell. He became quite worried when he did not find him, and intensified his search. As he returned to the house overcome with concern, Sue was laughing on the front porch, pointing at the roof of Eric's car where Reb had lain all the time!

There were advantages to boarding Reb in Georgia. No more chewed up shoes right before inspection; no competition over who got the bunk or the floor. And no more embarrassing odors in the barracks, when Eric and Kazootch would look suspiciously at each other, only to find Reb to be the odorous culprit!

And, Reb had a country home, there with Sue. Everyone loved Reb. It wasn't long before boys were coming over and teaching this salivating scholar new tricks—even riding on the back of a motorcycle. So adept, Reb actually sat upright and could ride like a human passenger for hours.

Then one sad day Reb's toe got caught in the drive chain. It festered so, the vet could not save him. Gangrene claimed him. He was soon at such a level of suffering, the vet could recommend naught but euthanasia.

Eric was telephoned in Virginia. The sad scene was described. As if losing a close relative, Eric strained at the hard news; then with a heavy heart he consented to the inevitable, requesting cremation afterward. It is said that Reb's ashes were scattered atop Bald Mountain, Georgia's highest peak, above the Happy Hunting Grounds of Arkequah and Choe Stoe.

It is further said that Eric requests the same ceremony for him, when the time comes. Says Eric, *"I hope some of my ashes fertilize the herb patches up yonder; and that some blow down the backs of a few people who need an irritating reminder I was here!"* As for Reb's ashes, they honor the Hunting Grounds. His passing was duly mourned back at the Marksmanship Training Unit. His presence was vital; his absence was dismal. Never was there such loyalty between friends, nor witnessed any firmer devotion to the Corps, as shown by Reb to his personal Commandant, Eric England. After all, Old Reb was a good Marine.

CHAPTER TWENTY SEVEN

WORLD CLASS WINNER

CANADA was maintaining eminent international relations with England in 1969. Eric England, that is. For that was the year he won the Canadian Nationals, rattled the crown of the Queen's Match, then returned to fire Highest International Score in the prestigious Palma Match being hosted by Canada that year. He returned the Palma to America. The name of Eric England was becoming well-footed upon another country's sovereign soil, another step on his path to international acclaim as the greatest long-range rifle Shooter in world history.

The Palma is *la crème de la crème* of international shooting, reigning as the foremost long-range rifle match on earth since 1876. Founded by the National Rifle Association to celebrate America's Centennial of Independence, The Palma became *the* international match, open to all countries. The Palma is held every other year, in the country of the last winning team.

An individual fires one year, to qualify for his country's team the next. Eric has qualified four times and fired in The Palma twice. He missed one year due to service in Vietnam,

161

and another because no US military participated that year. Eric blew the top off of the scores in 1969, on the winning US Team; and as a civilian in the 1976 Palma which was the Palma Centennial as well as the American Bicentennial. Thus making the 1976 Team was a distinctive honor, and winning The Palma Trophy back for America that year was of paramount importance. Officials of the NRA made certain that Eric England was going to be available to participate.

Special match-grade ammo was made: the shells were stamped, and the boxes printed, indicating they were made for that prestigious match year. Any cartons or unexpended ammo became instant collector's items. Fans even grabbed up casings, as Eric and selected others fired in a tribute ceremony.

US Marines who have fired in The Palma read like a *Who's Who* of Distinguished Marksmen, the tight circle of the world's elite Shooters whom Eric calls his friends. Don Bartlett, Robert Partridge, Bob Goller, D. I. Boyd, Greg Connor, Danny Sanchez, Kenneth Erdman, Thomas Holcomb, R. F. Seitzinger, Don Smith, Earl Manning, Emil Blade, Jack Caseman, Roy Combs, David Luke, and Dana Dennis are prime examples. Other branches, and also civilians, have fired superbly in The Palma. But the impact of the US Marines—cemented by Eric's team-promoting savvy—was momentous.

Eric is also honored on a special Palma roster of "Those Who Have Represented America More Than Once." Had duty and circumstance not interferred, he may have been the only one on a roster of those firing in four Palmas. Long retired and with one eye nearly blinded from a fishing accident, the US team still requested him to coach their 1999 team, the last of the century.

The premier British armorers, Parker-Hale, produced a special red-white-and-blue "Palma 1976" engraved Winchester .308 rifle in limited quantity, strictly reserving them for each country's team of twenty Shooters plus their coaches and administrators. Even the most astute firearms collector is hard-put to locate one today, let alone persuade their owners to sell theirs. Thus The Palma represents eminence and distinction unparalleled. It generates an air of dignity. A bond of brotherhood is shared by the teams, which is accentuated by the wearing of Palma blazers, ties, and emblems during the ceremonial events.

The Palma mystique is compounded by the "vanishing trophy." Created in 1876 in the form of a Roman Standard of Triumph, its artistry is equaled only by the precious metals of which it is comprised. This coveted icon has been housed in the most honored edifices of each respective winning country, from the Lord Mayor's Mansion in London, to the Smithsonian Institute and the Pentagon in the US. From earliest times, it would be proudly depicted on the front pages of the winning country's leading newspapers. The Palma Trophy spoke for itself.

Then several years ago the honored memento disappeared! Its whereabouts is rumored: some suggest it is in a secret vault in the Smithsonian, or a secured nook of the Pentagon. Still others say it is in a private collection somewhere.

Hopefully the historic treasure was not melted down for its gold and silver!

Even with The Palma Trophy missing, its spirit seemed to continue to thrive. It remained essential to win this trophy—or its soul and essence—back for America in its Bicentennial celebration in 1976—and in 1969 within Canada's borders where the honor was last won, and where Eric had already won The Canadian Nationals.

Subsequently, a new Palma Trophy has been created, modeled after the original. It is every bit as beautiful and representative of The Palma, as is the original. It is well guarded.

Of all his individual honors, nothing compares to the designation of Palma Match Distinguished Shooter. It is tantamount to an Olympic title. Participation therein marks the culmination of a truly accomplished shooting career.

Long-range categories in The Palma include 800, 900, and 1000 yard competitions. Eric averaged 96 to 99 percent of his rounds striking perfect bullseyes. In the 1969 Palma, Eric's total score was 214, highest in the world that year. And the winning American team's overall average was 202.9.

There were four Marines on the US team, constituting 20 percent of its makeup. Included were Don Bartlett, Earl Manning, and David Luke. In the 1976 Palma, Eric and one other Marine, Robert E. Partridge, were still gunnin' 'em big. Eric's scores again soared high: 97 percent of his overall shots were perfect bulls. And true to form, he helped galvanize the American Bicentennial and NRA / Palma's Centennial; just a little icing for Corps and Country.

Eric England, by his nature, defers the glory to his team mates and range-buddies. It is a trait which wraps well around the makings of an icon who, by his long-range shooting performance, earns the distinction of World Class Winner.

CHAPTER TWENTY EIGHT

THE PRESIDENT'S HUNDRED

THE HUB of Washington with its whirling wheel of ambiguity can at times generate a surprise element of logic. The President had some useful ideas for Distinguished Shooters. Nearby Quantico USMC Base with its world-renowned match ranges was home to Eric England in 1958. He was coming to stride as a reliable Top Shot. Other notables were forming up teams with him, including the Marine mainstays Kozuch, Bartlett, Davenport, Knapper, Pietraforte, and others. Eric was an Old Salt by now. Future buddy and Shooter legend Carlos Hathcock was going through The Boot. Ike was in the White House and keeping an eye on these marksmanship marvels. It was a favorable year for the formulation of destiny.

During the Postwar years, Eisenhower still showed a keen interest in the USMC's top Shooters. Marine Snipers were deployed with great success in World War II. Quantico's Colonel Walter Walsh was highly instrumental in that undertaking. Other legendary Shooters such as John Boitnott launched Marine sniping toward a more permanent posture during his exploits in the Korean War. Washington had the presence of mind to keep these formidable crack-

165

shots close by—at HQ-USMC, the Pentagon—and at Quantico.

Eric England has referred to Colonel Walsh as his competition mentor, and Boitnott as his hero. The "Rugged Gentleman" and "The Father of Modern Shooting," Walsh had the foresight to develop sniping at an early stage, clearly mindful of its future usefulness in defense of country. Boitnott gave Marine sniping a permanent respect.

John Boitnott's effectiveness with a sniping rifle was dazzling in the hills of Korea. Marines had been taking many hits from North Korean snipers. History takes note of Sergeant Henry Friday, courageously (or outrageously) running along a trench line to draw enemy fire. John would see vapor trails left in the humid mountain air by enemy bullets. Scoping in on the origination points of these tell-tale "fog tracers," he could see the culprit rocking another round into his chamber. He would zero on him and take him out of action before he could fire another round.

After taking out nine key enemy snipers with nine shots, each averaging over 700 yards, John was suddenly called back to his Corps Commander's HQ. The Major General was so impressed with this young Sergeant, he had him set up a USMC Sniper School. "Class is right here. Graduation is on the battle front!" the General ordered him. And a new chapter in military history was born.

John relates the incident with candor and modesty. In Washington, he is still being discussed as an example of a model Marine. He was in almost every battle—twenty three campaigns and as many battle stars—from Pearl Harbor to Tokyo Bay. Then he survived the nasty Korean War with a combination of battle savvy and pinpoint sniping skills. He was such an innovative strategist and so adept at communicating and implementing same, he was made a Sergeant Major and sent to work at the Pentagon.

John worked directly with USAF General Paul Tibbits of Enola Gay / Hiroshima fame. Their job: to create the modern strategic communications system still in service today, the National Military Command Center. On a more personal note, prior to the Pentagon he was training Eric England on the fine art of enemy sniper detection and counter-sniper elimination. By imparting his sage and war-tested advice, he indirectly saved Eric's life—and earned the title of "hero" in Eric's estimation.

Eric and many USMC Shooters were training heavily in Sniper warfare at Quantico. They were linked to a concentration of Top Shots in the Washington region. There was a reason for this.

There is a highly honored distinction known as "The President's Hundred." This elite group is a selection of the choicest, highest-scoring Shooters in the US, from all military branches. They are the first to be called up in time of critical need—as bodyguards and defense tacticians for the President of the United States.

Eric qualified for this distinction four times. This is a lesser-known fact in the Marine Corps partly because of its privileged status; and because unlike other branches, the USMC has never gotten around to approval of wearing the special engraved epaulet which reads, "The President's Hundred." But all the important people knew he had earned it, including Ike.

Cousin Harry was in Washington in 1958, visiting his brother Edward. They paid a call on Eric, who took them around Quantico. Harry, although out of the Corps seven years, found his name still remembered by some of the Marine Shooters in Eric's fellowship. Eric was introducing Harry around as the man responsible for instigating his own shooting career. The men urged Harry to come back in—take a commission even—and by all means get on their rifle team! They assured him they had sufficient connections "all the way up the line" to secure the deal. Though honored, Harry knew he must decline, being the head of a family now and in an important career position.

Harry turned his attention back to Eric now. "Ol' Georgia Boy here will carry on the tradition! I hear he's even got the attention of Ike now. On his list of Top 100!"

"Aw," Eric responded. "Ike's an Army man. 'The Hundred' is an Army badge. It's just an Army thing!"

Eric and Jesse Davenport would soon after visit Harry at his lakeside Hiawassee home. Again the subject arose: would Harry join the Match Team? Harry looked at his kids playing

Marine with toy rifles, and said, "Nowadays, it's just a civilian thing!"

Harry's kids became expert Shooters. And Harry enjoyed watching his "recruits" grow. That was just Harry's thing now. Eric went on to be the President's No. 1. That was just an Eric thing.

CHAPTER TWENTY NINE

PRESUMED DEAD

VITAL yet deadly was the Hai Van Pass, situated not far from the Phu Bai airfield, and leading to the life-line of Da Nang. Through it, the serious flow of convoys could not afford to be imperiled or delayed. Despite Marine bunkers and strongpoint security presence there, *beau coup* VC had taken the offensive in harassing and ambushing US and allied vehicular movement in the crucial land channel.

A particular VC strategy was to forego the temptation to display any strategy at all. Rather, they would dig in days before the expected convoy activity, then on sizing up the tactical factors related to the procession, would shift the ambush toward one end or another of the pass. Usually this was merely sniping the lead vehicle as it neared the notorious and treacherous hairpin turn. If there were a 5-ton truck in the convoy, it may have to slow to a mere 5 MPH at that point.

Much of the sloping terrain lay windward of the South China Sea, where vegetation was sparser. Then westward the foliage became lusher. Initially the pass was on the windward slopes only, nigh impossible for ambushes of consequence, but never immune to enemy sniper fire. At many points farther into the pass, strong teakwood trees provided excellent cover. It was difficult to determine just where along the lengthy corridor an assault would be, or how severe.

Sometimes the unsuspected steeper slopes of the sawtooth ridges would hide Charlie in substantial numbers. Charlie's escape was often spotted by FAC's, LOH's or OV-1's, and promptly snuffed. But what of the hard-chargers who burroughed down and lived out the mouse-hunt without breaking brush? This rugged solitude also represented exactly the extra mileage Eric and fellow Phantoms would go to observe and outgun the grassroots foe. Charlie was not accustomed to regular troops being as willing to dig in and mold with the native soil as long as he did. Charlie had nowhere special to go; no shower to look forward to; no club; cold cokes. But to the mountain-Marine hard-holder—the backwoods contender—the hunting was good. This element of surprise and counter-logic gave Eric precisely the edge he needed to outlast, outmaneuver, and outgun Charlie on his own turf.

The strategic problem was that no one ever knew when or where to expect an ambush, of course. Despite aerial and ground reconnaissance, Charlie was seldom caught in his sporadic incursions into the Pass. When he did ambush there, however, two tactical patterns were beginning to be noted.

A traditional full assault was rare due to strong US presence and tactics, and the limitations of the Hai Van's steep slopes. Instead, as a convoy approached an open, straight section, dropping its guard with a sigh of relief, remote-fire mines and rocket-propelled grenades would take out the lead vehicle. Then the rear would be devastated, corking them up. Machine-gun mounted jeeps, APC's, and other escort vehicles, would thus be blocked for the hit. Fire would rain from VC on both sides initially, then would alternate to give the illusion of shifting or withdrawal or being eliminated. Then as VC on one side concentrated fire, distracting the convoy's fire to them, the other VC opened up on their backs, but seldom charged them outright. It hit hard and it hurt bad, but Charlie got his "rear-guard" whupped enough to ease him off.

In a more newly developing tactic of harassment and interdiction, the VC would dig in at varying elevations, achieving two to three tiers of well-concealed combatants. Or Charlie merely posted one or two snipers. Alternating their fire made them difficult targets, and likewise difficult to register for air or arty support. Moreover, artillery was for the most part impractical for firing into many segments of the Pass. Only with devastating air support and helicopter-inserted ground reinforcements, could a stalled convoy ever hope to leave the Pass again. Many wounded, unable to benefit from medevac, would die needlessly as their comrades were pinned down. But in the Hai Van Pass, it was mostly nagging by sniper fire.

As the convoy ambushes were sporadic and hard to forecast, US forces even tried driving empty fuel tankers through as juicy decoys for saboteurs, after leaking intelligence of when they would be running, their destination and priority. Heavy backup would stand by, especially at the infamous "hairpin."

Local traffic would be stopped by MP's. Then as the trucks raced through the Pass, their cabs reinforced with steel plate and sandbags and additional fire-power escort, Charlie would be a no-show. It became evident that the under-supplied Charlie was stockpiling his arsenal with unpredictability, a weapon he used against US planning, clarity of objectives, and morale.

As security increased in the Pass and pressure mounted to reduce friendly casualties, a single convoy personnel hit by a sniper or landmine could be as morale-lowering as a status-deep-serious ambush was in times of heavier fighting there. And the effect was the same: supplies or vital movement was curtailed.

The scenario was being discussed at the USMC Sniper School at Phu Bai. "Could any pre-emptive action be taken against such unforeseen enemy operations?" and "Could Marine Snipers be deployed in such a way as to spot and suppress enemy effectiveness in the Hai Van Pass?" were questions Eric and team were being handed by the brass. "Gotta ride the ridge early, to see the hawks dive!" and "We'll have to slither out and scalp 'em before they send any more saddles home!" were typical responses being handed back by Eric.

Gunny England and his elite *confreres* studied on the situation day and night. Air-supply could keep the Americans in Phu Bai sustained, but that road needed to be kept open. And it was a matter of principal: the Comanches couldn't be allowed to harass the Santa Fe Trail!

The conversation arose with freshness among the school's NCO's and officers, with news of any convoy ambush anywhere. If a technique could be developed here in this spur of the Trung Son Mountains, it could be deployed regionally as well. The 1st Division Sniper School had been founded by Distinguished Shooters: George Hurt, to whom Eric still refers as "the most squared-away Marine anyone ever knew;" and Jim Bowen, the crack shot who would storm the Nationals with astonishing scores—Don Barker, who made the first VC kill by a Marine Sniper—Billy Savelle, the first-rate armorer who made history in the first Marine landing at Tourane and crafted the School's first sniper rifles—and their OIC, Bob Russell. The school was still run by Distinguished Shooters, all buddies from the competition matches back home, and still turned out the finest rated Snipers in history. Eric wanted to apply their expertise to alleviate some of the Charlie factor holding sway in weaker segments of the Hai Van Pass.

But any mission into the Hai Van would require too much time and risk to involve Division Sniper School students. The experimental task, if it could be carried out at all, would be up to the seasoned pros—the instructional cadre themselves. Eric thought and sketched and played out a multiplicity of strategic ideas, based on humping, overflying, or driving by the Pass—and poring over all recon photos, maps, and after-action reports he could lay his hand on. Contacts at Intel were pleased to share data with him. They didn't ask, and he didn't volunteer info in return—until after a mission was complete. And they knew how he relished his study time: let him ponder it all out, like a hungry hunter. Finally he arrived at a fresh insight into an old adage.

He approached his NCOIC and long-time pal, G.B. Merrill. "We gotta fight Charlie up yonder, dog to dog. Sniff

172

out his trail, and get to the feed bowl first," he related. "Just like we always do, but really fight surprise with surprise. Use nature, the elements, foresight—and Charlie's own tactics—to our own advantage. Turn the checkerboard on him!"

G.B. Grinned. "With you so far, Moonshiner! You're trying to *git thar fustest, with the mostest,* like your ol' Redneck Rebel, General Forrest, would do," he divined. G.B. knew his partner well—trusted his life to him frequently—and trusted his way of thinking. He knew Eric would not act without all angles being accounted for, and all Marine lives safeguarded. And that he would bag his limit.

"Well, lay out the facts: Charlie has been taking three to six weeks to plan an ambush in the Hai Van.
"So, we light out early?"

"Roger that. Get harbored up, and wait for *him* to saunter his half-pint hiney up or along those slopes. He has to be coming from the ends or the back sides of the ridges. So, we arrive early enough with a recon team who can mine and booby trap all the logical approaches to Charlie's kill zones."

"Sounds massive already."

"Naw, we keep it simple. Go in early, lose the recon escort. Recon sets the traps while we move on ahead. They can provide a blocking force at the same time, if interdicting fire is needed. Or they can follow Charlie to his lairs if undetected."

"Okay." G.B.'s grin grows and glows. "Now, Snipers. Where..."

"Turn-to, about zero-dark-thirty. Get a good blind, harbor up good n' gungy. Dig in as high up the ridges as possible. Charlie never assaults from 'way up yonder, 'cept maybe sometimes snipers. Might have him an observer or scout up there. But too far from the road, in most cases, or a bad angle to the road. I think Charlie's shooters are digging in—spider holes—further *down* the slopes. They're watching for our flying bird dogs. We mostly observe; call it all in, in code, when they look like they're setting one up. Two of our Snipers atop each ridge..."

"Man, what a sea story this will weave!"

173

"...then we look for heavy weapons bearers, radio men, cut them off right at the start—their skills will take a long time to replace. Look for snipers and spotters. Watch them a long time, study their ways and means and their foul-ups too. Then snipe them as needed. Or just roll frags down the hills. Drive Charlie down to the road. Cap off both ends of their escape route—and *then* lay siege to any exposed positions left over."

"Seems strategically sound, at first look. OIC will be pleased to hear anything that sounds like a solution, to hand up the ladder."

"Most of all, we move out well ahead of time, under cover of heavy monsoon. Real *Marine* weather. Command the range."

"How do you expect to get back?"

"Meander back slowly. Try to catch a monsoon cover, and move by night. Route us away from our traps."

"And recon?"

"Aw, forget re-con or lurp's at that point. They'll be too busy interrupting Charlie's lines of commo, supply, and retreat. And Charlie? No sweat. He'll have forgotten us by then. Whether we have to dig in a day or two, or scoot like a scalded skunk, we'll be off their minds as they deal with the traps and patrols. Many will've already been shot to shreds once they're driven down to the road. Any convoy target, real or dummy, won't even need to close. We'll expose Charlie before he hears Detroit Drums!"

"By the numbers!"

The plan formed up well. As a sign of merit, the OIC echoed credence from the powers that be. The overall strategy was hailed as being as comprehensive and effectual as any one or two men could ever hope to achieve. Within twenty four hours the final script was approved, although Eric had already initiated rehearsals. In another twelve, it was implemented. Curtains up. The monsoons were rolling in hard and heavy.

"One more thing," G.B. pointed out. "Got to spread the spirit of *The Phantom* in all this. Our students have started to run with the ball that you and our buddies pitched in. Your mark is everywhere."

"*Our* mark."

"Let 'em know The Phantom of Phu Bai has struck! Strike a stake through their evil, cunning hearts."

Eric and his spotter, a Buck Sergeant some called "Gator Hide" due to his toughness in moving through rugged terrain, loaded up with a recon team in a Huey UH-1 bound for the back side of the far ridge of the Hai Van Pass. The recon moved with them the first night, in pouring monsoons that chilled the bones and mired the feet. At times they felt like they were using their knees for feet, and their hips as propellers. Next night, the patrol withdrew into the ambiance and the Sniper team slowly and cautiously advanced up the stern back side of the ridge.

Reaching the crest required three nights of steady effort, on short rations. But they were alive, and were well situated with a crow's nest view of the pastoral scene which could spasm into one of blood and death. They selected a depression in the earth just behind the lip of the ridge. Feeling for booby trap wire and noting that the cavity had apparently never been occupied as a sniping hide, they spent the remainder of the night constructing natural cammo for themselves to supplement their cammo clothing and face paint.

Though they had brought seven days' limited rations, they could only carry two canteens each. Gator Hide constructed a trap-basin of broad green leaves for collecting rainwater. Eric bunched up a section of his rubber poncho and braced it up with twigs, just beneath their cammo canopy, for like purpose. Now, they wait.

And wait they did. The team plan was to remain in place three days max, then withdraw at angles oblique to their original approach. They were reasonably comfortable for the first while, but they could not move significantly. Any movement on their part could fix them as a target for Charlie's woodland scouts. Then the cold rains began to pound down on them all the more, as they struggled to keep their weapons dry.

After several hours the nagging old sensation came back—that 'Nam-*esque* way of wondering if they had outsmarted Charlie, or if Charlie had detected them and was slowly turning the tables. After all, they were deep into Injun Country—and this time, they were taunting Cochise himself.

"Looks like Charlie's gone out with another gal," Gator whispered after two days of damp. To help keep the natural shivers down, they curled up around chemical heating pads obtained from the Corpsmen. "Wonder if Charlie can hold his entrails as long as I have to."

"I'm more worried about yours!" Eric scoffed. The Phantom continued to scan the area, then went on, "We're so well set up here. And he hasn't seen us, thanks to the rains. Too bad we can't rotate off, sneak in fresh men every few days." He paused and sighed. "But we gotta move."

"Roger that! We'll die of pneumonia, or else sneeze our cover away!"

"Yeah, and our escape route is only effective as long as we're not spotted! Otherwise, we could be trapped up here forever, like a cold, hungry poacher watching the game wardens climb up to his roost!" Scanning the kill zone a half hour longer, Eric reached for the radio. "Reception committee—return to ballroom," he murmured.

The order given, they began to emerge from the muddy hole at sundown, worming their way down the back of the ridge and into denser foliage. They slithered almost 200 yards before daring to move by foot, still making little progress, but exploiting the slow pace to listen and observe for enemy presence.

On the morning of the fifth day they were burroughing in to take turns getting some sleep, when to their restrained surprise a squad of VC came running up a trail they had been watching. And in the distance they could hear what sounded like several approaching vehicles from a southerly direction in the Pass.

"Man! Gotta get 'em, Gunny!" Gator hissed.

"Naw, wait," Eric interceded. "They're just riflemen, a small lead element. 200 yards, lotsa cover. Let's wait and nail any heavy weapons bearers that may follow. If no other VC show up within a quarter-hour, we'll track 'em back up there and throw a surprise party for that rifle squad, *and* cut off their retreat!"

176

They laid low as the squad ran by them, turning toward the south end of the ridge where it dropped in elevation. Then sure enough, within minutes three VC came plodding up the trail, one lugging an 81mm mortar tube and rounds, another one toted its base plate and a slung AK-47, and the third one was humping even more mortar rounds.

By now Eric and Gator had moved into a hidden swell obscured by vines and a stand of young, thin bamboo. The VC were easy pickings. The Phantom scoped the lead one with his .30-06, slamming a round squarely through his heart at 50 yards. Gator swiftly dispatched the other two with his M-14.

"Wish we could go down there and destroy that tube," Gator mumbled.

"No sweat, Swabbie!" Eric replied with a salty grin, scanning for it through his scope. "You nicked it, good. Nonfunctional surplus!"

"Better make like elbows and shoe soles, eh Gunny? That rifle squad will disperse around us, or give chase. Ya reckon?"

"Yeah, they'll withdraw from the ambush site. And they didn't go near as high as they looked like they would. We'll set up on down the slope a piece. Pick off as many retreaters as we can. Really spook 'em good. They'll think we're *ever*-whur!"

Sure enough, a convoy could be heard rumbling by. But no hostile fire. He radioed that no enemy operatives had reached the strike zone—Eric's economics sparing heavy US firepower. Then they resumed their own stealthy withdrawal.

Soon they cringed in their tracks, at the blast of a mine 300 yards distant; likely VC nibbling on recon's bait. Listening for breaking brush in their own sector, they tuned out all others and moved on.

Then came the droning of a C-130, trailing a gaseous cloud.

"Defoliant!" croaked Eric. "No way! They ain't due for *this* A/O! Who in the *wild-blue-yonder* coordinated *that* dirty-bird?"

"Radio it off?" whispered Gator.

"Naw! It'll pinpoint us for Charlie! But we gotta scram 'fore that poison hits us! Gotta make a run for it! Charlie's running 'way ahead of us by now anyway!"

Moving briskly as their undernourished legs could carry them, they were separated briefly. Gator Hide slipped down a muddy slope and broke his lower leg. Eric popped his thigh with a little morphine syrette issued to them by their senior Corpsman. He splinted him, slung the M-14, and plotted a mental map to the extraction LZ. Gator would have gritted his teeth and grunted on, but the extra noise would be deadly; or he would die of shock, or impact his fracture. Soon the morphine put him down. Eric slung him in a fireman's carry and plodded on, maintaining a focal point of trying to tote a huge buck to a pickup truck while dodging game wardens—guerilla game wardens.

Twice he had to squat in the bushes while VC ran by. Then onward again. Abandoning any hope of chopper extraction now, he meandered toward Phu Bai. It took nearly two more days on quarter-rations to reach the flats. Gator's leg was swollen and on the verge of gangrene. No morphine. They could not make it over the open terrain. Eric radioed for a chopper.

In camp, Eric was surprised to see his gear packed for shipment. Those who knew him darted around for a second look, aghast and sputtering, "England! Gunny! 'Zat *you? Can't* be!"

"Why, s'me as ever *was* me!" he snapped back.

Back home, a Marine officer was calling on his folks to deliver the regrets of the President and the Corps: *Eric England is dead.*

CHAPTER THIRTY

A THORN IN THE FLESH

NEWS of Eric's demise on the field of battle spread through Blairsville like wildfire. His folks were deluged with spontaneous tears and buckled with faint spirits as the officer related to them that Gunnery Sergeant Eric England was killed in action. But their initial devastation was soothed into a state of mystified hope, when sister Edie noticed a discrepancy in the Marine serial number and other identifying data on the Department of Defense forms. His devoted fan since childhood, she knew Eric's records and personal data about as well as he did.

Her observation prompted the DOD's own inquiry into the matter. Still, before the report could be confirmed, the word buzzed all around Blairsville and two neighboring counties that the supposedly invulnerable Eric England had gone the way of Davy Crockett at the Alamo. People fell into a quiet stare, a sort of attentional salute, at hearthsides and fishing streams and 'lightenin' stills and race tracks—at general stores—on tractor seats—and behind the wheels of deputies' patrol cars. Their own hero and brother of the common bond—could he be gone?

Within two days the Marine officer, in a mixture of embarrassment and great joy, returned to their home to report the mistake. The folks could only stare in wonderment;

179

then after his departure, collapse in a fusion of relief and unreleased grief.

Half a world away, the false report was also circulating among the VC and NVA operating in I Corps, hoping the unseen Deliverer of Death—The Phantom of Phu Bai—had indeed gone the way of all KIA. The mystique was only promulgated all the more, as his sure mark continued to be emblazoned upon their war dead, either by his hand or that of his many unseen protégés. Enemy intelligence had felt certain that the reported KIA was their own Phantom. Their fear and ironic respect for him grew with every well-placed USMC Sniper round still being incurred.

Then came the wound. The Phantom's reach might have been finally curtailed by the wound. His momentum only stretched in spite of it. It was early 1967. Mortar attacks were not exactly news. But they always announced themselves as heavy headlines. Mortars began to rain upon Phu Bai. *Again.* The stunning thud, then *"bah-woompf,"* compelled men to cover.

Eric's reflexes were as well-conditioned as they had been in Boot Camp. He was down and behind sandbags before the second round hit. But not soon enough to escape a needle-sized sliver of white-hot shrapnel piercing his lower abdomen, zinged at him from the first round.

In the excitement of the moment he had failed to fully notice the pin-prick wound, searing as it was. After the attack was over and the all-clear was sounded, he attempted to resume a standing position. But now he winced suddenly at the sting burning his lower belly. There was minimal blood on his green trousers. Personal examination revealed something like just another thistle puncture, a way of life for him.

He treated the puncture with a Band-Aid, and felt no need to report for medical aid. Soon he was in his stride again, albeit with a mild limp which he craftily concealed. But the little foreign object began to intensify as a veritable thorn in the flesh, painful, and encumbering movement. He toughed it out.

He had no intention of reporting the minor wound, since news of it could be exaggerated and alarm the homefolk—or Charlie. His buddy Carlos Hathcock had already been identified by the enemy thanks to an overzealous reporter headlining his Sniper exploits. Soon after, Ho Chi Minh made it a personal goal to have Hathcock's scalp. And now more than ever, Eric needed to be in the field—young Marines depended on him.

But due to this nagging little prick of a wound, some field duties were becoming more difficult to fulfill. He did not want to endanger a spotter or a student in the wilds of the Vietnam bush. He feared above all an assignment to "a desk full of memories." He was not ready to harbor up. He was in his prime. And he always worked faster and more efficiently alone.

So naturally, he began to venture out into Injun Country solo, more than ever, to enhance productivity. He knew his potential to contribute outweighed his time. His war was ending, but not his fight.

Many Americans initially entered Vietnam assuming the natives were all primitive and ignorant. They soon learned that Charlie's intelligence-gathering prowess was formidable, equal to his stunning cleverness in guerrilla operations. Still, it came as some surprise to Eric when a recon patrol reported overhearing VC mention him by name—pronouncing it phonetically as *A-Wick Ain-Lan*. The Marine grunts killed the passing three-man VC recon, who died with Eric's name on their lips.

A daily camp laborer, a Mama-San washwoman, had been overheard at Phu Bai Village passing information to a suspected VC. South Vietnamese Intel also heard her mention the name of *A-Wick Ain-Lan*—*Ma Quai Phu Bai!* The traitorous woman escaped as the VC suspect was arrested by Intel agents. She was pursued by ARVN MP's of dubious loyalty, who may have allowed her to escape.

When word filtered down to Gunny England that he was the subject of enemy espionage, considered important enough to have his name on their worried breath, he only grinned. And shook his head. G.B. at first looked concerned for his buddy, but soon regathered his confidence in him, knowing of his mettle.

"Not worried are ya, G.B.?" he pried. He was also dredging for any additional Intel data on himself, of which he should take note.

"Not especially," G.B. replied in good spirits. "Least not, knowing *you*! You'd probably invite yourself to Ho Chi Minh's garden party, and probably get out alive, too!"

A renewed grin restored Eric's focus. His confidence chimed through. "Well, I reckon we'd better close ranks awhile, and keep our powder dry."

"Turn invisible, you mean! Remember when Carlos Hathcock was in-country? Charlie put a big price on his head, they say. Most likely offers a rebate on ours."

"Sha, I know for *reason*! Even put up wanted posters on him. But they never got him. Made his focus sharper, is all."

"Well, we need to rotate you around more. Keep you from getting targeted. You let it *sag*, you get it *bagged*."

"Just like a fat-n-sassy possum." Eric stood up from his cot, and stumbled slightly.

"Did I see you limp?"

"Naw! Just one o'them *phantom limb* reactions you hear about!"

G.B.'s chuckle failed to fully mask his worry. "Well, maybe stay outta the field for awhile—much as you can! You're too valuable a teacher, to get wasted by those Skunk Squads. Just watch out for Mama-San assassins in camp! Boy-San *hit men*."

But Eric did limp. He struggled to conceal it while instructing. He ventured to mask any semblance of physical limitation around the cadre. But now a vital mission needed to be undertaken and executed, one he sensed growing and pulsating in his bones, muscles, nerves, and viscera. His sinews twinged with the current. He knew there was one more "big one" to carry out. Command wasn't cognizant of its existence or import. But Eric knew it. Like a phantom, he fully sensed the need to scout the peripheral terrain for any encroaching enemy who may be intent upon eliminating any USMC Snipers, their schools, or their effective operational status. And if they were coming for *him*, he needed to divert them away from his unit and his buddies.

The instinctive awareness that some enemy commando operation was afoot in the area, directed toward the Sniper School, would not cease its nagging. It was no grandiose ideation. It was a prescient red-alert to protect Marines, manifesting itself not only through Intel data, but through all the senses, tingling the hairs of the back of his neck. This may be his last mission. He was going to plan out a one-man long range recon patrol—a slow sweep—a scouting survey of the flats and ridges surrounding Phu Bai. It would be his farewell gift to I Corps.

He would alternate between being a solitary observation post by day, and a prowling deadly reptile by night. A few extra rations, water purification tabs, and a little first aid gear would be all that he added to his routine equipage. That, and an extra issue of faith and esprit.

He would not maneuver his way out from the base, into any awaiting traps. He would insert far beyond the ridges, then work his way back. He would become a worm in the woodwork, scouting the periphery of peril; detecting enemy positions or activities, and eliminating as many as may prove propitious. He may be limited to one crucial shot per day, then move by night and set up for the next day, and so on. Charlie would be waiting for him to exit the base via traditional routes, or by chopper insertion, and would deign to be ready for him. But he would rout Charlie with a sweeping rearward movement, get behind them and flush them forward like game birds, in startled confusion. He would be The Phantom.

Catching a ride out on a convoy at sunrise, he had already gained unit-level clearance to be out a few days. He hopped off the convoy at a bushy curve of the road and darted into natural cover, working his way obliquely up a ridge. He got atop the crest and surveyed from within the scrub brush. By 10:00 it was already a hot day.

The camo face paint was not supposed to fully clog the pores, but it was uncomfortable enough. He remained calm and motionless, minimizing the generation of body heat. He regulated his breathing after the vigorous climb, to be long, slow, and deep, to conduct heat out of him by the respiratory process. He conserved more water this way. The high-potency vitamin tab made him slightly queasy, but this was good; this reduced the sense of hunger. But it also caused his skin to emit a tell-tale scent, which he masked by slowly rubbing non-toxic leaves on his appendages and chest. He lay keenly observing, like a rock with eyes and ears.

All ID had been left behind. No insignia of any sort. Not even his usual rifle, to avoid the serial number being traced. He must not be identified if captured or killed. They could await MIA reports, to guess who he was. Or they could send a fingerprint—or a fingertip—to Hanoi, for analysis in cooperation with a covert contact in Washington. They could eventually determine who he was. But he delay their probing long enough to overwork and logjam their intelligence operations—and prolong the mystique.

He faced north, to minimize solar rays within his visual field.

He scanned every ravine, vegetation clump, and deadly inch of valley for movement—for matériel—anything out of the ordinary which may suggest preparation for enemy operation. He calculated windage and elevation at potential target areas by observing temperature, slope, rising heat waves, and breeze. Despite many years of practice and firing 1.5 million rounds on rifle ranges, his hearing was still sensitive to every snap of a twig and rustle of a leaf. Given a repetitive sound pattern, he could estimate height, weight, and direction with stunning accuracy, much like sizing up game back home. After all, the average Charlie weighed about the same as the average white-tail doe.

The perch was too exposed to sun and breeze. There was no water source, and little tree cover. He needed to move down. Toward late afternoon he crouched up and worked his way eastward along the ridge, slowly scanning for elements of concern, moving at a snail's pace and with the gracefulness of a battlefield ballet. Then cautiously turning about, he began to inch his way diagonally down toward the mid-elevation point. As he approached his new hide facing north by northwest, he arrested his body's impulse to leap, duck, or fire. For his visual alarm rang clearly through his finely tuned optic nerves, detecting an animated object moving up a tree, with apparent purpose in mind.

Eric slowly sank into the cover of bushes, pulling his binoculars surreptitiously to his eyes. A little raven-haired man clad in the standard black PJ's, and "Ho Chi Minh shoes" made of old tire tread and innertube, moved cunningly up the arboreal spire with a captured US 20x spotting scope slung on is back.

Once perched atop the tree, Charlie fixed in on Phu Bai with his powerful scope. The Phantom watched Ranger Chuck as he watched for evidence of The Phantom. His AK-47 was leaned against a tree trunk. He was an easy kill at 300 yards, and an important one since he was a spy or artillery surveyor or scout. Then Ranger Chuck pulled a US-issue grid map from his shirt and began to make calculations on his fingers, "walking off" distances by forming two twigs into a compass. He seemed to be taking notes and comparing them to other papers he held. He was obviously skilled and dedicated at killing the good guys.

Eric had him crosshaired in his scope—observing, waiting, plotting—then Ranger Chuck folded his notes inside his map and began feeling for footholds, apparently satisfied with his findings. His elimination was necessary.

However, to shoot him now would only alert other VC in the area, getting himself surrounded and captured at a vulnerable point on the slope. He knew Ranger Chuck would not move toward Phu Bai. His arty comrades, with rocket launchers at the ready, would surely be behind him or to his flank. He may have an accomplice, and they would surely return to the rocket launch site. And they may be passing directly toward him!

Ranger Charlie, the little spy, angled up the ridge toward a clump of heavy brush at the top, and moved along it until he reached his cover-man—his back-up. Though 200 yards above him, Eric could hear them chattering with excitement. He had been stealthy enough, surely, not to have been spotted by these VC. Yet this VC rear guard was also concealed, and Eric had no idea just where he was, or what he could see. Holding his fire had extended his own war and life at least another few minutes.

The tides of war, at least for a Scout-Sniper, diminish into whirlpools of complex, individual battlefields.

The two VC chattered some more, then moved together through the bushes, edging onto the back side of the ridge. Eric resented having to work his way back up in daylight, but did so, moving at first in an opposite direction, then doubling back to the crest to observe them.

He was surprised to see them descend the ridge and move southward through tall grasses. At first their movement in the elephant grass was easily detectable, but then a moderate breeze stirred up the sea of grass, extending their lives. The sun was crouching lower, on its first backward glance of the day. The VC were moving into its rays. He needed to stop these intelligence-gatherers. He kept a vigil to his flanks for any VC trying to trap him. Were the two below leading him into a snare as their silhouettes blended with the solar beams? He would rather risk capture or a shoot-and-evade field day, than to allow the varmints in the grass to escape with their ill-gotten goods.

He scanned the waving grasses with his scope, knowing the window was closing, narrowing into a peep hole with each vital second. Then two dark figures emerged at a point over 1100 yards to the south, where they began to ascend another ridge. It was now or never.

Eric labored to stay within his Shooter's bubble, hampered by sharp pain throbbing in his lower abdomen. He was so self-masterful, he subconsciously regulated the flow of sweat which threatened to obstruct his eyes and hands. And he absorbed the pain; quarantined it for future reference.

The VC moved slowly, but in a jerk-and-halt gait, as though carrying something. He had only a moment. He had to take his due course. The crosshairs of the 10x scope he kept aligned on the top of the bobbing head in back. Once it paused long enough to cause the lead man to also halt, a match-grade .30-06 round riveted the rear VC perfectly between the shoulder blades. Forward and down he went in a flash. The lead VC heard nothing more than a sudden *thoop*, and turning to look downward in horror, may have just heard the faint and distant report which had propelled it. Already Eric had smoothly chambered his second round. The surviving VC flailed his arms and looked frantically all around for a logical path of escape. Eric could make out the spotter scope dangling from his neck.

Ranger Chuck had lost the composure he had exhibited in his spy perch earlier. He was jumping about so furiously, he made a poor target until he seemed to freeze, signaling to an unseen comrade. He made himself a lateral target. Eric wanted to strike his chest in hopes of damaging his notes. He waited until Ranger Chuck raised his left arm again, beckoning to his comrade—just long enough for his personalized projectile to find true its mark—directly through the left ribcage, blowing out bone, heart, lung, and all. He would not be talking now.

His unseen pal now ran over in a crouch to his fallen frame. From the cover of chatter, he probably didn't even hear the shot that ushered his comrade on the express train to purgatory. No matter. Stopping to assess the horrific damage, he hastened his own demise—got his ticket punched—as yet another well-placed round tunneled his cranium, ear to ear.

Three rounds from one hide, midriff of the back side of a ridge with low cover, nowhere near water, and in immediate need of crossing back to the opposing slope, he knew that like a good Phantom his next move was to utterly vanish. Dig in and lick the morning dew from plants if necessary—or squirm like a limp lizard toward friendlier lines—but make himself scarce. His pain was in clear focus now; he fought it off like a Marine as he scrambled. He silently praised Providence that the VC had not inculcated the art of tracking with dogs. The only trick a Vietnamese dog learns is to "roll over and stay dead," while being prepared for dinner.

Then after crawling 300 yards in a diversionary pattern, intense pain burned through his belly and thighs. Was he hit by a distant round? Stabbed by a bamboo spear or pierced by a booby trap? His body would not move! He ordered it into action, but it was insubordinate. He felt for blood. None. No, he knew the source of his debilitating pain. His little wound had so weakened his muscle tissue, that he had acquired a hernia!

In agony he inched forward. Every centimeter of ground was excruciating, draining his stamina, but not his nerve. By focusing on Boot Camp cadence he once called out as a DI, and the honor of his Appalachian roots—and abiding visions of returning to sweet Sue there awaiting—drawing deeply from the well of soul, he advanced with steely determination. Over stones and mud, through thickets and streams, he out-crawled a torturous night of agony laced with hazard, chilled by the foul breath of looming death, until within US patrol zones surrounding Phu Bai.

Day would dawn within the hour. He could now lie still until spotting friendlies, then radio in code back to Operations, where a message could be relayed to pick him up. Or he could lie in the weeds through the new day, and struggle on through stealth of night as an infiltrator into his own base, risking friendly fire as an unfit curtain call on an already tragic play.

But vivid memories of Marines captured in this sector, mutilated and slain and mutilated some more, motivated him to grovel on until he could wobble up to the main gate. A sight for the guards to behold, he was a walking piece of the bush.

Yet he was back to the bush in days, toughing out field instruction and gun position check-overs. Then on a three-week scout-solo, it hit again. He made it back. But his war was over.

CHAPTER THIRTY ONE

KAZOOTCH

KAZOOTCH is a phenomenon in his own right: Kazootch the Sniper—Distinguished Shooter—renowned combat Marine. Jerry Kozuch shines among the primary facets of the dazzling Marine Shooters' world, and features prominently in Eric England's remarkable career. "Kazootch," as Eric calls him, brings to bear the essence of the world in which Eric the Shooter budded, bloomed, and grew to his place in history. That their careers would parallel so closely and frequently as they did, alludes to the destiny that molded these great men and the distinction they came to embody. This applies to highflyin' hijinks as well as sure-fire shootin'. History bears this out!

Kazootch—National Open rifle champion for twenty two minutes, defeating the national record held my team mate Don Bartlett—only to be beaten by Eric England before he could fully savor the victory. All three men on the same team; all three world class Shooters; all remembered forever as among the pioneers of the USMC Sniper program in Vietnam. Destiny was ringing their doorbell.

Kazootch is as Yankee as they come. His juggernaut Jersey accent has never lost its edge after years of military and public service, living all over the world and in the spotlight of acclaim. He is a self-contained entity; so why give up anything? That he ranks among Eric's and Don's closest and most respected friends attests to his salty savvy as a true Marine. As a match Shooter, Kazootch is world class. As a combat Shooter, his accomplishments are still talked about. He sniped with everything from a rifle to a 106mm recoilless. He generated combat strategies that helped cast *"the mystique."*

Their mystique—the shadow of the Sniper Phantasm—was generating among them long before actually seeing Vietnam.

They had begun honing it on the Marine Corps Rifle and Pistol Teams since the early 1950's. They kept hound dogs together at the Camp Lejeune range barracks, and hunted together to the point that they had trained one another almost as well as their dogs. They lived for cultivating their art of hunting perfection. The impact this would have on the enemy in Vietnam, and the entire future of US military sniping, was momentous.

They left for Vietnam together, too, receiving simultaneous promotions to Gunnery Sergeant. Assigning them to serve as Scout Snipers in Vietnam was tantamount to sending a Major Leaguer to pitch for the Little League. The skill and long-time *esprit de corps* of they and their fellow Shooters was perhaps the key element in formulating the mystique. These were a brotherhood of arms—a breed of target masters—a tradition. And tough. Charlie did not know what was coming.

Eric and Kazootch shared a friendly rivalry of course, especially as to who was the better shot with a .45 pistol. In 1959 at Lejeune, they had gone to the North Carolina woods to target shoot, and perform quality-assurance tests on samples of "Lightenin' Elixir" imported from North Georgia. Both had fired High Expert and won several matches with the weapon. Both had been known to have held a .45 upside, firing from the hip and triggering with the little finger, while rapid-firing a tin can into a death-dance. Now Eric formally challenged Kazootch to a two-man showdown.

Reeling from "Appalachian Windage," they were several knots adrift. They had blasted all their targets with precision throughout the day. Now as dusk enveloped them, Eric proposed a grand finale match.

"Betcha can't hit the reflectors on that old junk car over yonder, across the grass," he challenged.

"Step it off!" Kazootch answered the dare. Eric tried to walk but his feet were now off duty, and his bearings had gone TDY. Regaining his balance, he warbled, "Hundred yards—all clear, down-range!"

Eric proceeded to empty a clip of seven rounds, slowly and with feigned attentional acuity—in the direction of his own new '59 Ford!

"Cease fire! Cease fire! Score the targets!" Eric bellowed, slumping down to a more restful position.

Kazootch had his turn on the line. Slowly, methodically, he fired off a full clip, achieving a group spanning several feet—as tight a group as Eric's. The two pistol experts had established a new mark. Of sorts.

The match was over as soon as it started. Kazootch wondered where the ground had been all this time, and was glad to find it again. *"Gotta find my car, and get us back to base,"* Eric kept muttering. They grappled with consciousness, until finding the riddled Ford and, once minimally sober, the wherewithal to start the car and coax it back to base.

On exiting the barracks the next morning, Eric let out a yelp that could have awakened the next time zone. Kazootch came running out to see what bear trap Eric must have stepped into. Eric yelled, "Lookee here! *Some*-bidy's shot my *car!* Who in th' *world's* done shot my *car!*" The answer to the question proved just as shocking as having found the new car peppered with huge bullet holes. Slowly, the memory of the Midnight Match began to filter back into Eric's mind, and he simmered down to a low boil, then hid the car and tried to keep cooling down to a stoical avoidance of the incident.

Kazootch was one of the grand ones in I Corps. He mapped new A/O's and plotted death traps for Charlie which have gone down in history. Yet like Eric and their contemporaries, he shrugs it off, paying deference instead to the feats of others—of The Team. But he has been there. His skills were not wasted in Nam.

191

Jerry's actual duties in Nam varied. At times he set up a blocking post to the rear of a patrol, to await possible VC trackers. Or he may have to worm his way along a ridge to take out a machinegun nest. There was occasion to maintain vigil over open valleys of rice paddies, popping away at the many VC coming through. Or he may have to perch atop a hill, manning a 106mm recoilless rifle—a rifled *canon*—overlooking the infamous Elephant Valley. Charlie's presence there was a reliable liability. Just a year earlier their buddy Carlos Hathcock and the late hero John Burke pinned down and wiped out an entire company of NVA in the gory glen.

Nearby stood Hill 55, a large forward Marine encampment which housed Hathcock. Unknown to Carlos or Jerry at the time, Eric's second cousin—Harry's stepson Martin—was helping them. Also known as Jim, Corporal James Martin Brown, Jr., protected the perimeter of Hill 55, and also went on force-recon missions to insert and extract Marine Snipers. Jim knew Carlos Hathcock in his second tour, but they never realized how much they held in common via Eric. Jim recalls Carlos as appearing emaciated and gaunt, and wire-tough, after two tours of crawling after the Charlie-bug like a gung-ho lizard.

There were times when Jim and Kazootch probably fired on the same VC, as they rotated or overlapped A/O's. On another day Jim saved a convoy bringing supplies to Hill 55, with his quick eye and steady trigger finger. From the perimeter he noted dust popping along the side of the road, suspecting rifle fire. His ears tuned to the clack-clack sound an AK-47 makes from afar.

Next came the pop-n-puff of distant grenades, and then a truck exploded. He turned his .50 calibre machinegun toward the bushes on the roadside, and ripped away. In moments he could see VC fleeing in panic, before they could inflict many serious casualties on the Marines. The driver of the exploded truck leapt to safety, and seeing this, Jim provided cover for him by following the escaping enemy and whacking the bushes with the mighty .50. Kazootch heard of the incident, but could never have suspected that his next load of rations may have been secured by Eric's second cousin from Georgia.

News of fellow Shooters, however, traveled fast, as they generally operated in close circles. Don Bartlett even slipped up on Kazootch in the bush one day, to pay a casual visit which utterly astounded Jerry. News of Hathcock's dreadful wound by a 500 pound landmine while riding a half-track, reached his buddy Jerry Kozuch with swift sadness. Then he learned of Eric's being gone from Phu Bai for a month, and found the means and connections to get loose and go check on him. Along the way, he heard tales ranging from KIA to POW to hernia. At Phu Bai he was told, *"Gunny England is once again either dead, wounded, missing, sightseeing in the DMZ, or teaching the VC how to fly-fish..."* but that, *"this time, we understand he is definitely probably dead. Or, you might try the Naval Hospital at Da Nang."*

Already Charlie was passing the word: "A-wick Ain-Lan is dead! The Phantom is deposed!" Still, Charlie was too unnerved to step into the open for at least a week, in case it was all a ruse to draw them out. Charlie's line of intel confirmed that Eric England was in the Naval Hospital, down but alive. A reflexive flood of VC claims boasted of having put him there.

Down but alive is how Jerry found him, after a long and draining search. Charlie began to embolden himself, increasing operations near Phu Bai where the Phantom was feared the most—then fanning out across other A/O's in I Corps. Just as soon, Eric's colleagues and protégés carried the torch right back to Charlie, in the deadly art of elimination so reflective of Eric's style and savvy. Charlie only came to perceive him as being all the more ominous. Charlie could never quite escape him.

But Kazootch found him. Bracing himself to face the worst, he was at least gladdened to know Eric was listed as alive. But on seeing him, he still wasn't so sure. He was emaciated, pale, scarcely able to stand—and the living image of death. Skin was sloughing off. He was sick, and hated that it showed. They stared at each other in a moment of disbelief, then both grinned. Then they laughed, until Eric moaned, grabbing his side with a fearsome grimace.

"Well, I see *you're* all harbored up!" Kazootch joked, to ease the tension. Two Navy nurses walked in to give him meds, and to hassle him with taking his vital signs. "Or, a POW," he laughed. *"Prisoner Of Women!"*

"Aw, down like a snake-bitten dawg!" Eric grumbled. "Back to duty soon, though!"

The little wound had festered. The hernia had developed. Now the surgical sutures seemed to be festering. They had to cut Eric open time after time to inspect and clean the wound, and reclose it. He got more infected, and sicker. Sicker than he ever thought he could be. Charlie's little wound was spreading like the insidious bacteria of Communism itself. He wished the antibiotics could take it out like a Marine Divisional offensive.

The Marines' premier Shooter, known for taking out Charlie with pinpoint accuracy, had been felled by a wound of pinpoint proportion. It vexed and rankled him. But he would bounce back. He always did.

Added to Eric's pleasurable visit from Kazootch, was the simultaneous visit by Blairsville friend, Leon Berrong, brother of his gal, Sue. Leon, who would retire as a USAF Chief Master Sergeant, was in his first of three Nam tours, and at that time was in the Army. He had finagled a way to get from II Corps up to Da Nang, to check on his buddy and future brother-in-law.

Leon's trip was as hazardous as anything in his tour to date, facing untold dangers and culminating in an ambush on the convoy he was riding. The truck he was in was riddled with bullet holes. Then as he arrived at Da Nang, he had to dive for cover from an attack of incoming 122mm rockets. The barrage was intended to keep choppers from flying to aid in the raging battle at Pork Chop Hill. There were so many medevacs flying in, however, that they could not even land them all at Da Nang.

Bedraggled and war-weary, Leon stumbles into the room, and Eric brightens up and then grimaces in one expression. But it was a most encouraging reunion.

194

A nice photo of Sue stood on the nightstand. Kazootch remarked, "You'd better turn that picture around, Eric! You'll get distracted, and go AWOL!"

"Belay that talk!" Eric admonished. "This-here's her own brother, sittin' here!" They all had a good laugh over that, until the laughter made Eric wince again.

The first thing Leon did was take photos to send to the home folk, to assure everyone he had seen Eric in person, and that his bulldog determination would see him up and around soon.

But the photos revealed Eric was in too sick a state to ever send to the worried. All caution was exercised, at Eric's insistence, that nothing be mentioned about the wound, or his ever having been in grave danger in his duty. The secret was so well kept, it was not divulged for three decades.

"C'mon, Eric, you'll be up and outta here soon," Kazootch encouraged. "Try to get orders for us to do some huntin' together! Got everything we need—even permanent licenses—just no dogs!"

Eric appreciated the cheery words, responding, "Aw, we got plenty of *two-legged* dawgs over here. But they look too much like the *game!* And the real ones, the four-legged ones..."

"They get eaten by the *two-legged* ones!"

"Ha-ha-oooow! Don't yuns dare make me laugh!"

"Heh-heh. Yer gettin' the fire back in yer boiler," Leon assured.

"You'll be shootin' game and takin' names again in no time," Kazootch consoled.

But Eric continued to have complications. His outlook became grave. He was transferred to Naval hospitals first in Japan, then San Francisco. He would not see Kazootch or Leon again in the Nam. But having their visit as a parting memory of that hellhole was a blessing.

He would not be seeing G.B. in-country again, nor the A/O's they hunted and mastered. His war was over. He was abruptly whisked from the profoundly exotic, perilous, and intrinsically engraining other-world dimension called The Nam, back to a place he had remembered as The World—

TURNER

America—Land of the Big PX—*home*. Now, all he could do was hope others made it home.

CHAPTER THIRTY TWO

THE WALKING WOUNDED

LETTERS from home were being returned, stamped "Marine Casualty." Few items could evoke as much anxiety and anguish, as a serviceman's folks finding such an article in the mailbox. It was some time before the family could track Eric England down. He was becoming the Phantom of the Postal Service. Soon they were receiving letters from his sickbed, however, at the USN Hospital in San Francisco. The exact nature and seriousness of his malady continued to be the subject of wide speculation.

Eric's condition worsened. He was very ill and debilitating. But his only focus was outside himself, writing more letters than at any point in his life—letters to comfort the folks—to keep abreast of his buddies' fate in the Nam—and gradually, to begin inquiring into alternate career routes in the event he was forced to take a medical discharge.

His mother and sister did not believe the hernia part, feeling sure he was masking some dreadful combat wound. Their prayers were answered, however, on learning he was recovering. Their letters showered him with love and comfort. Sue also kept his spirits high with letters of dearest support.

His father, the crusty and spirited Arizona cowboy, was deluged with emotion due to the returned letters, and the gnawing uncertainty; and then relief, on learning his prized son was in the US and was alive. On first receiving word from Eric himself that he had indeed survived, he wrote him back:

"Dear Son – I was so happy to get your letter, and to know at last that you are okay. I had to come back upstairs. I was so happy, that I cried. I poured a shot of Old Forester—one for you, and one for me. God only knows how happy I am..."

A.L. closed with these words:
      "...all my love and best wishes, to my son, a fine Marine—and the best son a man ever had."

Eric stayed busy. And he kept everyone else busy. G.B. was shipping his personal effects to him, and updating him on the progress of the Sniper School and the combat action. Stateside buddies were keeping him posted on the latest match results, NASCAR races, hunting and fishing events, the outlook for potential civilian occupations, and the moonshine industry. He had Sue and his mother and sister Edie keeping him advised of social and family happenings. His dad, A.L., he kept busy scouting out a pair of the finest pedigreed hound pups in Ohio where he was working; he could look forward to training and breeding a new hunting team.

Fellow Shooter, Bill Dunham, had been in the San Francisco hospital, compliments of Charlie Cong. He wrote to Eric advising him of facilities, services, contacts, and programs in the area—including the hospital swimming pool, which they had stocked with fish for patients' recreational use. "If you catch one," Bill added, "the mess staff will cook it for you!"

G.B.'s letters were cheery and encouraging, though some revealed he was on the cutting edge of war action in I Corps. With time, his letters began to reflect that he knew Eric was not returning—at least not any time soon—and how he regretted it, missing his buddy and ace Shooter. He was needed in Phu Bai.

THE PHANTOM OF PHU BAI

A typical letter from G.B. would read:

"Dear Eric – We sure miss you here. Hope you are improving. It is impossible to find a replacement for you. We hope you can come back to Phu Bai, but if you can save your health by remaining Stateside, then by all means you'd better do so…"

But then the subject would invariably turn to sniping efforts:

"…staying busy as ever: Dong Ha, Chinook, Cam Lo, Gia Linh, back to Chinook, back to Phu Bai—down to Da Nang, back to Phu Bai—all in five days. Starting the new Counter-Sniper Recon Class, and sure could use you! We're keeping your weapon active and in good use, as you would've wanted it to be. They are really catching it over in Khe Sanh, your old stomping grounds. I was supposed to go there, but

I got a lucky change of schedule: The Rough Rider I was supposed to go out on, got ambushed. Seven killed, four wounded."

A somber note is sounded with news of a closer death, inflicted by a VC counter-sniper:

"This next part I hate to tell you, but Sergeant Major Robbins got killed the 18th. He went out to check his gun positions, and took a single round through the head."

James Walter Robbins of Dallas, Texas was forty eight. He was born April 14, 1919. He rose through the rough-n-ready ranks of the Old Corps, to attain the rank of Sergeant Major. He served his country and his Corps with dedication. He gave his life seeing to the security of his men. Though still relatively young, he was well over twice the age of most of the Marines in his care—as well as most of the VC's recruits. On May 18, 1967, after twenty six years as a loyal Marine, he was simply gone. His name would stand as a monument to patriotism. (His name would also come to grace Panel 20E, Line 35 of the Vietnam Veterans Memorial Wall.)

With resumed tranquility in his pen strokes masking the feelings in his words, G.B. goes on:

"Dodged lots of incoming up at Gia Linh—we suffered several KIA. Then we got hit hard down here at Phu Bai with mortars last week—68 wounded, no killed. Man, we really need you here! But you just get well for right now. That's your main priority. Your old buddy, G.B."

Eric got all the news—who was hit, who went home, where the action was—news of Carlos Hathcock's slow recovery from his serious burn wounds. The brotherhood of Distinguished Shooters kept up with each other, always. They would crawl through hills of broken glass to help one another. But all the Shooters could do for Eric was provide moral support, as his nagging wound threatened to pull him down and out.

Then finally the culprit was found: a piece of gauze had been left inside Eric's wound, which had become infected. After a long wrestling match with the tag-team of mystery and near-death, he could begin recovery. He worked at being well. He wanted like the dickens to get back to Nam and save Marines.

In time he was stable enough, or at least he told them he was, to enjoy liberty on base—then in town—and gradually improving until his reassignment to the MTU at Quantico. Still, he was a continuous outpatient at Sick Bay, for care of the perpetually nagging, festering wound. Only the most rugged and determined of men could have endured and pushed himself to the point of range instructing and match competition, as he did. Despite the pain of prolonged hours in grueling positions, it was actually his motivating factor—his carrot on a stick. In combat medic terms, he was among *"The Walking Wounded,"* or those casualties who could walk by themselves back to the rear lines for further medical care. He was home and on duty, but he was not well. He was still Walking Wounded.

Only the gungiest of the gung-ho survive and overcome such an ordeal in time to re-enter the match circuit. And as the months wore on, he was appearing in the 1968 Nationals hosted by Ft. Benning, Georgia. He would fire in one relay, go behind a shed and swab out his still-open wound, restrap into the tight and stifling sweat suits and "leather harness" firing jacket, and perform dramatically in all firing positions. Maintaining his "bubble" despite the searing pain was exactly the kind of professional soldiery that kept him effective and alive in Vietnam.

Eric and Kazootch had durn-nigh missed a date with destiny, so hindered had Eric been that morning with cleaning and dressing his wound—so abiding was his malady, as he continued to tough out his arduous duties. Men in the showers would nearly faint as they watched him plunge the long cotton swabs deep into his raw, abscessed flesh. Today the pain was as bad as ever, and he had to give the performance of his life.

They couldn't find the range. They raced about in their USMC pickup, bouncing all over the back country of Ft. Benning, arriving just in time to learn that Eric had missed his firing relay! The jostling had aggravated his tender wound beyond description. Now a "hard-Corps" chewing-out could be added. Not since stalking and evading VC with his sudden hernia had he been under such pressure, from so many angles, to perform as a Spartan—as a Marine. Even if he could finagle another chance for a firing relay, he had to make it his best ever. He had to make a show. He had to be full-Eric as he had never before been Eric. It was an absolute imperative. To the Corps!

Kazootch pondered how lesser men would have succumbed to the agonies encumbering Eric, as he stepped to the pits. His admiring team cheered him on, aware of his sacrifice for them.

Kazootch grinned and quipped, "Show 'em how it's done at Phu Bai!"

Don Bartlett was enthralled in mixed feelings: he was encouraging Eric and the team on, while facing the fact that Kazootch had just beaten his all-time National Open record of .994, with a .996. Within 22 minutes, both outstanding records fell, as Eric fired a grand aggregate of .998, which stands over three decades later as the all-time highest score in America, military and civilian. Still, he bowed to the Team. They all paid deference to each other, always. He was happy to retain his place among them.

TURNER

His career arighted, his future re-secured, The Walking Wounded emerged from a hold-over wound and the withering fire of personal turmoil, to win the day. He has never stood so tall as on that day—rising from chaos and despair, to achieve the highest rifle performance in history. He was walking tall.

CHAPTER THIRTY THREE

EAGLE–EYE OKIE

IT IS SAID that an eagle can clearly discern game as small as a mouse or salamander, from 300 yards. The ratio could not vary significantly in the case of a man who can visually identify a moving adult human being at over 1000 yards with the naked eye; or movement of the mere shadow of a deer at 200 yards, bare-eyed. Or place twenty high-powered rounds, without a scope, into a fixed group the diameter of a pie pan—at 800 to 1000 yards.

The ranks of enemy forces diminished significantly due to the totality of Eric England's shooting aptitude, enhanced by his genius for distinguishing blending objects at great distances. More important than numbers killed, is the impact of the "quality" kill, or eliminating vital operatives among the enemy. One well-executed kill of a key enemy figure could prove detrimental to the fighting effectiveness of hundreds of his subordinates. The ability to not only shoot, but seeing whom and when to shoot—*or not shoot*—are the hallmark of a Top Shot.

Lives have been saved due to Eric England's precise optical analysis. The errant Marine at Camp Chinook who almost died by friendly fire, an incident which would have set awry a major skirmish, probably never knew the debt he owed Eric's discerning eagle eye.

But there is a noted case in which the deepest possible gratitude was indeed felt, compliments of his not shooting.

There are people in Okinawa who are forever grateful that Eric England stopped off for temporary duty there, enroute to his second tour in Vietnam. Don Bartlett and Bob Goller were officers at the Camp Hansen range, but were due to transfer back Stateside. Their Colonel was livid about getting a rifle team together for the 3rd Marine Division. Don got word that Eric would be changing planes in Okie, and turned a page in history.

Don and Bob excitedly got their Colonel to effectuate a change in orders through HQ in Washington. Eric would be the Colonel's coach. It was arranged before Eric even landed on Okinawa.

"He'll be great," said Don, to the Colonel.

"He'll be irate," said Bob, to himself.

The Phantom of Phu Bai was now Range NCOIC at Camp Hansen. But part of the deal was, he would transfer to Camp Pendleton, California with the 3rd Division Rifle Team that he whipped into shape. As a dubious bonus, he would be on-call for special assignments in Vietnam.

He was training Shooters one day on the 1000 yard range when suddenly, just as they were prepared to commence firing, he abruptly ordered, "Cease fire!" before a single round could be discharged. For within his constant visual analysis he detected foreign objects—movement—down-range near the targets!

Securing the range and jumping into the red range pickup, he sped out to the target pits and took into custody two small Okinawan children, playing innocently as certain death loomed at the thin veil between time and eternity. Eric turned the kids over to base authorities, who returned them safely to grateful parents.

Few men would have been so constantly astute, monitoring down-range for hazardous oddities, let alone se two small children down on the ground with the naked eye. Yet this heroic action came as a typically reflexive action to Eric. Such conscientious use of perceptual skill was put to good use many times, but never so well as on this day.

His newly formed 3rd Division Rifle Team took the Regionals in California. And naturally, Eric took Regional Champion in long-range rifle competition.

Meanwhile, back in Nam, Charlie was getting intelligence reports that a certain *Awick Ainlan* was again in the Asian neighborhood. Would he be back? Was he ever really gone? He was an undying enigma. His intrigue plagued the enemy.

On Okie, Eric found his warring legends still unforgotten. And in making extracurricular TDY tours in and out of the 'Nam, he was back on campus to teach Charlie a refresher course—a Conqueror-on-Call——flunking out Charlies, and bewildering their classmates.

Few others could have maintained the nervy equilibrium to perform in such a complex role, while bouncing in and out of the murky entrapments of Vietnam like a ballistic bolo ball. In a diplomatic and strategic career-balancing act, he now had his feet in the US, the Pacific, and Indochina.

The covert missions were now even more precise, more high-level, more crucial to the bigger picture of international developments, yet were of necessity mentioned to no one. They were not officially logged. Eric, in his own modesty and sense of duty, uttered nary a word. The complexity of his new roles was met and managed by his hustle-n-savvy—his genius for duty and mastery—his forte of victory with dignity.

They called him Eagle Eye, in Okinawa. If the eye is a window to the mind and soul, then conversely he projected his genius and inner-self outwardly, through this window—through the eye of an eagle.

CHAPTER THIRTY FOUR

DUMPY AND THE SCOURS

SHOOTING across America's northern border at British Loyalists in the Canadian provinces was once commonplace. But shooting in the 1969 Canadian Nationals was an invitational goodwill tour for USMC Top Shots. Canadians have become America's closest international friends, and their mutual shooting was likewise becoming fraternal.

The Marine Team was a veritable lineup of All-Pro Super-Shooters welded into a formidable contingent by Colonel Walter Walsh. All were long-time champs, yet were never more in the prime of their unbelievable shooting careers. And all were Snipers—mostly Vietnam—though Walsh began in the 1940's.

Colonel Walsh, who in his 90's still competes in the Senior Nationals in pistols and black-powder guns—and who originally taught Eric England the rigors of competition firing—is also America's only Triple-Distinguished Shooter: Distinguished Rifle, Distinguished Pistol, and Distinguished International Pistol. He has always stood as a rallying emblem for shooting excellence and Team morale. Moreover, it is said that the only reason he did not make the rank of General was due to his honesty and his loyalty to his men.

Don Bartlett, Eric's long-time shooting partner, was naturally on the Team. Don was and still is World Class—and the first Marine to ever win the Interservice Match, with a perfect 500 out of 500. He still wins the Senior Nationals whenever he wants to. Don was born to it.

The entire Team was primed for a joint performance expected to border on awe. Spirits ran high. Eric had recently set national and international records. The entire team was world class; a no-nonsense mechanism of power and prestige, representing country and Corps with distinction and decorum.

The entire pre-match setting was taking on a cheery atmosphere. The Marine Team freely complied with every opportunity to build a diplomatic trust with the Canadian marksmen and hosts, inclusive of attending festivities to which they were extended the heartiest of welcomes. It felt good to be appreciated for what they were, as the US military and the Vietnam War in which they had so gallantly served grew immensely unpopular down home. Now, the Canadian government and military were treating them to banquets, speeches, and other merriment. No one among them was cognizant of just what a "corn bock" was, but the friendliest insistence of the Canadians convinced them that they should indulge themselves fully therein.

Don Bartlett, now a Captain, elbowed Eric and urged with a hearty grin, "C'mon Eric! You're sure to love it. It involves ale—and *corn*—substances you are right at home with!"

"Not to outshow you West Virginians by any means," Eric harped, grinning equitably. He and Don had stood shoulder-to-shoulder as NCO's, and their camaraderie held fast after Don's commission. Eric wasn't even sore about Don getting his orders changed, from Nam to Okie. It led to even more opportunities.

The competitive spirit between them was good-natured, and actually fostered morale. After all, most of their careers they had been paired as shooting partners. They shot alike. Their rounds grouped alike. They thought alike. Their humor was symbiotic and their respective accents not far adrift. Their careers ran an uncanny parallel; naturally their personal lives did also.

When Eric ceased smoking, Don tried to also. But when he saw Eric's modality of smoking cessation—taking a chaw o' terbacka—he understood why Eric had stayed off cigarettes when he could not. Eric would grin and chew, covertly still having his tobacco, and now even on the firing lines.

One day in the Quantico firing pits, Don discovered the evidence. In mock seriousness, he confronted Eric with, "Now, *Gunny England*, I've never pulled rank on you before, but I am giving you a direct order to take your firing position to my right, so that when you spew tobacco juice to *your* right, it will be down-range from *my* right!"

Eric merely cracked a leathery grin, and chomped on his plug while assuming a position to Don's right. He did it ostensibly to oblige an old friend, but actually to buy time while he formulated a come-back. He knew rank did not factor into the equation at all. It was just an unexpected ribbing. He knew he had to reciprocate one on old Dumpy.

He got his chance. As the pangs of tobacco withdrawal gnawed away at Don, he reported to the range the next day with his own chaw secretly affixed between his molars. He hoped he could be even more covert about it than the adept chawer Eric had, but the sickening sensation of this novel vice had him spewing more frequently than he expected. Firing had hardly begun when, between rounds, Eric dryly quipped over his shoulder, "*Captain* Bartlett, a new directive's been handed down: pending demonstrated proficiency with chawin' terbacka, *officers* will position *them*-selves to the right of *all* chawers with seniority!" And his Comrade Captain complied.

In 1969 their careers, and humor, were in full stride. Every aspect of their lives seemed flavored with a series of challenges met with victories which, if not occurring naturally, were contrived, when necessary, to convert boredom into exhilarating action. Thus a *corn bock sudden-death playoff* was to them a natural course of events, and presently as vital and urgent as competing in the Canadian Nationals next morning.

Soon they had rapidly consumed over a dozen ears of boiled corn apiece, washed down with ample quantities of ale. They began to slacken the pace, but neither would back down, eyeing each other's progress and endeavoring to persevere. The formation of a crowd of cheering onlookers rekindled the momentum. They were in it now; they were committed.

"What if it's all a trick, to get us sick?" Eric mused aloud, gnawing into his sixteenth ear.

"Trick *is*, to keep up with *me!*" Don chuckled back.

On and on they ate. And drank. Appetite had long since vacated. Stomachs hinted at mutiny. Eric kept up a visual surveillance of Don's progress. Don had hidden a couple of his expended cobs behind his big bowl. Eric took a tally, counting to himself as he finished off his twenty-fourth ear.

"Twenty four for *you*—and *there!*" he said, with a gloating sigh of relief. "Twenty four for *me!*" Any draw, if resulting in relief,
was as good as victory at this point.

"Aha!" Don bellowed, as he slid his two hidden cobs from behind the bowl. "*There!*" He chortled. "Twenty six *X's*, and all clean-through, perfect group, no Maggies!" ("*Maggie's Drawers*" is the traditional Marine Corps term for missing a target completely, followed by the scorers waving a red flag.)

Eric grumbled, "Aw! Yours was all s*mall*-bore! Mine was all *40mm* cobs!"

"A win's a win. Oh-ho! Read the manual!"

"Hmmmpf. You've just been feedin' at the trough a lot more, is all. No *wonder* they call you *Dumpy!*"

"Okay, *Fruit Jar!*" Just 'cause *you* think corn is only a drink!"

The friendly banter went on long after they left the corn bock pavilion. Those unfamiliar with them were convinced that this Gunnery Sergeant and Captain were genuinely embroiled in a prelude to fisticuffs—and subsequent court martial. An international incident may even develop, some concluded. Those who knew them laughed inwardly at their verbal antics, while outwardly playing along and reinforcing the apparent animosity. Tensions were relieved to see the two laughing and slapping each other's back.

Come daybreak, all hands were on deck, and geared for the historic events about to unfold in Ottawa. The USMC Rifle Team had all its cogs intermeshed and its inner-workings well oiled. Don appeared no different than usual, his winning smile and indomitable spirit shining through for the benefit of all. Eric wondered what the gimmick was— Don looked so buoyant.

Eric feigned this spirit, as inwardly he drew on the spirit of the Spartan. Not since General Puller had pricked his chest with the medal fifteen years earlier, had he had occasion to summon so much ceremonial endurance. Winning the 1968 National Open with festering stitches ripping out of his flesh was child's play, compared to this day. For today, he had an acute and undeniable case of— *the scours.*

Appropriately named, he knew this malady would not run its course until thoroughly scouring the gastrointestinal tract.

He felt certain it was all a Canadian trick. He kept his eye on Don, the Corn Bock Champion; no sign of scours from *him.*

But Eric exuded signs a-plenty: his face awash with pallid trepidation; skin cold and clammy; stomach well past queasy and nearing calamity. His plumbing needed tightening. His agility seemed intact, but for his gait: he displayed a new way of walking—more like shuffling—with minuscule steps and minimal hip movement. But he fired. And he fired again. Flexing all muscles in line with the snugging-in of the rifle, he must now absorb the recoil of the weapon—notwithstanding its urge to *loosen up and let go.*

He had difficulty remaining in his bubble of concentration, and in swallowing the lump of Shooter's anxiety. But he fired and he fired, true to form, winning the 1969 Canadian Nationals and further qualifying for the prestigious Queen's Match. He was a dead ringer to win, scours or no, his bubble intact. As the day passed, it all came down to a runoff between himself and a crack Canadian

Army marksman. Eric could have sailed on through it, but began to sense a breakdown of his bubble.

An errant round resulted from this impending onslaught of terminal-stage trots. It was just enough to cost him first place in the Queen's Match. The Canadian won, and his countrymen rushed up and tossed him into the air, jostling him on a rocking chair, parading him raucously through the jarring crowd.

Eric winced at the sight and thought, "Sure glad *I* didn't win first place, if *that's* whatcha gotta go through!" He scouted around for any available facility for attending to his pressing malady. Just as he stepped from the pits, someone grabbed his shoulder and pulled him back, exclaiming, "C'mon, Eric! They're calling for you to come accept your award!"

This moment proved to be the most excruciating of the entire malaise. With caution in his stride, he awkwardly yet stoically climbed the steps to the platform, suffering patiently through the attention and delay until finally the Canadian government presented his award along with a check for $11.00 in prize money. He would have traded it all for a bottle of Pepto Bismol.

He never cashed the check. He had more serious matters to attend. He keeps it as a reminder of one of the fiercest battles he ever endured—and of the day a royal case of *corn-bock collywobbles* cost him a royal accolade.

CHAPTER THIRTY FIVE

COMMANDO ON CALL

GLOBAL fame, or infamy, did not hang about the grisly neck of Khe Sanh until the cresting point of the Vietnam War—the 'Tet '68 Offensive. But Khe Sanh had been a veritable hotbed of warfare, both conventional and guerilla, for years. That was the way Eric England found it in 1966, though he left it better gunned and better guided after imparting his shooting savvy to the Marines there.

Eric was back—again—to a place he hardly recognized. Tet '68 was now a memory. War had torn the hide of the landscape. The base was a parcel of desolation. Despite US victories there, the hills of Khe Sanh were again infested with enemy vermin.

Picking off NVA observers, infiltrators, and snipers from the Khe Sanh perimeter was old-hat to the Phantom. He had not been called back there on TDY for that purpose, but the situation called for it. Within two days of plinking and zeroing, he saw to it that six surplus NVA were dispatched to their Comrade Cong in the Happy Head-Hunting Grounds.

He never cared for Khe Sanh. It was nothing more than a fortified dirt clod serving as a buffer between South Vietnam, and North Vietnam's main entrance to it via Laos. He was glad when the staff convened to review his mission. He wanted to get done, and get gone.

212

What was desired was a test case, a probe of advance Snipers being deployed as cover for recon and MACV-SOG patrols. Scouting out data for Intel would be an added benefit. As the strategists jabber-jawed, Eric and his selected spotter, a Buck Sergeant from the Tennessee hills he called "Hooch," shook their heads in disbelief.

"They're all wondering what we can do from *Tiger Mountain!*" Eric whispered to him during a break. "We know better than them, what we can do. Why not take it a step farther, and go on *past* Tiger Mountain..."

"You mean, cross over into *Laos?*" Hooch interrupted.

"Affirm! We set up *behind* the NVA, watch *them* watchin' *our* guys!" Pop a couple of top officers..."

"From *behind* their lines, you say!"

A big salty grin preceded the confident reply, "Why, sure thang! Why not? They'd wonder *what-on-earth!* And then the US can always claim it must've been friendly fire from the NVA's own ranks. I know for *reason!*"

"You mean—mess their minds up good!"

"Ha ha. Yeah." Eric shook his head dramatically, and spewed a stream of 'backer juice, arching it over and beyond the sandbag wall they leaned on. "Imagine them, expending all the resources in the world, tryin' to figger out what hen's a-layin' rotten eggs in their own barnyard! And the cost to us? A few cents worth of lead."

"Hee hee! *Man*, Gunny! What a scheme! But what about your escape?"

"*Our* escape? Well, sha, Marine! They got lotsa land in Laos. How much does a bush-crawler need? They got lots less booby traps too, too. Harbor up awhile. Live on snakes like Captain Knapper did, if we hafta. But it *is* a slim slot getting' back to Nam, for sure." Eric grinned and his eye glistened with amusement, as he spewed another arch over the sandbags. Hearing a passing Lieutenant exclaim, "*What th'*...", he and Hooch slipped around the sandbags and stepped lively toward another bunker.

"But there's beau coup NVA surveillance all over the bush, in Laos, I bet. A close-up NVA could hear your shots."

"Say, lookee here—what about a silencer? It would be a big help."

"How you gonna accomplish that? The only silencer a Sniper gets, is distance!"

"Dumpy!"

"Huh?"

"Ol' Don Bartlett! His first tour, he rigged one. Took a pint cleaner can, filled it with shavin's, covered the end with screen, inserted a piece of water pipe. Weren't bad, say, 400-600 yards. Maybe 300, in some cases. He specialized in enemy patrols. He could get up closer with that piece of plunder, then pick off the last man in line. Clean through the ears. Then go search him. The patrol might not miss him for hours."

"He was a Captain, *and* a Sniper in the field?"

"A mustang. Why, he *invented* the field! He practically invented *shootin'!*"

"And never got caught. Nabbing patrol humpers like that."

"The patrols seldom even noticed the shot. A few hundred yards off—silenced, even if crudely—then Don and them would scamper down and search the little squinty-eyed devil for maps, papers. Ol' Dumpy, he's a mustang, ya know. The *best kind* of officer. For *us*, anyway. I'm sortin' these officers out here, lookin' for a mustang to help us get thangs done right. Or at least one who knows the taste of blood."

"So this Bartlett—one smooth Commanche, huh! And he never got caught?"

"We all run in a pack back home. A howlin' pack. But over here, we play Phantom!" The grin and swagger could have been coveted by Chesty Puller himself. But no one would covet a mission into Laos, on the best of days. No one except the *Phantom of Phu Bai*. He invented missions."

Eric had his say in the planning and operations hooch. Too politically sensitive, the proposal to go into Laos—though admired by the brass—was officially scrapped. Unofficially, it was kept in the top drawer.

"Too many surveillance specialists in the area from Hanoi, China, even the USSR. Wouldn't do to get spotted,

captured, photo'ed, ID'ed," the strategists explained. *"The Commies and the liberal press would have a field day— make it a scandal. They could have made Washington's crossing of the Delaware look like a vicious atrocity. Officially, we have no personnel in Laos."* It was all rear-guard rhetoric from the bureaucratic brass. He had heard it all before.

Then afterward a Lieutenant Colonel looked around, and pulled Eric aside. *"Officially, we have no personnel in Laos."* He winked and repeated, *"Officially."* With a look of confidence which failed to mask a deep strategic concern, the LTC added, *"Officially,* Chesty Puller never rode a horse in Honduras. You *savvy,* Gunny?"

"Uh, yessir, affirm! By the numbers!" Eric had roped his mustang.

"But you can *officially* come as close to the Laotian border, and The Trail, as you may deem appropriate. *Officially,* your mission proposal will be filed and kept for consideration, perhaps, some other day. With the shifting fortunes of war, that day could soon arise."

"So get there *'fustest with th' mostest'*..."

"Or at least, with the best! What I'd give to go with you. Korea was my crawl-n-kill zone. Learned from a hot-shot named Boitnott..."

The two salts found plenty to talk about; much cud to chaw over.

Later, he was going over plans with Hooch. Suddenly he was preoccupied, a trait for which Eric may have to ground him from incursion missions.

"You with me so far?" Eric inquired. "What'cha stewin'?"

"Are the people really protesting us back home, Gunny? I mean, riots, and all that?" Hooch surprised him.

"Aw!" Eric spat out. "Let 'em come on over here, and watch these divisions of Commies crossing international borders! Killing babies if their mamas don't help them kill the Americans who are feedin' and protectin' 'em! *Then* who'd they riot on?"

"Too late, I hear—their pinko minds are made up— sayin' *we're* the bad guys in all this!"

215

"I read somewhere, '*Chase a Mouse into Laos, catch Chaos from the Mao's. Pursue a Pest across a Border, ya Best be a Reporter!*' But I reckon if the Marine Corps wanted us to have an opinion, they'd *issue* us one."

"And look at all we've done so far—so much blood..."

"And so much victory!" Eric got straight in his face. "Victory is a personal virtue. A private choice. You are here. You are your own commander. What's yer choice?"

"Charge like the wind and don't look back. Buds first, duds last."

"Aye, buddy." The alliance was sealed with a hearty handshake.

There is a ridge in the A Shau Valley known as Tiger Mountain. From this vantage point one could easily see the NVA amassing over the line, in the *officially* neutral Laos. They could not be fired upon, however, except in strictest self-defense. But few if any liberals protested the NVA being there, even dispensing artillery fire from within the forbidden zone.

Getting to Tiger Mountain was no casual task, without alerting the many eyes and ears of enemy recons and listening posts in the area. Helicopter insertion was risky. And it was doubtful that a Sniper could get much done there, and escape to tell about it. The way in was with a friendly patrol or recon team. There was a slim margin of friendly territory, though it shifted like wind-driven dunes. But the recon escort for this mission knew its turf. They were seldom out of the field, and they knew Charlie like a pinball knows its flippers. It was the recon's turf—they lived on it. They saw to it that Charlie died on it.

As a professional, Eric was pleased with the extent of knowledge and intelligence-gathering the recon team had achieved. His life depended on it as well. What impressed him the most was the Montagnard joining them on the mission, with his expertly handcrafted crossbow. He walked on the jungle floor with ballet-like finesse, his feet trained since infancy to feel their way over twigs and traps like air over a feather. He could prove essential in the silent elimination of singular enemy.

Eric could only observe, not make notes. The team leader discouraged him from writing down any data he collected for himself. They valued him highly, however, and frequently sought his opinion on field and tactical observations. He was like them. They wanted to see this grunt-n-gun-'em genius at work. Their orders: scout and reconnoiter—gather data—apply limited interdicting fire if the outcome justified it. But no ambushes, no firefights. No drawing Charlie into a fight. Avoid detection at all costs. All the while Eric was keeping mental data as well on the Montagnard tribesman-archer, a sort of Vietnamese Apache, calculating how best to use him in creeping into a good position, by silencing pesky VC.

They found a heavily wooded promontory ideally suited for overlooking a key segment of the Ho Chi Minh Trail. The recon divided in two, sweeping around both sides of the base of the leafy perch. Slowly they worked upward, diagonally, taking over an hour to ascend 40 feet. A VC sentry, in the fork of a tree 50 feet overhead, had dropped his guard long enough to stuff a fist full of rice into his mouth. As he did, the Montagnard zinged a swift dart of death squarely into the VC's throat. The enemy fell back against the trunk, his neck impaled to the tree.

They waited half an hour, then resumed their cautious advance. The archer skirted around the crown of the knoll, almost joining up with the other half of the team. Then he launched another arrow at a VC sitting in a foxhole, observing with binoculars. Again, directly through the throat—no screams of pain, just a brief gagging sound—and the crest was secured.

The Sniper team wormed into the woodwork, atop their new vantage point. The recon team remained halfway down the knoll, observing. A tall, narrow slot of an opening between the trees, some three feet wide, provided a clear shot at a long stretch of road, ("*just over the line, in Laos,*" as the team leader said. But Eric knew they were *in* Laos.) It was straight, but it was distant. For Eric, that was perfect. He wanted no tell-tale close-up shots—not in these circumstances. The enemy must not hear or even suspect

217

American sabotage. The oncoming NVA must be halted or curtailed, and confused. Anonymously. But how?

Hooch scoped and calculated the ranges and zones. Eric selected several potential target spots on the road, ranging from 900 to 1100 yards. He had hit targets at 1400 yards before, like truck engines, but impact was less effective at that range. The 10x scope brought Laos so close, most men would have allowed the jitters in. Instead, he channeled that energy positively, cementing his bubble. He was on the job.

One of the recon men left the little perimeter on the slope, and burroughed in lower, in the Laotian direction, as a potential blocking force—or as fate may demand, providing a rear guard. The Marines ensconced themselves and attuned to the cacophony of sounds about them, singling them out—analyzing for hazards afoot—struggling with insect bites, heat, and the intensity of agitated boredom. Night wore on, senses wore out.

Toward the pre-dawn hours their expected visitors began to arrive: a full battalion convoy of NVA—troops and munitions—confirmed earlier by Intel. The low rumble of slow-moving trucks, paced well apart for safety, was faintly audible. The Marines strained to see the convoy's subdued headlights. There being a full moon, the lights would likely be turned off altogether except while under a thick tree canopy. They would soon be pulling over to hide for the day. Action time: *now*.

A debilitating shot at a large target was needed. An explosives truck? A fuel tanker? Too hard to make out. Then Eric remembered a more humane methodology for deactivating an enemy vehicle. He flashed back to Georgia—and the time he had driven home in his green Marine utilities, and stopped off in the mountains for some quick trout fishing. Army Rangers were conducting war games in the area, and took him prisoner!

Grabbing him in midstream, the camo-faced commandos cried out, "C'mon, troop! You're captured!"

"Th'...*what!*" Eric spewed back, slinging them into the water, then scuffling with a squad of on-rushers. He fought a good fight, fending off an entire squad and pounding serious memories into the noggins of half of them, until he was subdued and cuffed and tossed into a jeep like a newly-shot deer. Or wild boar.

He was hauled down the mountains to the Union County jailhouse in Blairsville, which provided cells for the war game "POW's." Not until the Sheriff recognized Eric, did the Ranger trainees let him go. A good laugh was had by all, except Eric.

Driving the old ridge roads that week, he stopped to scan a broad valley with the scope of the .30-06 he invariably kept in the car. Laying across the hood, he slowly surveyed the distant wood line. A grin coursed his lips as he spotted an Army jeep 800 yards distant.

"Careful aim, augmented by unresolved justice, *could* just compel this ol' 173 grain projectile into that hostile jeep's renegade radiator, and likely burrough a substantial depth into its engine block as a bonus," the *Mythical Muses of Marine Marksmanship* tempted him. A personal victory would be achieved; a private glory!

But tonight the vehicles approaching were far truer enemies. No good-old-boy lawmen to rescue him here. He listened for the sounds of the approaching convoy, balancing his attention with the immediate proximity. Was Charlie creeping up on them? Were they surrounded? Not so important as stopping that convoy. Death ironically takes a number and waits when there are other lives to be saved.

Just how much damage could he actually do to a big convoy? He was sure he could take out the lead vehicle; even if he only made them pause to check out whatever was "popping under the hood." He regretted the Marines could not mine the road and ambush the trucks outright, it being regularly patrolled and guarded. But if he could stall it long enough to register artillery or an air strike on it, a goodly dose of heavy explosive and antipersonnel ordinance, the mission would be well worth it.

Seizing a rare moment when a number of slowing trucks could be seen in a straight line ahead of him, he methodically drilled three well-placed rounds through the engines of as many NVA trucks, all in under seven seconds, all over 900 yards. The convoy was soon sputtering to a confused halt. The fourth, an armor-piercing round, punctured a fuel tank. He held the fifth round, to preserve arboreal anonymity.

But then a mild explosion, followed by a huge one, rocked the convoy's middle segment. Munitions began to fling like fireworks, apparently in reaction to one of his rounds. His night vision was about to be flared out; he took the fifth shot, aiming farther up the road where the convoy curved slightly, striking fear into the Hanoi Hobos of yet another truck, which had veered out of line trying to pass the wreckage. There were no confirmed kills in the hail of lead. Yet by the time the NVA could assess just what had happened, make repairs, and ponder the intelligence value of it all, their fresh troops and their damage to Allied forces would be delayed for days. Several crucial days.

There were road repair supplies stationed all along the Ho Chi Minh Trail, which at its widest part was actually a network of odd trails and roads some nine miles across. But there were few resources, if any, along this jungle path for making truck repairs. Of course, they were nearing the juncture where the NVA and their VC helpers offloaded their gear, mounting up to 500 pounds onto single bicycles, humping it into South Vietnam.

But that was for Intel to ponder. For now, the recon had some serious withdrawing to do. "Phu Bai Eagle Eye" would serve as their call-sign on many future missions after Eric had left them—to stir up the mystique—to let Charlie's eavesdropping radios know that The Phantom would never forsake them.

CHAPTER THIRTY SIX

HAUNTING UNCLE HO

IT IS NOT exactly a scare. It may be a spirit. But there is an electric sort of twinge that runs through the military psyche when a sense of high caution or supreme battle urgency surfaces. Transcending every rank and position, this *krieggeist*—Spirit of War—taps the central nerve of all combatants and direct support personnel whenever a "big one" is in the works. It distills collectively and crystallizes individually. You can feel mortal movement coming. You know it is in the mill.

Eric England felt the icy hand of *der krieggeist* tap his shoulder. It reached for him from Vietnam to Okinawa, as he was whisked abruptly from the range at Camp Hansen, and found himself suddenly strapping into a C-141 transport plane enroute to Da Nang. There was that distinct sense of urgency, to be sure. His perceptual expertise struggled to define it. It was icy, and bore an imperative momentum. This sensory momentum is seldom one-sided. It usually occurs in reaction to *der krieggeist* emanating from the ranks of the adversarial forces. Eric sensed it. He followed this unseen call to duty, and "assigned" himself to take "weekend hunting trips" back in the 'Nam, based out of Okie. It was easy to get aboard the many military aircraft enroute to Da Nang. It was even easier to check into his former "hunt club" at Phu Bai, draw "hunting gear," and bag his limit. Then back to Okie before 0700 Mondays, back instructing on the range with no one the wiser.

He imagined trying to explain his activities if he were ever questioned. He daydreamed about being officially assigned to these freelance heroics, about how the topic might go down. He pictured himself with an S-2 Intel officer, in fatigues bearing no insignia whatsoever, unstrapped and went over to sit by Eric. He opened a green canvas portfolio case.

The man's presence would prime Eric's erupting curiosity. From the jungle brief case he would extract the answers.

"They're moving," he would begin, calmly and unaffected. "Huge numbers. They're just pouring through Laos. But nobody's *in* Laos, are they? Not officially, thanks to meddlesome press poagies…"

"R-E-M-F's, sir?"

"What's that? Oh, you mean the Rear Ech…"

"Affirmative. The—uh—*Rear Echelon Military Force!*" The spy-guy would show Eric maps and aerial photos— places along the ever-widening Ho Chi Minh Trail. There were no identifying notations. Only topographical detail.

"These maps are treated with chemicals that will cause their inks to deteriorate rapidly into indiscernible residue, if rubbed against each other. Have them in different pockets, maps in one and documents in another. If you face capture, wad them together briskly. Bury them if you can."

"Could I ask you just what in the mud patch you're a-*tawkin'* about?"

"As in, *what's the objective?* That's just it. There is none."

"Sir?"

"You create your own. You'll see what to do when you get to the zone. The less you know for now, the better."

"So it *is* Laos, then."

"Can't say." He would glance at his watch, the specialized dial indicating global time zones. "Not until this minute, did I even have clearance to tell you where you are deplaning. Da Nang, no big surprise. You'll be choppered out to a designated site. You may be choppered more than once. I cannot tell you. You will rendezvous with a recon team. The *team* will find *you*. You will not know where you are but you will know what to do. Questions at this point? Be mindful—highly classified."

"More by the minute!"

"I can tell you this: you *will* know what to do. Think about curtailment. Confusion. Think about *radiators*."

Eric would break into a startled grin. "Radi—you *know*—about the..."

"Radiators and engine blocks? Yes. In Laos, *and* in Georgia!" He would share a mild grin.

"Now that-un in *Georgia*, why—who ever claimed *I* done it?"

"We consider it a moral victory! Now, you will receive further orders at another point, in-country. Not much detail. Just an inkling of what we need you for."

"But why me? There's plenty of fine Snipers in I Corps."

"Who said anything about sniping?"

"Well, for one thang..." Eric looked toward the rifle case stowed aft.

"Oh, that. No wonder they call you Eagle Eye. Well, you're the talent we need. And you're close. Hathcock is back at Quantico, struggling medically. Jim Bowen, Bartlett, Barker—they're all stateside and busy. Merrill, Dunham, Hurt—they suggest you. They all do. You've got this *mystique—baffling enigma*—sort of a..."

"Reputation?"

"Rodge."

"We *all* built it. That's why it reaches so far. And the boonies over yonder are full of fine Shooters we've primed for the hunt."

"But the handle hangs on you. We want you to mystify these new waves of NVA. '*Whup up the skeer,*' as Lee used to say."

"*Keep* up the skeer. Forrest."

"Well, it needs whipping again. You know how to do it. Some sort of holy day is coming up for the Viets. The

223

Commies have a masked religious freedom among their peoples officially, but they're still inherently sensitive to the supernatural. Not sacredly spiritual as Americans know it, necessarily—more like a tendency to get spooked."

"*Oh yes, spooks n' specters. The Phantom of Phu Bai.* I figgered they'd of lost their fixation on that by now."

"The foundation is still there. We're whipping it up among the villages that support the enemy near the—well, nearest you're A/O. Been at it awhile, actually. Your actions will be the frosting on the cake. After all, you *are* The Phantom. And he still lives, eh!" Another mild grin. Then the imaginary spy-guy's countenance would grow taut again, as he realized Eric had gotten him to rattle off quite a good deal of classified facts.

Eric could only shake his head in wonder. "Of course, I'm all for it, sir. Going in gungy, green-side-out. I'll do it to save these young Marines who oughta be elsewhere."

He could only shake his head in wonder, as he snapped out of his momentary revery, glad to be freelancing and not having to go through all the rigamarole of real Intel briefings and controls. He inspected the gun in the case: an exact duplicate of his favorite sniping tool—the Winchester Model 70, .30-06 bolt action, Unertl 10X scope, fiberglas bed between stock and barrel. Match conditioned. Then there was a supply of match-grade ammo. Field gear, all prepared and stowed. Even beef jerky! They had thought of everything except the moonshine and photo of his gal, Sue. He wondered what they knew about his bootleg operations on base, Stateside.

It was 1969. Khe Sanh could not be used as a staging point. It had been dismantled after the US victory there the previous year. Its statement made, they simply struck camp. Apparently to inflict anxiety upon any snooping enemy eyes, today The Phantom was choppered from Da Nang, back to Phu Bai. It set the mood—and garnered the mystique. From Phu Bai he would chopper to a vague A/O far to the west, after zigzagging maneuvers to keep the trail dust down.

The night insertion would take place in a tight pocket of sparse foliage, between four wooded mounds within a hill mass. Swooping down on the narrow LZ, lights off, was a feat achieved only by top-gun chopper jockeys. Getting out of it within seconds was just as hard. They did not set down; the craft hovered at least 8 feet above the ground, forcing Eric to jump. Injury would have spoiled the mission and cost him his freedom and his life. But he landed so deftly, he was crouching and running for tree cover before the Huey could even ascend to tree-top level.

As the blades of the Huey beat a rhythmic escape, Eric followed orders, inching down the southwest slope until reaching a creek, following the left fork 500 meters. Harbor up; wait. That's all. But for how long? "Classified," they would explain—probably a word to use when they *couldn't* explain. He knew little more about this mission than the trees did.

It was well past 0200 when the recon team showed up. The gentle flow of the brook was disturbed by a rustle of leaves.

Then came an embarrassed halt, as the point man and Eric sensed each other's presence in the deadly dark. They strained to hear each other breathe or make a move. They played the waiting game. Finally the recon advanced, at a snail's pace. Once the point man had finally passed, Eric hissed, "All hands aft!"

The halt, the frozen movement of the death-brokers, exuded an almost audible inertia. Within a few breathless seconds the team leader whispered a reply, "Stand by for stowaway!"

The men exchanged brief verbal notes. They had to move with the night. "Charlie's everywhere," the young leader advised. "Gotta di-di-mau! Stop every 100 meters, all facing different ways. You face left at every stop, please."

"Affirm. Been there. With ya," Eric reassured. Eric was well over a decade older than the recon boys, and with nineteen years in the Corps already, but fully up to the midnight trudge. Just like a two-sided 'coon hunt. "Feels like rain. If it does start to rain like a cow leaking on a flat rock, how 'bout let's take advantage of the sound cover, and double time."

"Roger that. We got 6 klicks to make before 0400."

"Then let's skin some ring-tails!"

Descending almost into a valley, Eric could smell a river. On his unmarked map he had earlier noted what resembled the Xe Samou, running westerly, *inside* Laos. The terrain he knew would be rugged. He moved with caution, recalling "the cliff incident" near Phu Bai: Marine Snipers were following a recon platoon, and they all stopped while the point man checked out a hill mass up the trail. Jim Bowen and Hayden Russell saw Don Barker go down to his knees, feeling sure he had sighted a VC coming at them. The machine gunner flipped his safety off, which alerted the VC, who quickly stopped and crouched down.

Don saw the VC's Ho Chi Minh hat reflecting moonlight. Then the VC got up and crept toward him! Don saw a perfect opportunity to take him down with a stroke of his rifle butt, and claim a prisoner with obvious connections to clandestine op's. Then the thought of the VC carrying a grenade compelled him to go for the sure thing, and take a shot.

As unorthodox a shot as ever made by a Sniper—night shot, point blank range—was thwarted when the VC suddenly sprang up and ran toward Don, causing him to dodge and roll. The motion made the shot go high, entirely missing the charging guerrilla. Charlie, in reaction to the shot, likewise turned aside in the horror of the moment. When he did, he went over a cliff. Next morning, the body was recovered. Charlie was carrying three Chi-Com grenades. He had pulled the string on the first one already. Though it had been an apparent dud, the point was well taken.

No, the thing for Eric to do tonight, in the hills of eastern Laos, was not to encounter Charlie up close—not to evade him by cliff-fall.

Now the rains came stinging from the mountains. The men moved much faster, ever mindful of the many bluffs and ravines beckoning them into a death snare. Then the land form evolved into a narrow plateau jutting out toward a stretch of one of the series of roads making up the Ho Chi Minh Trail.

The recon stopped. The team leader whispered, "Okay, Gunny. You insert from here, sir. Solo. We harbor up and wait for you."

"And?" Eric whispered back.

"Orders are, you advance 100 meters west from right here. You are to observe. You will know what to do. Rendezvous back, 90 meters north of this spot, immediately after you do your business. Or, if we di-di, I'll come get you. But if we get hit, withdraw easterly, along the river, for five days. You'll find friendlies."

Once in position for almost an hour, Eric began to hear the distant rumble of motorized transport, and lots of it. Enemy night convoys! Visibility was fair to good, up to 400 yards with the scope, due to high lunar illumination. He could easily make out a lead driver if need be, but he may make himself too obvious if firing many rounds from this range. He knew his flanks were safe—the recon men could make quiet, efficient use of their knives. One even had a small crossbow. He retreat was secure. But a rifle report would make them all vulnerable. He sensed just how much the men respected his skill; they placed a great trust in him. He mastered many variables, not just the trigger-pull.

They could scoot like scalded snakes if overwhelming numbers of NVA had the insight and guts to scale this jutting spit of land. Or unable to evade, they could dig in and survive for days. The men were used to life as a lizard, and could subsist on roots and worms. Eric could do it, but preferred venison.

Scoping on the lead vehicle, he pondered a tire or engine shot in case he could not fix the driver in his crosshairs. Then a shiver ran through his veins. For on another ridge 300 yards to the southwest, over the river, a recondo released a helium balloon lifting an attached cassette player.

Once aloft, a recorded scream echoed as he held it in place by a string, directly over the convoy. Later, Eric would know this. But at the moment, in the naiveté of the dark, he was as stunned as the NVA in the valley below must be. He thought back to what the spy-guy had said about the spiritual spookability of the Vietnamese, and he grinned

227

to realize he was witnessing the unfolding of an exceptionally crafted tactic of international import.

The soul-chilling shriek was followed by an impersonation of the recently deceased Ho Chi Minh himself, pouring out woeful lamentations over the horrors he had perpetrated—urging the men to turn back to Hanoi to avert certain hell. Then the tape played the caterwauling of a Vietnamese funeral procession, the shrieking of dozens of professional mourners.

At this precise moment the recondo released another balloon with a bright red light. The devilish apparition flickered and flew away as the tape screamed one last, loud time. The mystic Asian symbolism of the color red accentuated the effect. A nuclear warhead could not be as devastating, if only for a frightening moment. And if only a handful of young Bo Doi recruits were shocked enough to panic, wreck, or flee, the convoy would be most assuredly in disarray.

Eric took his cue. For once, the military system had been right: he *would* know what to do in Laos tonight! And as trucks swerved all over the road, he rocked two full cycles of ammo—ten rounds of .30-06—as rapidly as he could work the bolt. Three trucks out of line, and a floating specter scattering NVA like scalded dogs, would prove a logistics nightmare. Add a few casualties due to falls, and this convoy would be a snail-trail.

Before the eerie airborne dirge began to fade on the wind, a fourth truck was in flames, as NVA fired wildly in all directions and at each other. Yet The Phantom—the *real* one—was already at the rendezvous point. The team leader tried to conceal the white of his grinning teeth, hissing, "Nice work, Gunny! Now, just two more of these ceremonies, and..."

"Two *more!* What th'..."

They moved on, west by northwest. They were in it, deep.

CHAPTER THIRTY SEVEN

A GHOST THAT NEVER DIES

RIFLES pointed at his head and back, the tattered American was gruffly marched through the tiny Vietnamese border village by a squad of angry VC. His hands were bound behind him. About his neck hung a dead chicken's head on a string. A VC political officer glibly denounced him before the curious peasantry.

"This is *Ma Quai Phu Bai,*" he snidely proclaimed. "You thought he was a phantom! Now, you see, he is just another captured American dog. Just another GI! He killed many of your revolutionary brothers-in-arms. We will remove this *phantom* from Vietnam forever!"

The squad leader took a knife and angrily cut away the American's sewn-on name tag, handing it to the village chief as a souvenir. His dog tags were yanked fiercely from his neck and tacked to a tree, hammered in with the butt of a knife.

Prodded along with rifle muzzles jolting into his back, the American was forced to march a few yards from the thatched hooches. Four VC leveled their AK's and SKS's at the doomed man. The political officer motioned for anyone who would like to take his pistol and join in the execution. But the peasants were still staring in slack-jawed awe. Finally

229

an aspiring VC boy came forward, about 15 years old, and took the pistol. As the officer signaled with a drop of his hand, the impromptu firing squad opened up on the American standing 20 yards away. The captive had struggled free of the cords binding his wrists, and as the fusillade erupted, he fell back against a tree, grasping his abdomen. Then he stood erect, opened his hands, and displayed several expended bullets in his palms—both 7.62mm carbine and 7mm pistol rounds. He threw them angrily at the VC, then chased toward them with a wild scream. They fired a few more rounds, then turned to flee him in wild-eyed horror.

The American screamed and screamed. The VC scattered in one direction as the villagers fled in another. The teenage boy threw down the officer's pistol, and evaded the screaming phantom on his people's well-known trails. The VC squad screamed like maniacs and ran for some 100 meters, then doubled back to a gathering point where they sat laughing with their pursuer, sharing canteen drinks and discussing final details of the day's masterpiece of psychological warfare. Their weapons were reloaded with live ammo. The "actor" placed bandaids on his abdomen and forehead where casing and wadding fragments from the blanks had peppered his skin.

The American and his "VC" oppressors were highly trained American and ARVN Intel officers. The villagers were now a mixture of new converts and revived congregationalists in the folk lore of The Phantom of Phu Bai, whoever or wherever he now was: for the Phantom had grown to be many USMC Snipers, in many places. The villagers could be counted on to spread this new page of the legend, into Laos as well as easterly back through upper South Vietnam.

The real Phantom, however, was over 100 kilometers away perpetuating the impact of his well-earned legend in his own way: sniping with a recon team. Yet another team was now working their way back through the jungles, toward the scene of the fake execution. Bringing the same Intel "actor" with them, in a few days they would make a vital stop at this village, where the supposedly invulnerable

230

Phantom Sniper would—on cue—pry the faked-up dog tags from the tree, and hang them about his neck as the villagers watched, stricken with fear.

As the recon team stood encircling the populace, eerie in their face paint, the team leader spoke in local dialect. The natives flinched in surprise. He called for the teen to come forth. Too fearful, he was finally dragged out by older, angry boys. He looked toward the ground in a mixture of shame and fear.

The leader told him in his own tongue, "This is, as you know, Ma Quai Phu Bai; The Phantom of Phu Bai. You tried to kill him. Because he knows you can never hurt him, he chooses to forgive you!"

The boy trembled with gratitude. The leader continued, As for the rest of you, your wisdom in cooperating is noted. You are spared by The Phantom. The Viet Cong may threaten you for declaring your allegiance to him, but the spirits will haunt you all forever if you stand in his way. Your ancestors can see through the spiritual veil, that *his* cause is *your* cause—your own *freedom!*"

The Marines vanished as quickly as they had made their startling appearance. The villagers were just isolated enough to buy the fake execution act, a variation on furtive white traders' trickery in the Old West, selling "ghost shirts" to Indian warriors. But the villagers would never have opportunity to disprove the trick, and their primitive jungle communication would reach, over time, as far and wide as a radio broadcast. The Phantom walked among them. They passed his mystique along, mouth to ear.

Such melodrama was often applied to a great many villages in the early years of the war, by the US as well as South Vietnam, on a variety of themes. The more remote natives often fell for it, or at least became more hesitant to meddle with the avenging Allies. By the time the stories filtered back to the more educated among the enemy, the effect was not so much persuasion, as a nagging kick in the pants from the Americans, who clearly demonstrated their ability to reach deeply into any lair of the enemy with effective impact.

TURNER

Morning broke crisp and new on the range at Camp Hansen. Okinawa was safely distant from the intrigue and misery of The Nam. The men being trained for the 3rd Division Rifle Team felt the competence of their coach. They grew with the greatness of his gutsy genius as the very essence of his presence distilled upon the morning air. Yet as he called, "...*all ready on the firing line—commence firing...*" they could not yet fully foresee the import and impact of the skills he imparted to them, and where it all may lead them.

But he knew. His feet were on Okie. But his sighting eye was hundreds of miles down-range, southwest of the pits—zeroed on a living range where the targets crept after *him*, able to return fire—where every native was both bullet-bait and ally—where the hand of democratic mercy grappled with the slithering hand of death—where a portion of his soul roamed hauntingly forever, and whose hell always trailed along behind him—a Marksman's hell called Vietnam.

CHAPTER THIRTY EIGHT

A BREED OF HEROES

TARGET competition is as old as archery or throwing stones, and as universal as the air we breathe. Combat scouting is recorded as early as the armies of Moses and Joshua. Sniping, considered an art of modern warfare, is surely as ancient as the first crude firearms created half a millenium ago, once they were refined sufficiently to place a round into a target from over 100 yards.

"But where is the heroism in taking a secret shot at an unsuspecting enemy?" some invariably ask. Sniping requires more personal heroism than the less-personalized long-distance death brought to bear by artillery, or aerial bombing. And Snipers live and survive on enemy turf.

Heroism is the act of applying skill against impending threat. Were Roosevelt and Truman and Bush not heroic in their remote-control application of bold, victorious warfare? They stood to lose everything if their delegated warfare failed. Was Carlos Hathcock not exceptionally courageous, being inserted into North Vietnam without a friend in sight, crawling for days to take out an enemy General with one perfect shot—not cracking under pressure and hardship—surrounded by enemy patrols, and the near-certainty of capture, torture, and mutilation? And there is the personal courage necessary to make *the killing decision*—that

233

moment of truth when the strategic Shooter must determine whether a silhouetted person dies, or lives.

Sniping is justified by the necessities of war which spawned it. Sniping has been practiced as a standard wartime and police tactic for centuries. One skilled marksman firing a single bullet can eliminate a vital threat which may have otherwise required the actions of a large ground or naval or aerial force, with an accompanying high number of friendly casualties. And the intelligence-gathering conducted by the Scout-Sniper is priceless as well. Heroism alone motivates and sustains him.

What makes for a good Marine Sniper? Since modern Marine Snipers were generated from the competition ranges, (their first love, to which they eagerly returned after the war,) the correlation between Match Shooters and Snipers cannot be dissolved. In a rare candid dialogue with Eric England, he related how he would select a candidate for his Sniper School, or Rifle Team. He would of course look for high-scoring experts, but most importantly for steady Shooters. He would rather have a lukewarm Shooter who is consistent, than a hot-shot who has cold days and a team-distancing ego. The lukewarm can be trained.

He sought out team-players. This element alone welded the Match Teams and Sniper Teams more effectively than any other aspect, and gave them the extra edge for victory after victory, and the strength to snap back after a reversal of fortune. A solo-Shooter who is only "into his own thing" will not shoot consistently, and he will disintegrate the team. So said Gunny Whitaker, now nearing 100 years old, Eric's first coach.

Eric looked for men who were stable. No blood-mongers or kooks. None but the most solid Marines and all-around Americans need apply. And there is the essential element which must be found to exist within the candidates: they must be genuinely dedicated. Brave, if you will; though bravery unfolds with circumstance. Bravery is not predictable. But dedication will override a multitude of shortcomings, and ultimately lead to winning in the face of tremendous odds.

The Shooters with whom Eric was associated throughout the 1950's, 60's, and early 70's were a rare conglomeration of heroes and super-talents, gathered into fellowship by Destiny's able hands. What they achieved was monumental. In terms of technique advancement, competition wins, interservice and international presence, combat success, and refinement of Scout-Sniper deployment as a permanent and respected facet of the US military, there was never a time in history to see their equal.

The Distinguished Marksmen and Snipers of the 1950's and '60s also drew on the capable role models of World War II and Korean War Shooters such as Walter Walsh and John Boitnott, George Hurt, G.B. Merrill, Henry Friday, and others. And of course they held in high esteem their hot-shootin' heroes of Old West fame. Wild Bill Hickock and Buffalo Bill Cody rose to the highpoint of that era. The twilight of their epoch was embodied in later notables such as Elmer Keith, the Montana cowboy who learned the rudiments by shooting the tails off cougars—and who by the 1950's was still firing in major rifle and pistol competitions. A chance meeting between Elmer and Eric was likely more a result of destiny than fortuity. For in that meeting was welded a mutual admiration which facilitated the passing of the torch, from the old to the new. Eric has lived true to the Code of the West inherited from Elmer Keith, as much so as to the Code of the Hills which Elmer admired in Eric.

Eric appreciates any true Shooter, any good ol' boy who shares a passion for keen-eyed shooting and the camaraderie which makes the moment linger. Training a Match Team in the 1950's, Eric could not resist turning about to share a courteous word with an elderly onlooker, who seemed expertly absorbed in their doings. There he met Steve Disco, Nationals champ of 1928. They became fast friends. Eric even bought an old revolver from him, a remnant of the past—a splinter from the passing torch. The blood of The Shooter ran in their veins. They were born to a select brotherhood.

Eric saw to it that Steve Disco was received into full fellowship among the Distinguished Shooters Association, where he rightfully belonged, attending reunions the rest of his years.

If Eric could build a monument to life, it would bear inscriptions of the many heroic Shooters he has known—from whom he learned—to whom he has taught—with whom he has shared—men who denied personal glory in the interest of the Team—who faced death fearlessly, for the sake of country and fellow Marines. Had Destiny not gathered so many heroes to create this lasting model of excellence, they would have formed ranks on their own—somewhere between the gunsmoke and the sunset.

CHAPTER THIRTY NINE

CARLOS HATHCOCK

ZEROED at 1000 yards, the one-man cannon made true its mark. Carlos Norman Hathcock, II was doing what he did best: efficient removal of deadly enemy vermin with a Winchester Model 70, .30-06, 10x Unertl sporting scope. Or a Remington 700, .308, would do nicely. The target, a Viet Cong terrorist who had to be curtailed in his filthy practice of killing good US Marines, was not so difficult a task for Carlos to take down. He had, only a few months before, won the Wimbledon Cup at the Nationals. It was the summer of 1965, and Camp Perry, Ohio witnessed the arrival of a National Champion, bar none, in the scoped gun / 1000 yard category.

He now stood shoulder to shoulder with the greatest Shooters in Marine Corps history. His good buddy and senior Shooter, Eric England, a Nationals figure since 1954, won the Leech Cup the same day as the National Champion for 1000 yard peep-sight bolt gun competition. They could scarcely conceal their grins when the Commandant came over to shake their hands; the grins lingered when the NRA photographer captured them for *American Rifleman* magazine. Eric was still grinning when he drove from Ohio to Georgia, and stopped by the Turners' in Rome to show Harry and the kids his photo with the Leech Cup.

A bullseye spanning 36 inches, at 1000 yards without a scope, might be compared to a 3.6 inch target at 100 yards. Extra points are awarded for hitting the V, or dead-center, which spans only 5 inches (.005 inches to the bare eye.) To strike this repeatedly and consistently with a high-powered bullet is the work of absolute champions—peerless paragons—even if meteorological effects did not factor in. Compound the mere shooting task with the tremendous physics and atmospheric challenges inherent over such a vast range, and the accomplishment seems humanly impossible.

It was not long until they and several peers were tapped for Scout-Sniper service in Vietnam. Before their tours were completed, *American Rifleman* magazine would publish a major article featuring these two expert Snipers, and the contributions of other National Champions including Don "Boo-Boo" Barker, to the war effort. Such publicity certainly added to the mystique of the Marine Scout-Snipers in Vietnam.

Carlos and his circle of Distinguished Shooters went to war on request of country and Corps, fulfilled a difficult mission, then hastened back to the world of competition shooting they loved best. Though Carlos would be too handicapped from wounds received in his second tour to compete effectively again, he would nevertheless remain on the ranges of Quantico as an instructor until his last day in the Marines.

To ask Shooters like Carlos or Eric about scout-sniping, they compare it to NASCAR drivers being sent on a temporary assignment to test-drive battle tanks. Or sending a deer hunter on a posse to arrest a terrorist. It was just a temporary duty. They were competitors, not killers. But as killers, they were the best. It all came from the discipline of the Corps, the matches and range life, and a deep-rooted heritage of hunting and survival. They followed their orders and did their somber war duty with such dedication and achievement, that they saved countless American lives, and won a permanent place among history's heroes. But they do not talk about it. It was a sad diversion from their first love. To listen to them talk, the dialogue is focused on the upcoming Nationals, who is still in, who is still alive. Gentlemen and sportsmen, all.

Carlos requires no introduction. His 93 confirmed and 400 unconfirmed enemy kills, his record kill at 2500 yards, and his solo mission into North Vietnam to erase a key NVA General in the security of his troops, are well documented in books, articles, movies, and videos. It is said that the enemy felt his impact so heavily, that North Vietnamese dictator Ho Chi Minh offered a reward of three years' pay to the Charlie-San who could nab him. Many tried, and many died.

The unprecedented level of popular and even military interest in competition marksmanship and scout-sniping can be directly linked to Carlos Hathcock, and his scholarly biographer Charles Henderson. Carlos can be researched on the internet, while any library of respectable size has at least one volume on him. There is hardly a gun show in America in the 1990's that does not have at least one booth selling Hathcock memorabilia.

The USMC has gone so far as to adapt its Scout-Sniper program, weaponry, and instructional curricula, to the data developed by Carlos and his colleague Snipers in the Vietnam War, and arms experts such as Colonel Norman Chandler. Colonel Chandler's renowned Iron Brigade Armorers created the Carlos Hathcock Sniping Rifle, a remarkable technical improvement over the military's M-40. The first one made was raffled off for a worthy cause, expecting to fetch $5,000—but easily netting $130,000. It is engraved with Carlos' name, and his Vietnamese nickname of *"Long Trang"* ("White Feather.") It is simply tops among precision sniping weapons.

Further research by any serious shooting scholar reveals Carlos is a prime integer among an elite circle of Distinguished Shooters, whose careers worked together like precision-matched parts. That Eric England and a host of other Top Shots congealed this brotherhood is well known by military historians.

But Eric does not exploit fame nor seek recognition. None of them do. Many of them got together to publicize Carlos' feats out of respect for him, and his losing his health and career due to wounds in Vietnam. They wanted him to get the recognition he deserved, and promoted a means for him to receive some income to supplement his disability pension. And they campaigned for him to get a Silver Star or Medal of Honor.

Though Eric does not choose to stand in the limelight, it comes to him anyway. Still, he tries to avoid it. He has actively opposed books and publicity about him since his retirement. And he does not exploit the fame of his buddies. He feels they deserve it, and he throws the focus right back onto them. He loves to boast about Carlos and others in their circle, but not to his own aggrandizement. To ask Eric if he knows the world-famous Carlos Hathcock, results in a response such as "Yeah, man! That Carlos! Poor feller's had some tough time with that MS. I talked to him and Jo last week. He's a real Marine, salty to the core. Let me tell you what he did one time..."

It takes some prying to get Eric to factor himself onto the stage. He will just grin and say, "Sha—we've been in a lot of axle-greasin's together!" Never mind that Eric was an Old Salt of eight years when Carlos was just getting off the recruit bus at Parris Island. He simply exudes that mountain humility that ironically attracts admirers all the more.

Eric may loosen up and reminisce, once it seems understood that he is not a glory-hound. He may relate a tale such as the time he and Carlos crashed his Vee-Dub under a closed bar gate, or revel in their hunting trips. He may touch briefly on a memorable sniping experience of Carlos', or his own, but then laments how Carlos never received suitable recognition or compensation for his valor and sacrifice. Carlos could have had plenty at the time of his wound from saving seven Marines, had he not humbly shied away from the attention and acclaim—as Eric and their buddies also typically did. But Eric takes it as a personal hurt that Carlos did not receive a Navy Cross or Medal of Honor. So Eric's focus is on the wellbeing of Carlos and Jo, nothing more. Eric and his breed take no liking to glory-hounds, nor those who come lapping at the heels of tall-walkers.

Still, the Hathcocks are gung ho. Although confined to a wheelchair, Carlos remains highly involved as a training consultant for the military, and crack police forces. He makes public appearances if it will benefit others, though it is painful to him. His manager, renowned armorer and Distinguished Shooter Richard Carroll, USMC, Ret'd., accompanies Carlos to numerous activities, remarking about the ongoing stamina Carlos displays considering his sufferings. Richard also tries to take him privately to gun shows and other events, such as watching his son, Sonny, fire in a match, but Carlos is always recognized. As the fans and well-wishers crowd around, the salty old Marine cannot stem the misty-eyed gratitude he feels for their genuine support. *[UPDATE: Carlos passed away from his war wounds on 22 February, 1999.]*

Billy Savelle, USMC, Ret'd., recalls his times with Carlos as among the most esteemed in his life. Billy was the armorer for the first USMC Snipers in Vietnam. He made match-conditioned service and bolt rifles for them, the very rifles that took out their first VC kills. He is currently armorer for the Federal Law Enforcement Training Center.

Billy recalls when Carlos was recovering from his massive burn wounds, then the situation being compounded by a diagnosis of MS. Even after he returned to range duty at the Quantico MTU, he was hard-put to perform under the heat and strain of the job. He recalls Carlos succumbing to heat exhaustion, becoming sluggish but hanging tough, as the staff would get him to sit down and remove the heavy firing jacket and layers of underclothing. Billy relates how at times Carlos would show signs of bleeding or skin breaking down. They had to cover for him, hide him out, and adapt the job to his disabilities. He was a hero and a friend in need. Still, Carlos would not quit. He fought the Medical Board reviews until they finally forced him into a medical discharge, ending his hopes of a full career retirement, which was only a year away.

Colonel Roger E. Knapper sizes up Carlos' predicament thusly:

"Champions of any other sport usually cannot perform as a Distinguished Marksman. Whereas an athlete performs outward physically, a Marksman must control and restrict all his body parts and muscles. The Marksman tightens himself up. He mummifies himself in layers of constrictive clothing topped off by a leather coat with several tight harness straps. He dons firing gloves that cover most of the arm. Then he stretches out in the boiling sun.

He constricts until he is as stiff and straight as steel pipe. The mental concentration and visual mastery are unsurpassed by any activity known to the human experience. Any laxness or variance in this rigidity, to within a fraction of a hair's breadth, cancels any chance of making the first-round cuts. The breakdown of muscle, skin, and nerve associated with burns and MS cannot be long endured under such conditions. Yet Carlos did so for years, masking his excruciating agonies until the Marine medicos finally drew the line. He is a Spartan—a genuine Marine."

Carlos Hathcock, the great American hero, knew about Eric England crawling around in Vietnam, chasing and evading Charlie, with a painful hernia tearing away at him. He was aware of Eric firing an all-time Nationals record while his wound was tearing open and festering. He knew of R.E. Knapper living on snakes as disease lived on him—being diagnosed at the brink of death, yet still an active threat to the Viet Cong.

The Marine Scout-Sniper circle kept up with each other, and stood tall in honor of each other. They still do, decades later. Carlos is certainly saluted by Eric and all their fellow Marines for keeping the faith—a salute which he returns to these great comrades—and that is good enough recognition for them all.

Eric likes to laugh about the spirited ruckus young Carlos raised the night before the Wimbledon, in 1965. "The Sergeant Major was peeved," Eric recounts. "He was going to order him back to base, off the team! Enough officers and NCO's pulled for him, though, that the top growlers decided to let him stay and fire on probation. He performed so well under this pressure, that even the Commandant wanted to be in a picture with him! He saved the team and his own hide that day. It was win, or die."

Unbeknownst to Eric, Carlos has a similar tale to tell on him. As the story goes, "Eric would've been in a bind at the '68 National Open, if he hadn't won! He nearly missed his relay, getting lost on Ft. Benning and tending that wound. But he buckled down real savvy, and kept the heat off— even set a permanent national record. Nobody would've griped after that!"

When the Hathcocks are asked for their most vivid memory of Eric England, they smile at each other, and Jo will jokingly say, "Well, what we'll always remember about Eric is hound dogs and moonshine!" Following a cheery laugh, they will add that Eric is the truest sort of friend they have known. Carlos will remark with solid decorum, "Eric England is a great man, a great Shooter, and a great Marine!" Jo will add, "We just love Eric. He means as much to us as family. Be sure and tell him that, when you see him!" Carlos reiterates, "One great Marine."

Eric echoes the sentiment, reflecting on the Hathcocks. He honors his friends with faithful concern. It has long been a source of regret that Carlos got no more than a Purple Heart for all his valor and sacrifice. It has galled Eric that "some military branches, maybe even a few Marine commanders, gave out medals like surplus grits. And here a feller like Carlos practically gave his life, and—well, he never sought after medals. None of us did. But we all want it for him, just to prove that the country took notice of what he'd done for us all."

Eric has not been alone in harboring these sentiments. What began as a low grumble among Sniper buddies over the injustice issue, began to surface as Carlos came into a position of national prominence due to publicity about his war achievements. Some of Carlos' techniques and experiences were even utilized in the making of the feature film, "Sniper." (Carlos recalls vividly the time he fired at a shining object in the jungle, after he and a VC sniper stalked each other for two days. His round went through the VC's own scope, killing him a fraction of a second before he would have fired through Carlos' scope! This feat was adapted into a key scene in the movie, a fictional film about insurgents in Latin America.)

By this time Carlos had so many admirers, that popular efforts began to sweep the country to urge the US government and the Marine Corps to award him a Medal of

Honor or Distinguished Service Cross or a Silver Star. The movement was greatly promoted by Norm Chandler, Jerry Kozuch, Richard Carroll, and others.

To Eric's great pleasure, the ardent campaigns culminated in a special ceremony held at Quantico on Veterans Day, 1996 to honor Gunny Hathcock. Like a Spartan, he rose from his wheelchair and stood to receive his overdue Silver Star for valor in Vietnam. He stands forever in our hearts and history. He is an eternal component of— *the Marksman Mystique.*

[Since the time of this writing, Carlos has passed in saintly review. He passed from our midst, for a time, on February 24, 1999 after a brave and lengthy struggle with MS. His legacy lives on; he remains a permanent American hero as a defender of liberty. He honored his Corps. He was Semper Fidelis— Always Faithful.]

CHAPTER FORTY

A LIVING LEGEND

ERIC R. ENGLAND retired from the United States Marine Corps on 31 May 1974, twenty four years to the day after first enlisting as a teenager in 1950. He was so devoted to his career as a Shooter, it is said that the venerable rank of Master Sergeant was as far as he desired to rise. Any further, and he would have been whisked away from the rifle ranges he so loved, to "a desk full of memories."

He could have been a Sergeant Major. He could easily have become an officer; there were many opportunities. But one truth always rang clear: he never saw any Colonels or Sergeants Major in the firing relays! Besides, he had his freedom, he was respected at every level of the Corps, he enjoyed more command and autonomy at the MTU and ranges and matches than most senior officers could imagine. After all, he was a legend. And like a true legend, he made his own breaks.

For Eric, looking back juxtaposes well with looking ahead. The old trails he trod led to an ongoing life of accomplishments, just as zestful and masterful as those going before. But one long look back provides a glistening image of the man who set inspiring records, who built ever higher upon every achievement, who won the respect of Generals and Privates and civilian shooting associations in many countries. This is the tale of a masterful man who inspired others on to mastery status—a modest yet talented

245

hero who frequently risked his life in order to save the lives of others. He shunned medals, but got them anyway. He won so many that one skeptical young Lieutenant stopped to ask the Old Salt what some of them were—engraved gold ones—rare ones—some he won even before the "El-Tee" was born.

"That-un there? Distinguished Shooter Medal, Lieutenant," Eric explained. (He resisted the urge to say "*I got it before you was even born;*" saying instead,) "I won that-un back in '52!"

"Very impressive, Master Sergeant," the young shaver replied. He was obviously reflecting on his math. "Non-regulation, though, isn't it?"

"Lieutenant, I assure you it is as regulation as this-un here, give to me by Chesty Puller."

He left the Lieutenant nodding in silence, a mixture of confusion and humility.

There is no medal that could completely capture the profile of Eric England, however. This is the legend of a humble mountain man whose genius and dedication compelled him from the obscurity of the sorghum-cane fields and pea patches, to become an international figure— whose bravery and cunning in warfare baffled the enemy to its highest echelons, and yet who generated more peace and goodwill among his fellowmen than is typically seen among human capabilities.

It is the story of a man whose technical achievements endure because they are etched in history, but whose personal history will perpetuate because it is so honored by those who were fortunate enough to know him. Yet in all, he fiercely rejects any tribute that may attempt to set him above his team mates. "You can't say anybody is *the* best," Eric insists. "Our *teams* were made up of the best. My hat's off to *many* Shooters."

By nature and not design, Eric continues to attract accolades after a quarter century of retirement. He was honored by the US Army at Fort Benning in 1996—the first Marine Shooter to receive such an award—due to the all-time record he set there in 1968. He is sought out for tributes from the UCMC Commandant and Sergeant Major of the Corps, the Governor of Georgia, Hollywood notables, many publications, and noted sports figures. The NRA Museum houses an Eric England display. The Veterans of Foreign Wars requested a formal photo-portrait in dress uniform. NRA and Olympics officials have researched statistics confirming his overall career scores in long-range rifle competitions are the highest in world history. And he has been sought out to coach the US international lineup in the last Palma Match of the century. To all this, he reacts with a modest shrug.

He remained active in pro shooting events, even the Senior Nationals, long after retirement. He could walk onto a range totally unpracticed for two years, and still fire in the top ten or so in the nation. Then in the late 1980's he seriously injured one eye with a fish sinker, while casting for trophy bass. He has not competed professionally since then. This did not prevent him from providing private shooting lessons to notables including NASCAR's Bill Elliott, or training local 4-H BB-gun match teams. Nor did it deter The Palma one iota from urging him to coach.

Perhaps his most satisfying post-retirement achievement was founding the Distinguished Shooters Association, the first assemblage of its kind in history. He never misses a reunion. At last count there are over 400 members. They meet in sync with the Nationals, and are always the highlight of events. Some say it is just another way of Eric keeping the Marine Corps supplied with white lightenin', though he grins and suggests that moonshine is a good ways back in his past. But another reunion he seldom misses is the North Georgia Moonshiners Convention, so the topic is open to speculation.

Eric shows no sign of slowing down. Men half his age cannot keep up with him as he scouts, hunts, and fishes in his Appalachian paradise. He wants "to see as much of what's left of it, before it's gone, or before he is." And in preparation for the old age which remains unforeseeable, he is busy transplanting rare and healthful mountain herbs, on the grounds of Nix Hall—the ancestral home which he now owns. His Grandpa's old fiddle music still sweetens the soul, if not the air, around Choe Stoe—Cherokee for *"Land of Dancing Rabbits."* This is the land where he learned to shoot his Great Grandpa's Civil War musket. He hopes to shoot there until all life's targets are down.

TURNER

Eric is equally content to be rocking on the Governor's porch or hunting with Bill Elliott, as he is with swapping tales with a cane farmer or a Bluegrass picker. He knows nary a stranger. He may be on the telephone one moment turning down a book or documentary offer, then the next call will be about the health of an old fishing buddy whom he will drive directly over to see. He will turn down a formal dinner or award banquet with a retired General or celebrity, if a sick buddy needs a visit—or if cousin Harold Harkins asks him to give a speech at his 50th wedding anniversary. And his 4-H BB team is as vital as any that ever shot.

Eric likes to drop in on his Arkequah cousins, like Harry's brother Edward. They talk about 'coon hunting, the sorghum crops—and battles they were both in when Ed was in his first tour in Vietnam in the Army. They recall the river crossings at Khe Sanh and the rockets at Dong Ha, and the numerous rumblings of the machinations of war which still echo upon the murky fields and up the hidden draws of memory only.

Eric keeps his eagle-eye out for adventure always, small or large. He has a way of turning the small event into a really big time for all. It is not unusual for Eric to be driving past an antique car show or parade, and impulsively enter his sleek red-and-black 1976 Ford pickup—and take first place among the classics whose owners have spent years in restoring them. It is typical of him to bag a record-sized bear or bass or trout, but not even apply for verification. "Don't need to be publicizin' my prime patch," he will explain, with a grin and a shake of the head. But it is expected of him to have the unexpected land in his lap. He has that sort of rare magnetism.

He strides confidently onward, and in good health, though fully mourning the numerous buddies who have "answered Taps." Part of his zestful living is in honor of them—carrying on the torch of gusto they once hailed. He hears the cadence, and marches on. But no one can recall seeing him with a jug of lightenin' in quite some time. The man who once kept Camp Lejeune so well supplied with the elixir that he was suspected of running a still on base, has apparently abandoned the stuff. "Sha, can't find any good stuff anymore anyway," he has been heard to moan. "Lots of it's amateur runs anyway, or made with chicken feed!"

But like a good NCO or combat trooper, he has cut back on anything that is starting to seem impractical. This managerial approach has even carried over to trout fishing. There are no more native trout, only hatchery specimens. And as cousin Harry says, "Once the native trout leave the streams, so will Eric." Yet he will not hesitate to take off to South Dakota to hunt pheasant, or to south Texas for the quail. And at 66 he is still trotting the steep Appalachian slopes where younger men fear to tread.

He has open invitation to private hunting grounds up to as large as 500,000 acres. His fame brings landed acquaintances into his path; his congenial frontier manner and humor earn him friends—and hunting rights unparalleled.

He takes his Distinguished Shooters roster on the road and keeps up with the fellers. There is always something new going on with them: D.I. Boyd, for instance, went from Marine Shooter to Olympics Coach. And there are ailing and aging Shooters to go check on. They all share an appreciation for the gusto Eric has lived by, a zest stemming from the days he and Harry and Harold rassled bobcats and future governor Zell Miller shared the sharpshooting dream with him. These are lifelong buddies who hold ranks and take care of their own, to the last muster. They are all living appendages of the *Phantasm*—all components of the *mystique*.

Eric knows no strangers. He *relishes* genuine people of any social stratum. He *tolerates* the amateurs and wanna-be's who talk-the-talk. He *rebukes* none but the intentionally cruel or phony. His hospitality is well known. But if anyone tries to buy a square foot of his mountain land, or approaches him with a book offer, he merely shakes his head to clear the boiling steam, and walks away.

Eric R. England has fought and won the final battle: Retirement! He has learned to revel in it. The first barrier was the realization that civilians are never on time; this took some getting used to. But he continues to carve a comfortable civilian niche with his soulmate, sweet Sue. His unalterable pattern of activity somehow jives with her tranquil spirit, and never prevents him from reporting dutifully home on time. The itch to travel and seek adventure never gets scratched away, much like the unending gusto of Davy Crockett of old. He has offers to participate in international security crises, and is consulted in an advisory capacity by more than one nation. Hardly a week rolls by that he is not sought out for sage counsel in military or sporting matters, or to speak as a celebrated legend at a prominent military or civic function. He enjoys lending assistance where needed, but shies away from events which may give him individual acclaim.

And he has never forsaken his first love: the Appalachians which spawned him. To approach his house, the visitor first notices half a dozen muddy boots—old Marine issue—kicked off in the carport. There's fresh game on the kitchen counter. Mementos from buddies and notables and the Corps adorn his walls, alongside old portraits of his pioneer ancestors, or his cowboy father or saintly mother. Between all these are punctuations of bass and deer trophies. The really big stuff—the Interservice Cups and Nationals and Internationals awards—emblems of actual fame—are used to hold screwdrivers, fishing tackle, loose change, and lost batteries, on basement shelves.

Nearby lie molded issues of magazines featuring him decades ago—commendations bearing the original signatures of past Commandants—and reams of historical documents portraying a brilliant career understood by few, but beneficial to many. Items of monetary value are in museums or vaults. He's really too busy to think about all those trappings these days, mementos once stowed in sea bags and footlockers, now retired to the basement. Sue has begun salvaging historic, Homeric specimens from the mold and mildew, and bringing them topside. "Old Yeller," the blond-stocked rifle he used to set the all-time record of .998x45, is museum bound. There is talk of a new Nationals trophy being created in his honor.

Finding Eric home by day is unlikely. He will be skinning a bear he shot, or conducting a private survey on trout populations or game migrations. Then maybe off to a dinner invitation at the Governor's Mansion, where the conversation is always on getting back to their good ol' mountains. In 2002, Zell Miller, now a US Senator, proudly recognized Eric in his keynote address to the NRA Convention, as did others.

A few years after Eric's retirement, his saintly mother Mary passed away. Then-Lieutenant Governor Miller was in attendance. Afterward he mentioned to Eric, "You know, Cuz, you've become a national treasure. You're an undefeated hero. You saved hundreds of American lives. And your example inspired me to become a Marine and a Shooter, where I gained the discipline that saved my own life and led to my career." (As Governor, Zell Miller also went on to institute the Boot Camp system for Georgia prisons, which has become a model to the world. His own model came from the USMC via Eric and Harry.)

Eric shrugged off the honors, and pointed a thumb toward their kinsman, Harry Turner, standing nearby. "There's the reason for it all, right there."

Harry grinned and shook his head, passing the accolade back to Eric. It is the Spirit of the Corps that matters to them, nothing more or less. Of Harry, another kinsman once said, "If Harry had stayed in the Marine Corps, he would have been famous." But to Harry, watching Eric's star rise in the illustrious sky of the Corps brings more satisfaction than any honor could.

Many things have been said about Eric, more than could ever be recorded in a single book. His name still buzzes around the ranges at Quantico and LeJeune and Parris Island and Camp Perry. He is still mentioned along the hallowed halls of the N.R.A., and around the campfires and fishing holes of many an Appalachian outdoorsman. Many things will still be said about Eric England for many years to come, some true and some enhanced by legend; for legend is perpetuated by those who are affected by the power of its very presence. But Eric would choose to be remembered simply as a good ol' Georgia boy and a good Marine. To Eric, that is honor aplenty.

Harry sums him up best: Eric is an approachable national hero, whose feet still itch to trot the globe—yet who keeps dodging the limelight—coming back to a homeland where he is just one of the folks. Eric never fully escaped

TURNER

Choe Stoe—but then, he never really wanted to.
~Finis~

UPDATE ONE

On February 26, 2006, Eric was honored by his hometown when a sculpture of him was unveiled in the Union County Historical Society Museum in Blairsville, Georgia. Keynote speakers were former Senator and Governor Zell Miller, and Maj. Jim Land (USMC, Ret.) of The National Rifle Association. Major Land is also noted for having been Carlos Hathcock's commanding officer and scout-sniping mentor in Vietnam, as well as a competition shooter.

Nearly two dozen of Eric's surviving fellow shooters and war buddies came from across the country for the historic occasion. It was the culminating event in a long series of honors which have illuminated his career trail.

In addressing a standing-room-only audience which flowed outside to the town square, Sen. Miller described the enjoyment of being near Eric when he visits the Nationals matches, and hears the world's most distinguished shooters excitedly whispering, *"There goes Eric England!"* and *"That's Eric England!"*

Maj. Land reviewed Eric's career, focusing on his undefeated record match scores, and how he terrorized and debilitated the enemy in Vietnam to the point that he came to be called "The Phantom of Phu Bai." Maj. Land added that Eric to this day defers credit to others, and will not take full honors for anything he has done. Even the "Phantom" moniker deflects off his humble armor, and settles upon the many noble scout-snipers with whom he served, whom he trained, and whom he inspired. That is the way he likes it: pass the crown of achievement to others whose lives he has touched. But he was very much part of it; he was and forever is the... *Phantom of Phu Bai.*

Master Sergeant Eric R. England answered "Taps" at the Veterans' Hospital in Atlanta on 7 April, 2018. He is interred at the Arlington National Cemetery.

Semper Fidelis

About The Author

Joseph Blair Turner, Ph.D., is related to Eric England eight ways. The closest is 1st cousin once removed; (Eric is his father's 1st cousin.) Dr. Turner is also related to Sen. Zell Miller seven ways, President Carter three ways, and distantly to Presidents Bush and John Wesley. He is a direct descendant of King Edward I, II, and III, Queen Eleanor of Aquitaine, William the Conqueror, and Emperor Charlemagne. He is proudest to be descended from the common folk who labored through the generations to keep their family lines surviving and intact.

He grew up in the shadow of his Marine heroes: Harry, and Eric. His earliest childhood memories are those of scouring over and through the Appalachian Mountains of North Georgia with them, regaling in high adventure and hearty anecdote.

Dr. Turner served as an Army medic in Vietnam when he was 18. He feels he more than earned his G. I. Bill, which paid for college. He studied psychology and English literature, then attended graduate school in management and rehabilitation administration. He is also a songwriter of some "note." Other books of military interest he has authored include *Victim of Valor*, and *Little War Stories*. He also wrote the short story, "The Battle of Widow Wood." His historic novel of the American Revolution, *Alamance!*, is a true story of his North Carolina ancestors' key role in the first actual battle between American Colonials and the British.

He is married to the lovely SaraEllen. They are the parents of seven children; and as of 2019, 21 grandchildren; all of whom love God, America, and family heritage. For this, he is grateful to the point of satisfaction.

He has also held a lifelong pride in Eric, and somehow knew from the age of 11 that he would one day write a book about him. When it came time to do so in 1996, it all formed together rapidly and phenomenally. He was humbled by the honor, and at the number of great individuals who were eager to assist in this worthy project. It is his earnest hope that he has "done right by him."

GLOSSARY OF TERMS

.50 cal large u.s. machine gun
.51 cal large commie machine gun
105 / 1-oh-5 105mm howitzer cannon, u.s.
81mm large mortar
a-4 jet fighter-bomber, u.s.
a/c aircraft commander
air strike jet attack, deploying bombs or rockets
ak-47 automat klashnikov, model 1947. russian &chinese rifle
a/o area of operation
arty artillery
arvn Army of the Republic of Vietnam; S. VN army. ("Arvins")
bo doi *vietnamese:* nva soldier
bubble shooter's mental coccoon of total concentration
by the numbers in order; effective manner
c-130 u.s. cargo and troop plane, convertible to command or ordinance platform
c-141 large transport plane, u.s.
c-4 plastic explosive
c-47 medium sized transport plane, u.s. (not ch-47)
ch-46 sea knight; large u.s. twin-rotor helicopter. compare army's ch-47 chinook
ch-47 u.s. army version of ch-46
charlie viet cong
chicom chinese-communist issue; *i.e.* a chicom grenade
claymore remote-control antipersonnel mine
cobra u.s. assault / tactical combat helicopter, issued 1967
commo communications
c-rats c-rations; canned food
crosshairs "plus-mark" shape in center of rifle scope lens
c-s tear gas
dai uy ("die-wee")—*vietnamese:* "captain"
deep-serious very deep, very serious trouble
di di mau ("dee-dee-mau")—*vietnamese:* "git gone!"

259

dmz   demilitarized zone between north and south vietnam
fac   forward air controller. similar to f/o, but for aircraft
f/o   forward observer; artillery scout who directs fire onto enemy
fire mission   artillery barrage, usually in support of ground troops
frag   fragmentation grenade; hand grenade or M-79 round
freq   radio frequency
green-side-out   wearing jungle cammies, as opposed to brown side
gungy   very, very gung ho
gunny   gunnery sergeant
hide   sniper's place of concealment
ho chi minh   former dictator of north vietnam
hooch   hut
howitzer   cannon which can fire at a high arc point for close- range targets in tactical support
huey   uh-1 helicopter, u.s.
I corps   tactical zone below dmz. 1st of I, II, III & IV corps regions
intel   intelligence department or intelligence data
kia   killed in action
l-z   landing zone
loh   light observation helicopter
lrrp / lurp   long range reconnaissance patrol
L-T / el-tee   lieutenant; (from abbrev., "Lt.")
m-14   automatic rifle, u.s.
m-16   automatic assault rifle, u.s.
m-203   a 40mm grenade launcher, usually attached to an M-16
m-60   7.62mm machine gun, u.s.
m-79   grenade launcher, u.s.
mad minute   defensive firing, full power all directions, for 1 min.
medevac   medical evacuation helicopter
minh oi   ("muhn-OY")—*vietnamese:* "ma cheri"
montagnard   ("MON-tan-yard")—french: "mountain tribesman"
m.o.s.   military occupational specialty; military job title
mtu   marksmanship training unit
nape   napalm bomb

nco / ncoic noncommissioned officer / NCO-In-Charge
nva north vietnamese army
old salt an experienced and time-proven marine
ov-1 a light observation or reconnaissance plane
pogie; poagie rear-echelon office personnel; clerk
px post exchange. a military store. also **bx** *(base exchange)*
recon reconnaisance; a snooping patrol
remf "rear echelon military force;" (slang.)
rough rider armed convoy or road transport in combat zone
rpg rocket-propelled grenade
s-2 military intelligence dept.
semper-fi *semper fidelis;* marine motto in latin. ("always faithful")
sks russian and chinese semi-auto rifle
starlight scope night-vision scope, u.s. introduced in vietnam
tdy temporary duty
the world the united states, as perceived by military in the bush
ti uy ("tee-wee")—*vietnamese:* "lieutenant"
uh-1 see huey
vc viet cong; pro-commie guerilla forces within south vietnam
wia wounded in action
willie pete; wp white phosphorous explosive, artillery, or frag
xin loi ("sin loy")—*vietnamese:* "sorry about that!"
zippo flame thrower

ADDENDUM

[From *The North Georgia News, Blairsville*]:

Eric England Sculpture Dedication

Union County native Eric England will be honored at a ceremony on Sunday, Feb. 26, 2006, at 2:00 pm, at the historic Union County Courthouse on Blairsville's town square. The ceremony will take place in the second-floor courtroom and will include the dedication of a new bronze sculpture of Mr. England as a record-setting marksman. A reception at the Old Courthouse will follow the dedication.

Mr. England is a retired career Marine who established a national marksmanship record at Fort Benning, Georgia, in 1968 that has never been broken. He served in the Marine

Corps from 1950 to 1974, including service in Vietnam as a sniper with the 3rd Marine Division. Mr. England retired as a master sergeant. **He has been called "history's greatest long-range shooter, and legendary scout-sniper."*** He also participated on two Olympic teams.

Zell Miller, former Georgia Governor and U.S. Senator, will commemorate Mr. England's service and marksmanship records; he will also unveil the new sculpture. Former Marine **Major Jim Land**, who served with Mr. England on the Marine Corps Rifle Team and in Vietnam, will speak about Mr. England's achievements. Mr. Land currently serves as Secretary of the National Rifle Association, of which Mr. England is a lifetime member. Music, entertainment, and tributes will be provided by Sam Ensley, Don Byers, and other friends and family members.

The bronze sculpture to be unveiled depicts Mr. England as a sharp-shooter, based on 1960's-era photographs of him in a kneeling-shooting position. Atlanta sculptor Andy Davis created the sculpture and will be at the ceremony for the unveiling. The sculpture will be donated to the Union County Historical Society in honor of Mr. England's outstanding service to his country.

* **[Proud to announce that this is a direct quote from this book, and its promotional website.]**

UPDATE TWO

In 2009, PFC Sherri Gallagher of the USAMU broke the oldest record in High Power shooting: the 1000 point aggregate. Gallagher shot a 999-67x to win the Remington-Bushmaster Open, breaking Eric England's 42-year-old record of a 998-45x. In perfect symmetry, both records were set on Easley Range, Fort Benning, GA. (Source: Union County Georgia Historical Society.)

NOTE: The author thinks it is important to note that although Gallagher technically beat his record of 42 years, she had a great deal of technical advantage.

Though she is surely a fine competitive shooter, the Remington Bushmaster she used is so high-tech, it does not even significantly kick. Moreover, it automatically reloads, keeping eyes and hands in the original firing position. It is a minimal-stress weapon.

Eric used a bolt-action, high-powered .30-06, which wobbles completely out of line every time the bolt is worked. To return to the "shooter's bubble of control", maintaining accuracy, and within the established time limit, requires tremendous skill and effort. To say Gallagher outshot him is like saying a 747 outflew a space shuttle. A great salute is due Gallagher, but there will never, ever, be another Eric England. Each deserves credit within their own sphere.

(Eric simply shrugs it off, and congratulates her for her achievements.)

A FINAL TRIBUTE:

THANK YOU, Esteemed Reader, For Honoring The Fighting Men Who Have Preserved Our Freedoms. Remember Also The Support Personnel, Who—With You In Mind—Hustled To Keep Them Sustained; And The Nurses, Red Cross, And USO Whose Superhuman Sacrifices Comforted Your Suffering Son, Or Kept Him Alive For You.

WAS IT WORTH IT? To The Families Of Those Who Lost Life Or Limb, We Owe An Eternal Debt. And As To Those Who Physically Survived, Remember That At The First Moment They Stepped Off That Plane And Into Harm's Way, They Too Had Already Given Their Lives For Their Country. They Knew Not Whether They Would Survive. And A Thousand Times A Day, For 365 Days Of Ghastly War In A Nightmarish World, They Continued To Give Their Lives. Then They Died A Thousand Deaths When They Returned To Face The Unfriendly Homeland Which Had So Freely Sent Them. Please Honor The

Vietnam Veterans, And All Veterans, Who Have Honored You.

A WORTHY CAUSE :

There Are Many Ways You Can Support Military Personnel. Write Them And Send Them Packages, Especially When Their Writing Drops Off. Visit Their Families And Cheer Them, Thanking Them For Their Contribution To Freedom.

Support Legislation Which Favors The Needs Of The Military, The Veterans, Or Their Families. Visit The Disabled. Organize An Entertainment Or Service Project For A Military Or Veterans Hospital.

Support Charities Which Have A Track Record Of High Service And Low Profit Incentive. As A War Veteran, I Cannot Adequately Express The Need To Contribute To The USO And The RED CROSS. How Many Times They Came To The Very Clutches Of Death Just To Cheer The Troops, And Pull Our Hearts From The

Mud. They Are The FIRST Support A Recruit Encounters Upon Entering The Military, And They Are Serving Him Or Her Until The Day Of Discharge. We All Owe Them More Than We Can Repay. The RED CROSS Is Also The First On Hand To Save Your Family Or Community In Times Of Disaster. I Endorse Them Wholeheartedly.

A DUTY
TO DEFEND :

Support The Constitutional Right Of Decent Citizens To Keep And Bear Arms. This Is Our Last-Ditch Defense Against Invasion, Crime, And Captivity. Rising Dictators Move Swiftly To Disarm Their Citizens. But Be Careful And Exercize Self-Restraint Pertaining To Firearms.

Please, Re-Educate Your Children On The Fact That The U.S. Was Not Defeated In Vietnam. Though This Is A Popular Leftist View In School Texts And Other Liberal, Anti-Veteran Venues Of Communication, The Fact Is That Our Forces Stemmed

Global Tyranny Despite Lack Of Support At Home, And Kept An Ungrateful World From Having To Learn To Spell Words Like "Proletariat" And "Bolshevik." The U.S. And Her Allies Won EVERY Battle In Vietnam, Often At A Casualty Ratio Of 30 To 1. We, And The Enemy, Knew That We Had Total Power. When Unleashed, We Were Always Victorious.

Two Years After The U.S. Left Vietnam With Honor, With The Agreement That South Vietnam Would Now Fight For Their Own Freedom, *They* Lost To The North Who, Along With Help From China And The U.S.S.R., Broke The Treaty And Re-Invaded The South. Though Countless South Vietnamese Served With Valor, Many Seemed Content To Let Us Spill Our Blood For Them While They Deserted. Teach Your Children That Freedom Is Purchased With Good Men's Blood And Good Mothers' Tears; Our Blood And Tears Are Not Proxies For Those Unwilling To Fight, Whether Fellow Citizens At Home Or Fair-Weather Friends Abroad.

~ The Author ~

~~~~~~

ILLUSTRATIONS

THE FOLLOWING PICTURES AND DOCUMENTS HAVE BEEN COLLECTED OVER MANY YEARS, FROM VARIOUS SOURCES.

THESE INCLUDE THE USMC, MANY ORGANIZATIONS AND INDIVIDUALS, AND FROM THE ERIC ENGLAND ARCHIVES.

WE WOULD APPRECIATE ANY HELP IDENTIFYING UNNAMED PEOPLE IN THESE PHOTOS.

SOME PHOTOS WERE FOUND DAMAGED, AND WERE RESTORED WITH TREMENDOUS EFFORT. THUS THE QUALITY VARIES. PLEASE ENJOY THEM FOR WHAT THEY ARE, AND WHAT THEY REPRESENT. WE ARE FORTUNATE TO HAVE THESE RARE ITEMS AT ALL.

THE GREAT MARKSMAN'S FIRST MARKS ~ 1950

Eric's Rifle-Training Notes From Marine Corps Boot Camp, Parris Island, SC

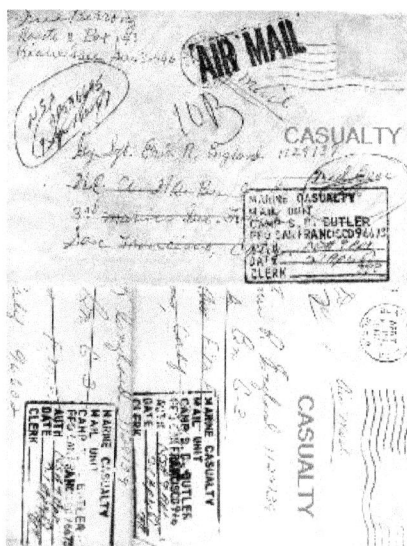

DREADED DELIVERIES

Mail Sent To Eric In Vietnam During His Mysterious Wounding Period Were
Being Returned, Marked "Casualty"   (1967)

LCpl. C. N. Hathcock, USMC   S/Sgt. E. R. England, USMC

TWO NATIONAL LONG-RANGE WINNERS ~ 1965
Eric England Won The Leech Cup For 1000 Yard Open-Sight Rifle Match
Carlos Hathcock Won The Wimbledon Cup For 1000 Yard Scope Rifle Match
The Double Feat Was A Resounding Victory For The USMC Team,
And Set The Stage For The Two Being Tapped Later For Scout-Sniper Service

Photo Courtesy Of National Rifle Assn.   Used With Permission

273

ENTRANCE TO HAI VAN PASS

WHERE SPORTSMANSHIP SAVES LIVES

A Small Section Of Eric's Hunting Map Of The Virginia Hills. Detailed Notations Show Deer Tracking, Sightings, Signs, Habits, & Kills… Total Professionalism Shown By Future Viet-Cong Hunting Legends Who Used This Very Same Map: England, Kozuch, Hathcock, Bartlett, Dunnam. Superb Outdoor Skills Contributed To Lifesaving & Combat

Survival

"A FISHERMAN'S DREAM"
(Caption In USMC Newspaper, Camp Lejeune, 1966.)
Shooting Legends James Zahm (L) & Eric England (R)
Extended Sporting Skills To Lunga Reservoir.
30-Lb. String Caught In 90 Minutes . Lures Were Made With Deer Hair

Photo By M. H. Kuzniewski, USMC

REGIONAL CHAMPION
Camp Pendleton, March 21:
Marine Master Sergeant Eric R. England emerged as Regional Champion during the 7th Annual National Rifle Association Tournament March 20-21. There were over 100 participants including 13 teams. MSgt. England took individual honors with a 5-match aggregate of 989-23X. He holds the National Open record of 998-45X. He presently serves as a marksmanship instructor at Camp Pendleton, and is the son of Mr. and Mrs. A.L. England of Blairsville, GA.
-Official USMC Photo / Kari Knocklem

BIG BARRAGE BETWEEN BATTLES
~ Eric Wins Regional Championship ~ 1969
Managed To Coach Winning Team At Okinawa While Serving Secretly In Vietnam... Then Returned With Team To California To Show 'Em How The Shootin's Done.   Never Missed A Lick!   This Gun Was Awarded To Him For High Score.

United States Marine Corps

Certificate of Commendation

The Commandant of the Marine Corps takes pleasure in commending

Gunnery Sergeant Eric R. ENGLAND 1129139, U. S. Marine Corps

for

Outstanding performance at the Eighth Annual Interservice Match at Marine Corps Schools, Quantico, Virginia, during the period 12-17 August 1967. His outstanding contribution as a firing member of the winning Marine Corps Team in the Interservice Rifle Team Championship Match is a credit to himself, his organization, and the United States Marine Corps.

11 October 1967

Date

Wallace M. Greene Jr.

Commandant of the Marine Corps

COMMANDANT'S CONGRATS

Gen. Wallace Green Thanks Eric For Winning 1967 Interservice Match

MYSTERY OF THE PALMA TROPHY

*"IN THE NAME OF THE UNITED STATES OF AMERICA,
AND THE RIFLEMEN OF THE WORLD"*

THE SYMBOL OF THE INTERNATIONAL PALMA MATCH ®
& Pride Of The National Rifle Association Since 1876

Eric Helped Win It Back For The U.S. More Than Once…
Though The Actual Trophy Had Vanished, & Is Still Missing!

Made Entirely Of Gold & Silver, & Displayed Over The Years In The Most
Prestigious Edifices   On Earth. The Priceless Trophy Disappeared
Sometime After 1950. Perhaps It Is Lost In A Storage Crate In A Museum,
Or Adorns The Den Of Some Greedy Collector With A Guilty Conscience.
Can *You* Solve The Mystery?

["Palma Match" & "Palma Trophy" Are Registered Trademarks Of The
National Rifle Association. Used by permission.]

278

THUỔNG CHO
GySgt England

« G'ah-N'e E'n-Lan »

« E'-Hu'ich E'n-Lan »

THƯƠNG TICH
100,000 PIASTRE

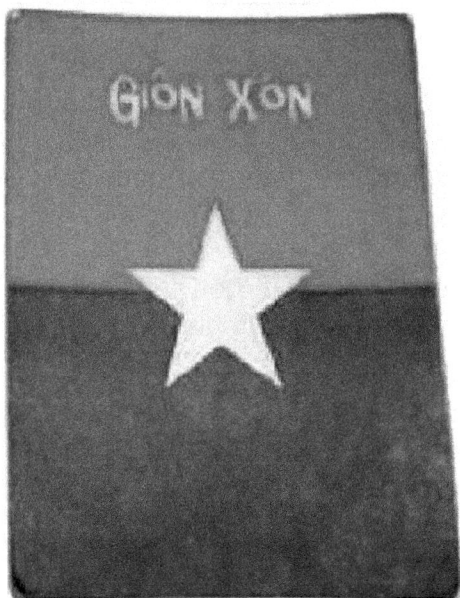

GIÓN XON

TURNER

PRECEDING PAGE:

VC / NVA REWARD CARD
OFFERING HUGE REWARD FOR "E'HU'ICH E'N-LAN"

Found By A Patrol Along The Trails Near Phu Bai

These Would Be Found Scattered In Town And Country, And Distributed Publicly.

"E'Hu'ich E'n-Lan" Is The Vietnamese Spelling Of Eric England. They Spell Foreign Words Phonetically.

Unlike Flyers Or Posters, These "Wanted" Cards Were Usually Left Along Trails For Both The Natives As Well As The Scout-Snipers Themselves To Find.

Some Cards Went So Far As To Offer US Servicemen A Bounty To Turn Themselves In, Promising Cash And An Exit From The War! It Is Difficult To Imagine The Folly Of Such An Unthinking Enemy, To Believe The US Marines Would Fall For Such A Ploy.

The Desired Effect Of Lowering Morale By Such Propaganda Was Never Achieved.

Around I Corps ...

USMC SNIPERS RULE THE FIELD

In a series of tactical operations, top USMC scout-snipers of the 1st and 3rd Divisions have practically ransacked a number of VC lairs while crucially interrupting key NVA operations in all sectors of I Corps, all along the DMZ.

With chilling efficiency in their craft, these unseen but ever-present purveyors of terror are unleashing the USMC's finest tradition of the frontier-like savvy and cunning so vital to winning guerilla conflicts.

Headed up by the finest marksmen in the US, the scout-sniper training programs take trainees directly to the fight. USMC scout snipers boost Corps morale with stunning impact and superior kill ratios.

Last week's after-action reports from all tactical zones near Phu Bai alone reflect as many as 48 VC and NVA dead, while in Cam Lo a VC squad was

Continued on Page 3

**WHY USMC SCOUT-SNIPERS
DO NOT RELY ON PROPAGANDA!**

Sample News Article Tells It All
"If You Can Read, You'd Better Heed!"

281

TOP BRASS WERE ALWAYS GRATEFUL
TO THEIR TOP SHOT

Eric's Competition Scores Enhanced Many A Commander's Status ~
And It Gave Generals Status To Be Associated With This Legend

ROUGH RIDER OF THE "RANGE"

Ever Alert, Ever Tough… Ever A Marine

DON BARTLETT, (R)
Eric's Lifelong Fellow Distinguished Shooter
And Past National Champion. His Great Renown
Lives On. Rose From Private To Major.

"KAZOOTCH"

MSGT Gerald John "Kazootch" Kozuch
Eric's Lifelong Fellow Distinguished Shooter
Held National Open Record For Several Minutes Until Teammate
Eric Came On The Firing Line

Jerry Answered Taps On 18 May, 2010
They Are Reunited Once Again

FAREWELL TO "OL' YELLER"
Eric Donates Record-Setting Rifle To NRA - 2002

**ERIC & CARLOS HATHCOCK
AT 1979 DISTINGUISHED
SHOOTERS REUNION**

The Group Was A *Who's-Who* Of
Top-Class Shooters, All Of Whom
Had A Place In History.

The Reunion Is Still Held Annually,
Usually In Conjunction With The
Nationals Match

Restored Photo

THE GREAT COMPETITOR, WHOSE LEADING-EDGE
SKILLS & WILLINGNESS
TO SERVE MADE GOOD MARINES & SHOOTERS EVEN
BETTER

GOV. ZELL MILLER & MARINE MENTOR

A CHEERY REUNION IN THEIR BELOVED NORTH GEORGIA MOUNTAINS, 1992

Zell Followed Eric's Example & Changed His Destiny By Becoming A Marine. Zell Learned Disciplines Which Later Inspired The "Boot Camp" Corrections System, A Model For The World. Zell Is A Top Shooter Too

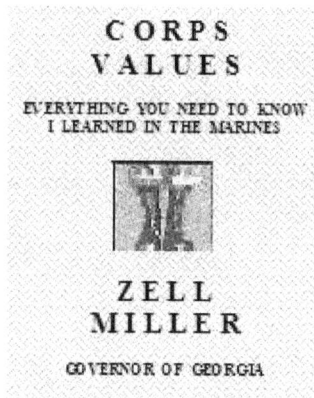

GOVERNOR'S BOOK CREDITS ERIC & USMC FOR HIS SUCCESS

(Can be Ordered Online At Amazon.com)

A PAIR OF LEGENDS WIN WESTERN REGIONAL
(L:) Mike Pietroforte   (R:) Eric England ~ 1970

Mike Was First Person To Shoot Perfect Score In Military Nationals
(1958) (Again in 1966)
Mike Now Has A National Trophy Named In His Honor

Official USMC Press Release Photo

THE DAY HISTORY WAS MADE
1968 US Open Match ~ (This Rifle Is Now In The NRA Museum)

(L:) Jerry Kozuch, Set New Nat. Record, Held For 22 Minutes
(R:) Eric England, Set *All-Time* Record Of .998x45
Also On The 5-Man Team Was Don Bartlett, Who Held Old Nat. Record

Historic Photo ~ Courtesy Of USMC

1965 USMC Crimson Rifle Team:
(L-R, Back:) R. H. Green, Carlos Hathcock, Mike Pietroforte (A new Nationals trophy is now named for him,) Greg Connor (Now with the NRA).
(L-R, Front:) G. Murdock, Don Bartlett. All Were Superhuman Champions

Photo Courtesy Of National Rifle Assn.   Used With Permission

WINNERS ~ 1965 US INTERSERVICE MATCH
FRONT CENTER: (L: Don Bartlett) (R: Eric England)
BACK CENTER: (L: Gen. Wallace Green, Commandant) (R: Col. Walter Walsh, "Father Of Modern Shooting")

MORE OF THE WORLD - CLASS SHOOTING TEAMS
WITH WHOM ERIC SPENT HIS MARINE CORPS CAREER

THEY STILL MAINTAIN A CLOSE BROTHERHOOD AND
CAMARADERY UNEQUALLED IN THE WORLD

THE "P. I. PISTOLS" PRECISION PISTOL TEAM
WINS ANOTHER MATCH

Parris Island Marine Depot, SC ~ The Early Years
By 19, Eric (2nd From Right) Was A Recognized Match Contender With .45

USMC'S .45 PISTOL "TOP GUNS," YEARS LATER

Eric (2nd From Left) Still At It Many Years Later

DUTCH MARINES TOUR WASHINGTON AND QUANTICO
Eric (L) Was Designated To Demonstrate America's Shooting Savvy To Official Delegation

ERIC RECEIVES NATIONALS MEDAL
About 1955

ERIC SURVEYS WRECKAGE OF HIS 1959 FORD
After Surviving Dramatic Crash Off Blood Mountain

A "SQUARED—AWAY" MARINE

Graduation Day,
Drill Instructor School

San Diego
1955

It Was This Ideal Marine Image
Which Inspired Gov. Zell Miller
And Countless Others To Follow
In Eric's Footsteps

Augmenting The Image Was
The Real, Inner Marine Whose
Talents Were Equaled Only By
His Dedication And Loyalty

293

TURNER

WINNER ~ LEECH CUP ~ 1965 NATIONALS

Eric Won The Coveted Leech Cup At Camp Perry, Ohio
Just As Dusk Set In. 1000 Yards, Iron Sights. The Glimmer
Of Twilight Distorted The Distant Target So Much That It Was
Considered A Miraculous Display Of Marksmanship Talent.

His Friend And Teammate, The Young Carlos Hathcock,
Won The Wimbledon Cup For 1000-Yards With Scoped Rifle The
Same Day. They Were Widely Heralded By The Shooting World,
And Received Personal Congratulations From The Commandant.

Firing a combined total of 992/105V, the Quantico MTU defeated the other teams for the winning trophy. Members of the team were from left to right; GySgt. A. Adams, SSgt. E. England, Coach SSgt. C. Galkowski, SSgt. W. Jones and SSgt. E. Manning.

SSgt. E. England studies his last shot through the scope.

WINNERS ~ 1966 EASTERN DIVISION MATCH

HISTORIC SCENES FROM
1ST MARINE DIVISION
SNIPER SCHOOL AT
PHU BAI - 1966-1967

SHOOTING LEGENDS
WHO BECAME COMBAT
LEGENDS, AT THE FRONT
OF THE CLASS

GSgt Marvin Lange Instructs
Use Of Rifle Scope.
Note .45 On His Belt...
War Was Everywhere.

Cpl. Ron Szpond Demon-
strates Snug Seated Position.
He Made History In Sniping
As Well As Close-In Combat.
Ron Has Been Featured On
The History Channel.

MSgt George Hurt, (Famed
Shooter & Eric's Buddy,)
Converting Match-Range
Skills Into Combat Kills.

THE PHANTOM OF PHU BAI

ERIC'S CORPS COUSIN ~ DR. J. HARRY TURNER

Former USMC
Weapons Instructor

Harry's Example As A
Marine Inspired Eric To
Enlist, Passing
The Torch And Setting
The Stage For Historic
Events

Harry Also Got Eric To
Re-Enlist In 1954, Con-
vincing Him That Eric And
The Corps Were Meant
For Each Other

This Kept Eric's Great
Talents And Gung-Ho
Savvy In Motion For The
Great Destiny And
Achievements That Were
To Be His

UNITED STATES MARINE CORPS ~ 1948-1952

FATHER OF THE AUTHOR, AND INSPIRATION FOR MANY MARINES
HARRY ANSWERED TAPS ON JANUARY 23, 2005

TWO BIG SHOOTERS SHOOT THE BREEZE
Eric England and Harry Turner's Last Picture Together
Taken In Their Beloved North Georgia Mountains ~ 1994

297

TURNER

1957 USMC MARKSMANSHIP TEAM

Eric: 4th Row, 2nd From Left

Many Notables, Including Walter Walsh, George Hurt, James Zahm

1957

EASTERN

DIVISION

CHAMPS

Another Impressive Score For The Records

Tight Team Work And Discipline Paid Off In The Matches, As Well As In Sniper Teams

Eric: 1st Row, 2nd From Right

WINNERS ~ 1958 ELLIOTT TROPHY MATCH
Eric: 2nd From Right

DRILL INSTRUCTOR SCHOOL GRADUATION ~ 1955
Eric Is Pictured Last Row, 1st On Left

He Would Prove Too Tough Even To Be A Marine D.I.

USMC SNIPER SCHOOL SEES BIG SUCCESS

SHOOTING LEGENDS WHO BECAME COMBAT LEGENDS, AT "THE FRONT" OF THE CLASS

The *Phu Bai Phantasm* Extends Through These Ace Students, Richard Morrison & Charles Harris, Who Got 18 VC In One Operation

LONG RANGE RECON PATROL PREPARES TO DEPLOY IN I CORPS

A "VC Hunting Club" Often Worked In Conjunction With Scout-Sniper Teams. The LLRP & Recon Teams Were A Vital & Dreaded Force In Cleaning Out Enemy Nests & Disrupting Operations

CANDIDATE FOR IN-COUNTRY SNIPER SCHOOL

Though Sniper Trainers Were Usually Match Competitors & Range Instructors, Students Were Often Selected From Active Infantry Units. The Rifleman At Left Is Picking Off A Running VC With A Standard-Issue M-14

300

HOT SHOOTING ON A COLD DAY IN TEXAS
Winners ~ 1968 National Infantry Team Match
Eric: Front Row, Center ~ All World-Class Champs. Eric Spent His Career
With Them. Fresh Home From War, Yet Rock-Hard And Range-Ready.
3 Future Nat. Record Setters On Team: Eric, Jerry Kozuch, Don Bartlett.
Next Month, Eric Set The All-Time US Open Record

COACHING A WORLD-CLASS RIFLE TEAM
Eric: Front, Right

301

DỞ PHẦN THƯỞNG
LINH DỒNG QUẦN DU KICH
THƯỚC VẺ BỀ
QUYẾT DÀNH THẮNG
100,000 PIASTRES

THƯỞNG CHO
THƯƠNG TÍCH

KHỔNG CỦ
DỄ QUỐC MỸ

ENGLAND
GIẮC MỸ XÂM LƯỢC!
LÀ KẺ THỦ KHỔNG DỘI TRỜI CHUNG
CỦA CHÚNG TA!
DỘI TRỜI CHÚNG CỦA CHÚNG TA!!

**AN ENEMY'S TESTIMONIAL
TO HIS FOE'S GREATNESS**

*Actual Enemy "Wanted Poster"
(PRECEDING PAGE, CONTINUED:)*

302

THE PHANTOM OF PHU BAI

Shown About 1/8 Actual Size, This Genuine "Wanted Poster" Was Authorized By Ho Chi Minh, Offering 100,000 Piastres (About $25,000) For The Capture Of Eric England. This Was Equivalent To A Lifetime Salary For A Middle-Class Vietnamese. For A Peasant, Who Earned About $100 Per Year, It Was A Staggering Fortune.

Truly He Was A One-Man Fighting Force, Of Such Importance That He Attracted The Attention (And Purse) Of The Leader Of An Entire Enemy Nation. Thankfully, No One Ever Collected On The Offer,

But America Can Never Fully Repay A Man For The Endless Dangers He Endured For The Cause Of Freedom. The Artist, Surely A Spy, Accurately Captured The Vivid, Penetrating Eyes Of "The Phantom!"

The Poster Generally Translates As A Call To Unite In A Popular Effort To Effectuate His Demise.

It says *"This Is A Reward For Guerillas Determined To Gain The Victory. P100,000. The Reward For Eliminating American Aggressors... They Are Our Sworn Enemy... Our Sworn Enemy!"*

(Seal:) *"National Front For The Liberation Of South Vietnam."*

[Thanks To Mark Andersen of MN, Who Obtained This From A Collector. It Was Found In The Locked Trunk Of A Former US Army Intel NCO After He Died, Who Had Secretly Brought Home Several Artifacts From His Tour In Vietnam. It Has Been Certified As Genuine.]

303

ERIC'S FATHER, (R), AUGUSTUS LUCIUS "Buster" ENGLAND
A Family Trait: Always The Adventurer

Somewhere In Arizona, As A Cowpoke & Range Rider In The 1920's

**DON'T WORRY...
IT'S JUST A
STUDIO GAG
PHOTO!**

ERIC, ABOUT 1980

**This Might
Be Posed,
But Who Would
Mess With
Any Lawman
Who Looked As
Serious As This?**

THE PHANTOM OF PHU BAI

WHO'S SLOWING DOWN FOR RE-TIRE-MENT?
Eric & Sue Check Out A Favored Ford:
Friend Bill Elliott's "NASCAR 9"

Contributed By Team Elliott

TAKEN AT TIME OF SECOND RE-ENLISTMENT, 1957

Returning One Day Past The Grace Period Cost Him A Stripe. He Soon Regained His SSgt Grade. His First Re-Up Was 1954, When Harry Turner Convinced Him He Was Made For The Corps. They Eagerly Took Their Hot-Shot Back, Despite Being 2 Pounds Underweight

305

THE EYES OF DESTINY

The Keen, Attentive Eyes Of The Fabled Hunter-Marksman (Left)
Are A Lifelong Trait, As Evidenced In His Youth (Right)

Photo: About Age 5, With Mother And Grandfather

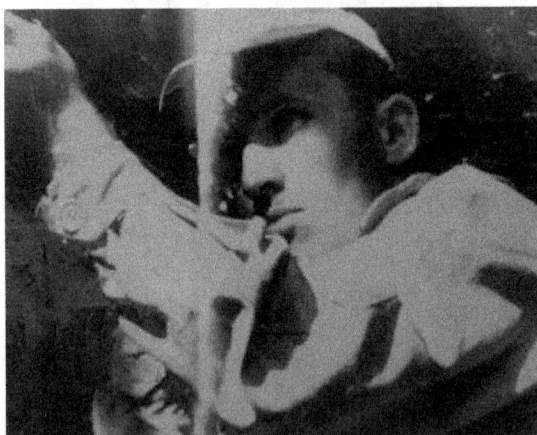

ERIC'S COUSIN HARRY TURNER, USMC WEAPONS INSTRUCTOR WHO INSPIRED ERIC TO BECOME A MARINE, AND TAUGHT HIM THE FUNDAMENTALS THAT HELPED HIM PERFECT HIS CHAMPIONSHIP RIFLE SKILLS.   USMC PHOTO

ON THE PERIMETER AT KHE SANH
WHERE ERIC TAUGHT 'EM HOW TO SHOOT FOR BLOOD

War-Weary Grunts Watch As A B-52 Strike Reduces The Flow Of NVA

Photo Provided By Jim Singer

NAPALM BOMBS VAPORIZE NVA & VC AT KHE SANH
Poor Grunts Outside The Perimeter Wire Facing Charlie Toe To Toe

Photo Provided By Jim Singer

307

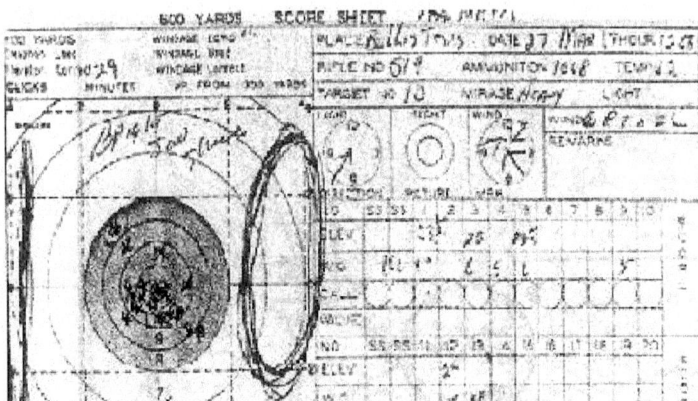

HOT SHOOTING ON A COLD DAY IN TEXAS ~ 1967

ERIC'S 600 YARD RAPID-FIRE BULLS

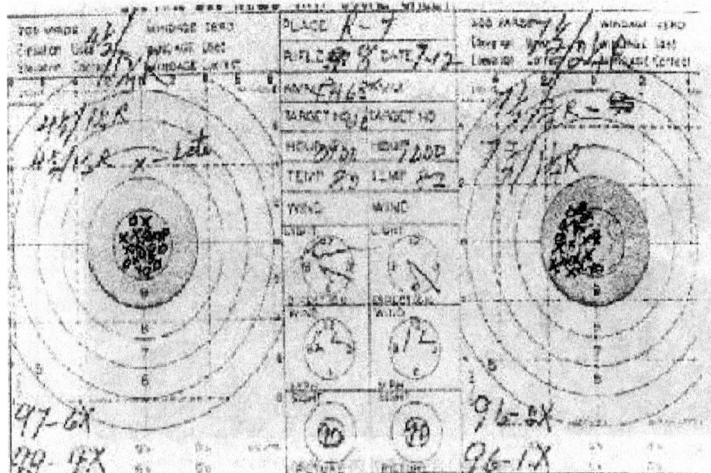

ERIC'S TYPICAL 200 & 300 YARD RAPID-FIRE
SCORE CARDS:
ALL BULLS & NO BULL

SNIPER RANGE CARD
His Spotter Usually Notes Positions For Him, Then Gives Shooting Directions

SNIPER RECORD CARD
As In Competition Matches, Effectiveness Is Enhanced By Keeping Records

THE TOP SHOT

**LEATHERNECK ON LEAVE – 1958
WITH COUSIN HAROLD DYER, WHO IN 1967
RESEARCHED RIFLE-SILENCING TECHNOLOGY FOR ERIC**
PHOTO BY HARRY TURNER

THOMAS JASPER NIX
Eric's Great-Grandfather

Jasper & Four Brothers
Served In 23rd GA Reg't
In The Civil War. Jasper
Joined At 15. Their Skill
In Woodcraft & Shooting
Was Inherited By Eric.

311

JOHN BOITNOTT ~ KOREA, 1952
9 SHOTS - 9 KILLS, AT 900 YARDS... KNOCKING OUT ENEMY SNIPERS

Eric England's Personal Hero

Fought In 23 Major Campaigns In World War II. Started The Marine Corp's Sniper School On The Front Lines In Korean War. Went On To Play Leading Role In Future USMC Scout-Sniper Training. Helped Train Eric At Quantico.

PHOTO COURTESY OF MSGT JOHN DAVID BOITNOTT

MODERN M-40 SNIPER RIFLE, BASED ON REMINGTON 70 / .30-06. HEAVY BARREL AND MATCH-CONDITIONED DESIGN ENHANCE STABILITY AND ACCURACY   PHOTO COURTESY OF USMC

BLENDING: A SCOUT - SNIPER'S ART

Planning, Preparation, Patience... Attention To Detail... Skillful Blending With The Environment... & Surgical Shooting: The Absolute Prerequisites For A Scout-Sniper Skill With Camouflage & Woodcraft Overall Are His Key To Success & Survival.

US OUTGOING ARTILLERY FIRE AT CON THIEN

Typical Scene At The DMZ Outpost Where Snipers Stayed Busy As Well

North Vietnam Is Visible In The Background

Photo Courtesy Of Jim Singer

TURNER

M-40 SNIPER RIFLE (US MILITARY)
Military Version Of Winchester Model 70, Match Conditioned And Adapted
For Heavy Field Use.   .30-06 Bolt Action

Lt. Col. Norman Chandler's "Iron Brigade Armorers" Created A Remarkably Accurate,
Precision Made, Limited Edition Version: "The Carlos Hathcock Sniping Rifle."
Unertl & Leopold Scopes Are Popular With This And Other Models

REMINGTON MODEL 700 / .308 CALIBER
An Equally Popular US Sporting & Military Sniping Rifle

MOSIN-NAGENT M-91/30 RUSSIAN SNIPER RIFLE
With Standard 3.5X Scope
Adapted From 1891 Russian Infantry - Standard Issue From 1891 To 1945

Sniper Version Used Extensively Throughout World War II, Korean & Vietnam Wars.
Standard Sniper Rifle For NVA & VC, The M-91/30 Was Remarkable Effective At 1000
Yards Despite Weaker Scope. This Was The First Russian Army Sniper Rifle. It Was
Developed During The Finnish War After A Single Finnish Sniper Was Credited With
500 Russian Kills In 15 Weeks. Still In Use In Some Countries' Militaries Today.

ARCHIVAL PHOTOS

MARINE SNIPER TEAM CHECKING GEAR IN THE FIELD
Survival Required Self-Sufficiency & Cunning Above All
USMC PHOTO

MARINE SNIPER HELPS DEFEND BUDDIES
He Hastily Assumed This Barely-Concealed Position As His
Patrol Came Under Surprise Attack

In Firefight Situations, Snipers Often Had As Many Kills As—Or More Kills
Than—Infantrymen Firing On Semi Or Full-Auto, Due To Trained Coolness,
Extensive Target Practice, And Mindset Of "Calling The Targets." The High
Discipline Of The Match Teams Contributes Immensely To Combat Accuracy
USMC PHOTO

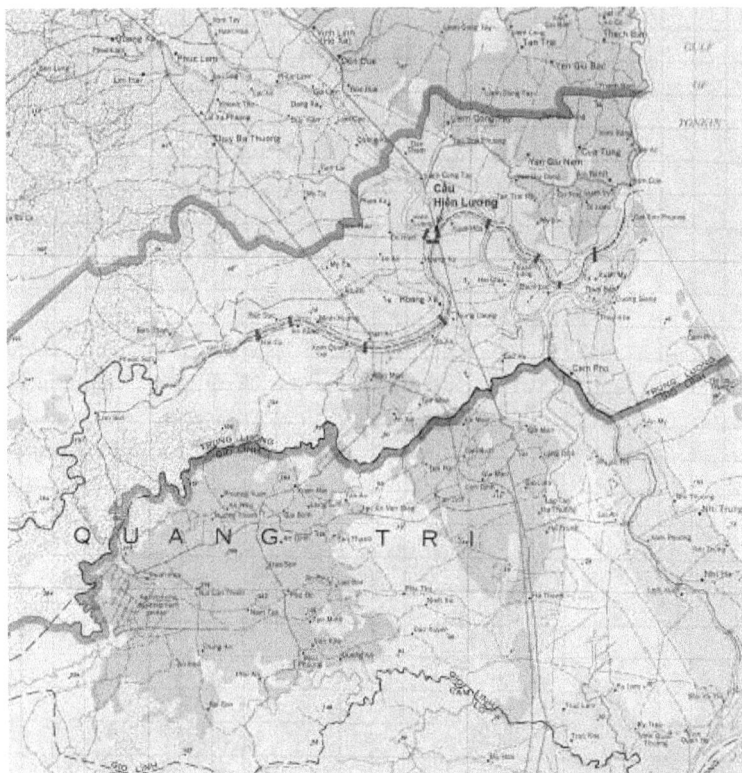

MAP OF THE DEMILITARIZED ZONE (DMZ),
SHOWING MANY KNOWN ENEMY INFILTRATION
TRAILS. MANY MORE BRANCH TRAILS ALSO
WERE IN USE. THE SNIPER'S JOB IN STEMMING
THE ENEMY FLOW WAS AS VITAL AS
ARTILLERY MISSIONS AND AIR STRIKES.

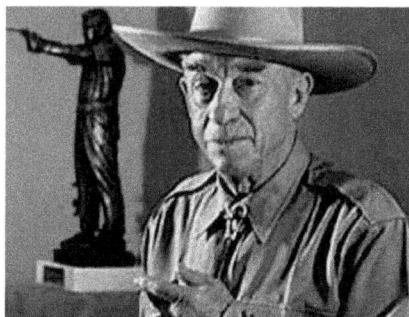

ELMER KEITH, "FATHER OF MAGNUM SHOOTING,"
WHO SAW THE LAST DAYS OF THE OLD WEST. WORLD-
RENOWNED MARKSMAN WHO DEVELOPED THE .357, .41.,
AND .44 MAGNUM PISTOLS. A CHANCE MEETING WITH
ERIC ENGLAND DEVELOPED INTO A LIFELONG MUTUAL
ADMIRATION AS DISTINGUISHED SHOOTERS AND
MASTERS OF THE RUGGED, ROUGH-AND-TUMBLE LIFE.
PHOTOS FROM PUBLIC DOMAIN.

ER

THE AUTHOR IN THE 'NAM AS A TEENAGER

THE AUTHOR'S BROTHER JIM, USMC, FOUGHT IN THE 'NAM, 1967-1968. HE WAS AMONG OUR VICTORIOUS TROOPS IN THE 1968 TET OFFENSIVE

USMC RIFLE RANGES, QUANTICO, VIRGINIA, OLD TIMES
AND NEW. ERIC'S FIRST LOVE! COMPETITION SHOOTING
DISCIPLINED U.S. SCOUT-SNIPERS BEFORE THERE WERE
SPECIAL SCHOOLS FOR THEM. THE TRADITION LIVES ON.
USMC PHOTOS

A LASTING LEGACY

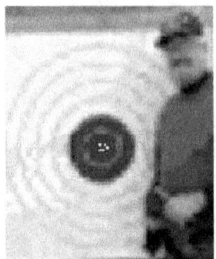

A WIDESPREAD INCREASE IN COMPETITION MATCHES, SCOUT - SNIPER TRAINING AND ITS HISTORY, USMC ENLISTMENT, ESTABLISHMENT OF PERMANENT SCOUT - SNIPER SCHOOLS, AND EVEN FILMS AND VIDEO GAMES ON THE SUBJECT, ARE TRUE INDICATORS OF THE LAST- ING EFFECT MADE BY THE CAREERS OF ERIC ENGLAND AND HIS COLLEAGUES

PHOTOS COURTESY OF NRA

PHOTOS COURTESY OF NRA AND USMC

The USMC's superb Scout-Sniper school is a well-established and permanent defense integer now, thanks to pioneering efforts and needs-demonstration provided by the heroes in this book. So much so, that the USMC now trains allies in sniping and woodcraft, as with Japanese troops above.   USMC PHOTOS

Images © and ®
Used By Permission Only

ERIC AT FAMILY REUNION, ABOUT 2000. STILL ROUGH N' READY, A QUARTER CENTURY AFTER RETIREMENT. HE SHOT A BEAR THAT YEAR SO HUGE, HE HAD TO BACKPACK THE MEAT OUT OF THE MOUNTAINS IN SEVERAL LOADS. PHOTO BY J. B. TURNER

1997 ~ Dedication Of Vietnam Memorial
Blairsville, Georgia

Still Fitting That Old Uniform
23 Years After Retirement !

Compliments Of Union County Historical Society

ERIC R. ENGLAND SCULPTURE
Unveiled February 26, 2006

(SCULPTURE, CONTINUED:)

Unveiling Ceremony Took Place
In His Hometown Museum

Unveiled By Cousin Zell Miller,
Former Governor & Senator

&

Major Jim Land (USMC, Ret.),
Sec. Of NRA, & Legendary Sniper

&

Cousin Sam Ensley, President of Union Co.
Historical Society. Sam's Bluegrass Band, "Roots And
Branches," Livened The Occasion By Playing The
Marine Corps Hymn In Bluegrass Time, Which
Brought A Standing Ovation.

Sculpture Was Created By Andy Davis,
Commissioned By Cousin Gary Harkins

Overflow Audience Witnessed Historic Ceremony,
Including A Score Of Eric's Old Match-Range Buddies
Who Traveled Across The Country,
Adding To The History Of The Grand Event. Base Of
Statue Is Engraved With Numerous Signatures Of
Colleagues

MAJ. LAND, SEN. ZELL MILLER STAND PROUDLY BY ERIC
An Unequaled Day In The History Of The USMC, NRA, And Georgia

ONCE A MARINE, ALWAYS A MARINE

2004 ~ 30 Years After Retirement,
And Passing The Torch

Lance Corporal Joe Telford, USMC,
With His Hero, Eric England, Before
Deploying To Afghanistan

*Eric Now Inspiring 3rd
Generation Of Marines*

PHOTO COURTESY OF JOE TELFORD

SPECIAL TRIBUTE:
COL. WALTER WALSH,

"FATHER OF
MODERN SHOOTING."

1907 - 2014

He And Eric Were Mutual
Fans And Heroes. Always
Relied On Eric's Skills.

Also The Longest-Living Olympic Shooter And Olympic Coach.

Was A Famed FBI Agent In The 1930's, Terrorizing Mobsters.

A Hero In The Pacific In World War II.

Col. Walsh Provided The Author With Priceless Memories And
Insights Into Eric's Career, And USMC Competition Shooting.
He Expressed Great Respect For Eric And Colleagues, Who
Likewise Spoke Of Him With Highest Honor.

Semper Fidelis To A True Marine, Shooter, And Friend